CHINA'S SPATIAL ECONOMY
RECENT DEVELOPMENTS AND REFORMS

CHINA'S SPATIAL ECONOMY

RECENT DEVELOPMENTS AND REFORMS

EDITORS: G. J. R. LINGE AND D. K. FORBES

Contributors

J. Fincher   D. K. Forbes   T. H. Hull   J. S. Hyslop
Li Wen-yan   G. J. R. Linge   Liu Yi   R. J. Nairn
Shen Wei-Cheng   D. Wilmoth   Chung-tong Wu
Xu Xueqiang   Zhang Lei

HONG KONG
OXFORD UNIVERSITY PRESS
OXFORD   NEW YORK
1990

Oxford University Press

Oxford   New York   Toronto
Petaling Jaya   Singapore   Hong Kong   Tokyo
Delhi   Bombay   Calcutta   Madras   Karachi
Nairobi   Dar es Salaam   Cape Town
Melbourne   Auckland

and associated companies in
Berlin   Ibadan

First published 1990
Published in the United States
by Oxford University Press, Inc., New York

Library of Congress Cataloging-in-Publication Data

China's spatial economy: recent developments and reforms/editors,
G.J.R. Linge and D.K. Forbes: contributors, J. Fincher ... [et al.].
p. cm.
Includes bibliographical references and index.
ISBN 0-19-585296-6: $34.00 (approx.)
1. China — Economic conditions — 1976- — Regional disparities.
2. China — Economic policy — 1976-   I. Linge, G. J. R.
II. Forbes, D. K. (Dean K.)   III. Fincher, John H.
HC427.92.C4514565 1990
338.951 — dc20   90-48095
CIP

British Library Cataloguing-in-Publication data available

Printed in Hong Kong by Calay Printing Co.
Published by Oxford University Press, Warwick House, Hong Kong

Man's social practice alone is the criterion of the truth of his knowledge of the external world . . . man's knowledge is verified only when he achieves the anticipated results in the process of social practice . . .
Mao Zedong (1965, p. 296)

The fundamental point of Mao Zedong Thought is seeking truth from facts . . .
Deng Xiaoping (1984, p. 141)

Preface

G. J. R. LINGE AND D. K. FORBES

F R O M the second half of the 1970s through to the late 1980s the People's Republic of China (PRC) experimented with new forms of socialism, including an unprecedented opening up to the West. Not only did this begin to change the economic and social structure of the PRC, but it also allowed Western and Chinese academics and consultants to discuss openly the kinds of problems facing China as the leadership strived to redirect the economy.

Unlike most of the many books and reports that have appeared in the last few years about China, this volume concentrates on recent spatial developments, highlighting the changing structure of the country's cities, regions, and spatial connections. It emphasizes how the operation of the space economy has acted and, in our view, will continue to act as a 'shock absorber' modifying some of the extreme oscillations in policy.

The volume is composed of contributions from both China and the West, notably Australia. Authors are either academics or consultants with recent first-hand experience of the problems of China's space economy. The chapters concentrate on the empirical aspects of China's space economy — truth from facts — and are skewed towards practical issues rather than theory.

It is important to explain some editorial decisions. Firstly, we have used the Pinyin system of romanization for Chinese words and names (see *Beijing Review*, 1979, 21(1), pp. 18–20). Where the features are better known by an alternative name, such as the Yangtze River, we have retained use of the Pinyin but included the alternative in brackets on first usage in each chapter. Secondly, readers will note that there are some statistical 'discrepancies' between chapters, including for example the proportion of the population described as 'urban' or regarded as 'floating'. At first sight these differences may seem to be a weakness, but in our view, one of the strengths of this volume is the diversity of sources to which the authors have had access.

Contents

Tables

Figures

Contributors

J. Fincher
Fellow, Department of East Asian History, Research School of Pacific Studies, Australian National University, Canberra

D. K. Forbes
Senior Research Fellow, Department of Human Geography, Research School of Pacific Studies, Australian National University, Canberra

T. H. Hull
Senior Research Fellow, Department of Political and Social Change, Research School of Pacific Studies, Australian National University, Canberra

J. S. Hyslop
Principal, Dwyer Leslie Pty. Ltd., Canberra

Li Wen-yan
Deputy Director, Institute of Geography, Academia Sinica, Beijing

G. J. R. Linge
Professorial Fellow, Department of Human Geography, Research School of Pacific Studies, Australian National University, Canberra

Liu Yi
Institute of Geography, Academia Sinica, Beijing

R. J. Nairn
Principal, R.J. Nairn and Partners, Canberra

Shen Wei-cheng
Research Associate, Institute of Geography, Academia Sinica, Beijing

D. Wilmoth
Associate Director (Higher Education), Royal Melbourne Institute of Technology, Melbourne

Chung-tong Wu
Associate Professor, Department of Urban and Regional Planning, University of Sydney, Sydney

Xu Xueqiang
Dean, Faculty of Geography, Zhongshan University, Guangzhou

Zhang Lei
Doctoral Student, University of Manitoba, Winnipeg

Acknowledgements

G. J. R. LINGE and D. K. FORBES wish to acknowledge the support of colleagues in the Department of Human Geography at The Australian National University, especially Carol McKenzie who did much of the typing; Ian Heyward and Keith Mitchell who drew the maps; Peter Shen who advised us about Chinese usage; Kam Wing Chan (Hong Kong) for his valuable comments; Christine Tabart who helped in many ways; and Jan Linge who provided both patient and painstaking editorial assistance.

R. J. NAIRN notes that material for Chapter 4 was collected during the course of several studies in China during the 1980s, conducted under the umbrella of technological co-operation between Australia and China. These include Maunsell & Partners Pty. Ltd. et al. (1986b); Pak Poy & Kneebone Pty. Ltd. et al. (1987); and Forbes et al. (1987).

T. H. HULL's chapter is based largely on work done jointly with Yang Quanhe for a project with the State Planning Commission and the United Nations Fund for Population Activities. While acknowledging their substantial research contributions, he accepts full responsibility for any errors of presentation or interpretation which remain.

J. S. HYSLOP thanks the Australian International Development Assistance Bureau, the Shanghai Capital Construction Commission, and the World Bank for making the project and his chapter possible. Mr Wu Xianling, the overall project co-ordinator provided considerable guidance in understanding the Shanghai system of planning and development. Colleagues Jing Qizhen, Wu Zhentong, and their staff at the Housing Management Science and Technology Research Institute gave the project team a good understanding of the housing system. He also thanks the other consultant team members, and Alison Cook who helped to produce the line drawings.

D. K. FORBES and D. WILMOTH note that their chapter is based on a report (Forbes and Wilmoth, 1986; Wilmoth and Forbes, 1988) prepared as part of the exchange programme between Tianjin and the Australian Institute of Urban Studies (AIUS). They thank the Tianjin Scientific and Technical Exchange Centre and other Tianjin agencies, the Australia-China Council, and the AIUS for their support.

Introduction

G. J. R. LINGE AND D. K. FORBES

FUNDAMENTAL changes occurred to the space economy of the People's Republic of China (PRC) during the 1980s. The economic reforms to rural production which began late in 1978 were followed by attempts to open up China to foreign trade and investment, rationalize the wage and price systems, and restructure the organization of production. Overall, these stimulated growth: increases of real national income rose from an annual average of 6 per cent during the 1952–78 period to 9 per cent from 1979 through 1988. The introduction of free markets for agricultural commodities in rural areas stimulated production and relieved shortages, and the 1984 application of a 'dual-track' price system in urban areas for manufactured goods (which thus became available at both fixed and free prices) made a wider range of products — especially consumer items — more generally available. The growth of net material product in agriculture rose sharply during the early 1980s but declined after 1984 because productivity gains due to organizational reforms (see Chapter 2) had largely been exhausted. Industry then became the main source of growth with the annual increases in net material product remaining at high levels from 1984 through 1988 (Table I.1).

The reforms were not entirely successful. The prices of energy and transport remained extremely low while those for manufactured goods reflected neither the scarcity of some raw materials nor their significance to the economy. The dual-track pricing policy helped to clog the railway system with fixed priced goods being sent to regions where higher free prices prevailed. Corruption, particularly by Party cadres, remained rife and diverted investment funds from essential infrastructure to conspicuous consumption (Chapter 1). The introduction of the 'contract responsibility system' to urban areas in 1984 did not achieve the expected gains in efficiency; irrational pricing led to wasteful investment in inefficient production lines which added to the over-supply of some goods that used scarce materials and imported components. In part, this was exacerbated by the poor articulation of the transport system which insulates regions from outside competition and, in part, by the longstanding jealousies of provinces each of which

Table I.1 Selected economic and social indicators, 1980–9

Indicator	1971–80 Average	1981	1982	1983	1984	1985	1986	1987	1988	1989
Growth rate of GDP[a] (per capita, per cent, per annum)	4.7	3.2	7.0	9.0	13.5	11.6	7.2	9.1	9.0	3.4
Growth of agriculture[b] (per cent, per annum)	3.5	5.8	11.3	7.8	12.3	3.4	3.4	5.8	3.9	4.5
Growth of industry[b,c] (per cent, per annum)	8.9	4.3	7.8	11.2	16.3	21.4	11.7	17.7	20.8	6.8
Changes in consumer prices (per cent, per annum)	1.4	2.5	2.0	2.0	2.7	11.9	7.0	8.8	20.7	18.0
Merchandise exports[d] (per cent of GDP)	6.4	8.1	7.9	7.3	8.2	8.9	11.3	13.8	13.5	11.4
Merchandise imports[d] (per cent of GDP)	7.3	7.5	6.3	6.6	8.2	13.5	12.7	12.3	12.1	10.2
Balance of payments on current account (US$000 million)	n.a.	2.1	5.8	4.5	2.5	-11.4	-7.0	0.3	-3.9	-4.0
External debt outstanding[e] (US$000 million)	n.a.	5.8	8.4	9.6	12.1	16.7	23.7	35.4	42.0	44.0

Note: [a] Per capita real GDP derived by dividing GDP in constant market prices by population.
[b] Sector growth based on net material product (not value added).
[c] Industry includes mining, manufacturing, and energy.
[d] Measured in f.o.b. prices.
[e] Short-term debt not included.
Source: Asian Development Bank (1990, pp. 223–40).

was determined to develop its own portfolio of economic activities. Fuelling these tendencies were the cheapness of investment funds (relative to the rate of inflation) and the irresponsibility of publicly owned enterprises (accounting in 1988 for 56.8 per cent of industrial output value, as compared with collective ownership 36.2 per cent, individual ownership 4.3 per cent, and others — including joint ventures with foreign firms — 2.7 per cent: Li, C., 1989, p. 20) which made decisions without regard to profitability. As a result it is estimated that nearly one-sixth of state expenditure in 1988 went into bailing out loss-making state enterprises — an order of magnitude borne out by Wang Bingqian's statement on the 1989 budget at the Third Session of the Seventh National People's Congress on 21 March 1990 (*Beijing Review*, 1990, 33(17), p. ix).

Higher rural incomes, rises in urban wages, excessive (and often unproductive) investment, and panic buying all contributed to a significant rise in consumer prices in 1988 (Table I.1) and, in turn, a further series of corrective measures by the government. These included the restriction of credit, the imposition of administrative controls on capital construction, the indexing of savings accounts, and the reintroduction of various forms of levies and price controls. In addition, government spending was curbed and the growth of enterprise wages and bonuses was tied to increases in productivity. This clamp on credit reduced inflation from a peak of about 25 per cent in April 1988 to a rate of about 20.7 per cent for the year as a whole (Asian Development Bank, 1990, p. 230). In an attempt to bring down inflation to less than 10 per cent and curb state expenditures the government in September 1989 cut workers' incomes and bonuses, and compulsorily invested part of their salaries (about 10 per cent) in government bonds. The resulting discontent led to a direction in December that state enterprises should pay full salaries even to workers who had been laid off (but had still been entitled to 75 per cent of their wages, therefore largely negating efforts to increase productivity). Not surprisingly, the morale of urban employees plummeted during 1989: the first eleven months saw productivity per worker increasing by only 1.5 per cent compared with the same period in 1988 (*The Economist*, 6 January 1990, p. 23). In October industrial production declined for the first time in more than a decade. Production declined again in January 1990.

Following the events of June 1989, Western countries imposed economic sanctions which reinforced China's own austerity programme. None the less, imports rose by 7.1 per cent compared with 1988 to US$59,100 million and exports rose by 10.5 per cent to US$52,500 million. Thus, the trade deficit, after deducting the value of materials supplied for processing, equipment imported as part of the investment in foreign-funded enterprises, and other imports — not all paid for in foreign exchange — was US$2,850 million. Foreign exchange earnings from invisible trade registered a surplus of US$3,000 million so that, contrary to expectations, foreign exchange reserves rose by US$150 million (*Beijing Review*, 1990, 33(17), p. iii). China's major trading partners in 1989 were Hong Kong and Macao (with two-way trade valued at US$21,400 million — much of which consisted of imported components and re-exported assemblies); Japan (US$14,000 million); USA (US$9,400 million); West Germany (US$3,310 million); and the USSR (US$3,180 million).

Uncertainty continues over the granting by the USA of 'most-favoured nation' (MFN) status to China's exports. Although this privilege was extended by President Bush on 24 May 1990 on the grounds that the USA had to weigh its 'impulse to lash out in outrage . . . against a sober assessment of our nation's long-term interests' (Awanohara, 1990), there are proposals before Congress to tie human-rights conditions to further extensions of MFN status. Ironically, were the USA to terminate the MFN agreement with China the greatest effects would be felt by entrepreneurs in Hong Kong that employ an estimated three million workers in assembly plants in the Special Economic Zones (SEZs) in southern China which are now less favoured by Beijing. In 1989 China's trade with the USA via Hong Kong totalled US$9,800 million.

Another problem for China is that in June 1989 the World Bank suspended seven loans worth US$780 million. On 29 May 1990, however, it decided to lend US$300 million for a reafforestation project. Only three other loans have been made (on humanitarian grounds) by the International Development Association, the World Bank's soft-loan affiliate: one was for emergency earthquake relief (US$30 million), another for an agricultural scheme in Jiangxi Province (US$60 million), and the third for a vocational and technical education programme (US$50 million). As a result the World Bank's loans for 1989–90 will be less than US$500 million instead of the anticipated US$2,500 million: this compares with US$1,100 million in 1986–7, US$1,700 million in 1987–8, and US$2,200 million in 1989–90 (Awanohara, 1990).

At its Fifth Plenum in November 1989, the Communist Party's Central Committee appears to have overturned much of the urban industrial and commercial reform implemented since 1984 (Delfs, 1989) and recentralized economic and fiscal power in Beijing. New restrictions have been applied to 'middlemen' (seen, by definition, as 'exploitative'), to small private enterprise, to the distribution of strategic raw materials like coal, and to imports of luxury goods and most electrical appliances. While the factory responsibility system remains (though the decision-making powers of managers have been curtailed), the dual-track pricing system is to be phased out by eliminating the floating price for goods produced and sold outside the plan.

One move towards this end and also to reinforce the revival of the centralized planning system was the introduction early in 1990 of a 'double-guarantee' arrangement whereby selected state enterprises in the north-east will be guaranteed supplies of energy and raw materials and communications and transport services. In return these enterprises will have to guarantee to meet state quotas for finished products, profits, and taxes. This attempts to counter the tendency for such enterprises to maximize the purchase of inputs at the lower state prices and the sale of finished products at the higher free-market prices.

Despite the fundamental nature of these changes, it is unwise to assume that future policy directions in the PRC are clear.

Linge and Forbes in Chapter 1 review the changes in spatial policy that have taken place since Liberation in 1949. While at one level these represented sharp changes in direction, their grassroots implementation cannot be divided neatly into periods. As this and several of the other chapters illustrate, 'top-down' and 'bottom-up' actions and reactions were not always in harmony. In broad terms, however, the last four decades have seen the emphasis change from the development of the interior for ideological and military reasons to the revitalization of the coastal region. The original concept of developing small and medium-size inland cities with more or less self-sufficient economies proved to be wasteful and largely impractical; in the 1970s it was replaced by policies designed to try to maximize regional comparative advantage. In particular, the 'opening' of coastal areas after 1978 was seen as a way of generating industrial growth based largely on imported production and management technologies. It was anticipated that these coastal dynamos would then stimulate activity in their hinterlands (which would be the source of energy, raw materials, semi-processed goods, and foodstuffs) and, eventually, in the more distant western regions. In practice, such an elegant developmental strategy has been proving less easy to manage. Thus, east-west transport links are having to be upgraded, provincial competition is only gradually giving way to regional co-operation, and investment priorities are being reviewed.

The spatial organization of China is put into a longer historical and wider political context by Fincher in Chapter 2. He uses a discussion of land rights and markets and of housing and other constraints on population movements to support a thesis that China's population is more urbanized — both physically and attitudinally — than many observers believe. The failure to recognize this has led to planning policies and instruments that favour rural areas and small cities and militate against the growth of large urban areas — a bias, he suggests, that is exacerbating China's social and economic difficulties. This view is not, however, shared by other scholars — as is noted in Appendix 1.

Intra and inter-provincial contrasts between living and development standards are pointed up by Li in Chapter 3, which emphasizes spatial diversity in China. He examines the spatial implications of four basic challenges: how to handle the relationships between national and regional economic growth, between the development of the coastal areas and the interior, between the specialization of the regional economy and its comprehensive development, and between urban and rural areas. A discussion of the diverse problems and potential of the various parts of the Eastern, Middle, and Western Zones leads him to the view that 'obeying rigidly one model of economic development or even a universal political slogan, and persisting in a one-sided approach to local interests at the expense of the national unified allocation of resources, are irrational strategies and hence harmful to the future of China's modernization'.

China's transport network is integral to any consideration of the country's spatial structure. Nairn, in Chapter 4, examines the relationship between freight patterns, passenger movements, and transport development between provinces, within provinces, and within the large cities. The important role of railways and waterways in China is highlighted, and the need for improved modal co-ordination is noted, particularly while the PRC pursues a strategy for increased regional economic specialization. Within provinces the use of road transport has increased significantly, putting new emphasis on road upgrading programmes, while in the large cities traffic management is stressed alongside infrastructure improvements.

Much of the discussion about the renaissance during the 1980s of coastal China has focused on the political and bureaucratic obstacles associated with its opening to overseas trade and investment. In

Chapter 5, however, Shen points to the practical problems created by the past neglect of the nation's ocean and river port facilities. Despite considerable investment since 1978, the absence of sufficient deep-water berths and bulk-handling facilities, continuing port congestion (especially in the Shanghai area), and the uneven distribution of ports along China's 18,000-km coastline continue to add to costs, inefficiencies, and delays. Of particular importance is the recent recognition that co-operative 'systems' of ports have to be developed and that port and urban planning have to be co-ordinated.

In his review of China's population policies, Hull in Chapter 6 provides in effect a background to some of the urban social issues that are examined in greater detail in the next three chapters. He is uncertain, however, whether the baby boom predicted for the 1990s will eventuate or whether government exhortations to limit family size, along with the problems facing the growing urban population, such as shortages of residential accommodation, jobs, and educational facilities will lead to a further fertility decline. The difficulties of interpreting likely population trends are illustrated by reports that female infanticide is increasing, that some provinces are barring marriages between close relatives and requiring pregnant women with physical or mental handicaps to have abortions, and that some sixty to eighty million people were 'floating' in search of work (*The Australian*, 21 February 1990, p. 90).

Wu and Xu in Chapter 7 take up this issue of the migrating population, some of whom are moving from relatively poor to relatively rich rural areas, and others from rural areas to small urban places or to large cities. Their 1988 sample survey of migrants in Guangzhou Municipality not only identifies some of the specific problems faced by these people but raises wider issues about the future of millions of rural labourers who are unable to find work either in rural or urban areas. This has been highlighted by reports early in 1990 that China has 300 million rural labourers but only 180 million farm jobs are available. In 1989 some 40 per cent of the rural workforce was unemployed. Li Peiyao, the Vice-Minister of Labour, said in mid-February that 'rural workers would not be allowed into cities because there were no jobs . . . instead, they would be encouraged to find work in agriculture' because it is time to 'cool down the overheated transfer of rural labour to urban areas'. According to the Xinhua News Agency (*News Bulletin*, 6 February 1990, p. 24), some ten million workers were recently sent back to the hinterland from urban areas.

The pressures on existing large cities, and planning responses to them, form the focus of Chapter 8 by Hyslop using the example of Shanghai. Since Liberation this municipality has been the subject of a series of Master Plans, the most recent of which was released in 1983. It especially sought to expand the area of the City and promote development on the periphery, and foster the formation of urban sub-centres within the City Proper, as part of an overall effort to reduce the very high population densities within Shanghai. Further studies have shown that, though very compact, the City is characterized by a mixed land-use pattern and therefore lacks some of the internal structural features which could be used as the basis for developing a modern rapid-transit system.

Forbes and Wilmoth in Chapter 9 draw attention to another of China's large cities, Tianjin. As a high-ranking industrial centre and port, located within the Bohai Rim Economic Belt, the municipality is at the core of urban-industrial development. Major developments include the formation of the Tianjin Economic Technological Development Area and extensive plans for the development of the major transport corridors within the municipality. These are to improve the linkages between the City and the port, and form part of a 'T' plan for guiding the spatial structure of the municipality. The growth of the City itself will be physically contained within a green belt, and the population limited in size, with some residents to be relocated to the port city of Tanggu. The recent greater attention being given to the inland areas of China will probably be offset in Tianjin's case by the renewed emphasis on the development of the northern coastal cities.

In Chapter 10 Forbes and Linge reflect on prospects for China's spatial development in the 1990s. Consideration is given to two divergent scenarios, the implications these might have for the spatial reorganization of the country, and the mediating influence of spatial structure on defining the possible range of economic strategies available for Chinese planners. International events, particularly in Eastern Europe, will undoubtedly influence the direction China takes, as of course will domestic pressures and politics. The existing spatial structure of the country will absorb and be changed by new policy directions, but will also slow the pace and soften the impact of future changes. Therefore, it is concluded, whether China moves in the direction of an 'opening door' or a 'closing door' strategy, it will ultimately have an important impact on the country's spatial structure through such factors as the regional focus of investment, the sectoral emphasis, attitudes towards the labour market and labour mobility, the role of large urban centres, and transport priorities.

In Appendix 1 Linge and Forbes try to summarize the data available about the urban population of China. Most countries have problems in defining 'urban' and 'rural' because of the difficulties of making clear-cut distinctions between the two. The interpretation of the published data is further complicated in China by administrative issues (such as the definition of people according to the status of their residence permits), and also by political motives including the emphasis on rural development during the 1949–76 period, on urbanization (equated with 'modernization' in the 1980s), and on the current concerns about the dangers of 'over-urbanization'. As they point out, boundary changes and re-definitions account for much of the sudden surge after 1984 in the number and proportion of the population defined as urban.

Appendix 2 by Zhang and Liu provides a brief case study of the industrial development of Liaoning Province, and emphasizes again some of the main hindrances to development — the shortages of energy and water, and the growing concern about pollution.

1 The Space Economy of China

G. J. R. LINGE AND D. K. FORBES

M U C H of the discussion about the People's Republic of China (PRC) continues to focus on the problems and potential of the economy as a whole and the role it may play internationally. The purpose of this book, however, is to draw attention to some of the spatial issues, not only because these have tended to be pushed into the background but also because they provide formidable obstacles to the pace at which the country can accommodate its economic and social goals.

Although the concern here is not so much with the physical geography of China, none the less it is important to stress the huge contrasts that exist in a country which covers 9.6 million km^2. This has been summarized by Chinese geographers using a line drawn from Aihui (Heihe) in the north-east to Tengchong in the south-west (Figure 1.1). This line, originally proposed by Hu Huanyong in the early 1930s, roughly divides China by annual precipitation (more than 400 mm to the east; less than 400 mm to the west), by altitude and topography (high mountain chains and plateaux, deep basins, and large deserts to the west; major systems of eastward flowing rivers and large fertile valleys and plains to the east), and by tectonic trend (west-east to the west; north-east to the east). When originally proposed by Hu, the western area covered about 64 per cent of China but had only 4 per cent of the population (although a much higher proportion of ethnic minorities). Following the 1982 census, Hu calculated, after allowing for territorial changes, that the western area covered about 57 per cent of the land area and some 6 per cent of the population (Figure 1.3). This showed that the population imbalance between east and west China had changed little during the previous five decades. In the meantime, however, surveys had revealed the rich mineral, forest, and water resources in the western area.

Crucial to an understanding of China's space economy is the strategy put in place after Liberation in 1949 that was designed to reduce the inequalities between regions and between urban and rural areas, and also to minimize vulnerability to external and, to a lesser extent, internal challenge.

The opening up of over 100 treaty ports during the second half of

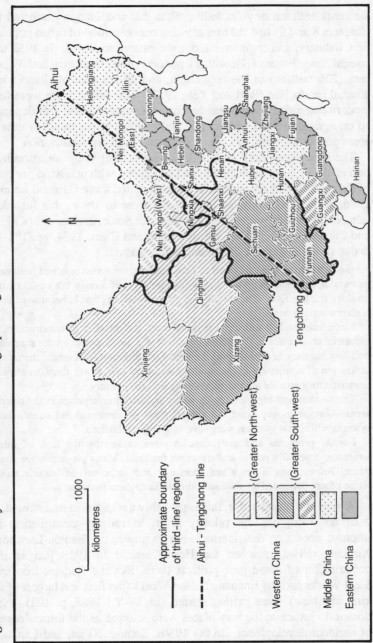

Figure 1.1 The three major economic zones for strategic planning

Aihui – Tengchong line

Approximate boundary
of 'third-line' region

(Greater North-west)

(Greater South-west)

Western China

Middle China

Eastern China

0   1000
kilometres

the nineteenth century (including Shanghai and Tianjin discussed in
Chapters 8 and 9) had led to a growing concentration of urban population, industry, and commerce along the eastern seaboard. In 1952 the
coastal zone (Figure 1.1), with 11 per cent of the land area, had 39 per
cent (225 million) of the population, and 68 per cent of China's industrial production (Roll and Yeh, 1975). Elsewhere, there were few
modern enterprises; vast areas had no industry at all and still depended on agriculture and handicrafts; and in some of the minority ethnic
areas people were still practising slash-and-burn-type cultivation.

The First Five-year Plan (1953–7) gave priority to the industrialization of the hitherto neglected inland provinces, with nearly 56 per cent
of the total capital investment being channelled there (Jao and Leung,
1986, p. 3). Ironically, as later events were to show, this included
'almost all the key projects built with direct Soviet assistance' (Kirkby
and Cannon, 1989, p. 5). One view (Sun and Chen, 1984, pp. 181–2)
is that much of this early investment was wasted:

As the enterprises were required to be scattered over a vast area and built near
mountains or in mountain caves, they needed a lot of money but could hardly
produce things. Even if some did, the returns were negligible because of their
high production costs.

Since independent industrial systems were sought after in construction of
industrial enterprises in these areas, there was a development in the machine-
building industry in disregard of the actual conditions. As a result, the rate of
utilization of equipment in the industry was very low, lower than the already
unsatisfactory rate for the industry throughout the country.

The sudden and big increase of heavy industrial enterprises in the remote
areas — some moved from the coastal areas — disrupted old coordination
systems while new systems were slow in being established.

Further problems and inefficiencies were caused by the lack of infrastructure, especially power and transport facilities. Many projects were aban-
doned before completion when economic and technical difficulties arose,
while others depended on state subsidies to keep them in operation.

While, in a literal sense, this is probably a reasonable assessment, it
does not recognize the priority given to railway construction to
improve access to the interior. For example, the Baotou-Lanzhou-
Xinjiang railway reached the Hexi Corridor in 1958 just as the
construction of some new projects there, like the Jiuquan Iron and
Steel Works and the Jinchang Nickel Works (the first and largest of its
kind in China), were getting started (Li, W-Y., 1988, p. 102). Nor
does it do justice to the way places were selected as the future 'cores'
of regional development. In the 1950s, Baotou, Xi'an, and Lanzhou
were chosen as the main economic, military, and administrative

centres of north-west China. Thus, when the Lianyungang-Gansu railway (the sole east-west trunk line) was extended in 1952 to Lanzhou, this city of 170,000 people (the capital of Gansu Province) was selected as the location for several industrial projects, including an oil refinery, a fertilizer plant, a synthetic rubber factory, and an aluminium smelter using hydroelectric power at Liujia Gorge on the Huanghe River. The completion of the 1,000-km Baotou-Lanzhou railway in 1957, the Lanzhou-Qinghai railway in 1959, and the Lanzhou-Xinjiang railway in 1964 made this city (with a population of 1.5 million in 1987) a major transport hub and the leading industrial centre of the north-west region (Li, W-Y., 1988, p. 104).

Although concerns were expressed during the 1950s about this investment in the interior — even by Mao Zedong — as much as 60 per cent of total investment outlays during the Second (1958–62) and 67 per cent during the Third (1966–70) Five-year Plans were directed there. Priority was given to heavy industry, particularly iron and steel which was seen as 'the key link', resulting in major works being built at Baotou, Wuhan, and Panzhihua. After 1958, twenty-eight provinces established their own iron and steel industries even though only twelve had adequate iron ore supplies. This was a costly exercise because the overall per-tonne investment in the interior was three times greater than that on the coast where much of the basic infrastructure already existed (Liu, 1988b, p. 113).

By the 1970s the diversion of investment from the coast was delaying the upgrading of existing industrial bases and jeopardizing the possibility of competing on export markets. As a case in point, during the 1960s construction west of the Beijing-Guangzhou line absorbed over 80 per cent of the nation's investment in railways, thus leading to the further deterioration of the transport system in the coastal zone. At the same time, the investment elsewhere was larger than could be absorbed with projects being suspended because of shortages of energy, raw materials, and even in some cases of food. The Fourth Five-year Plan (1971–5) therefore saw some increase in the proportion of all capital investment along the eastern seaboard (43 per cent compared with 33 per cent during the previous five years) and the hinterland areas able to supply it with raw materials.

The Third-Line Concept

During the Mao Zedong period (1949–76) there was, however, a hidden agenda in relation to the organization of China's space economy, the full extent of which has only emerged in recent years. The fear that the country might be invaded along the eastern seaboard, reinforced by border disputes with the USSR during the 1960s, led to the concept of the 'third-line' region, 'third front', or 'defensive heartland' (Figure 1.1). As a result, beginning in 1965, the focus of investment shifted to mountainous regions remote from the coastal zone and away from existing cities (Naughton, 1988; Li, 1990). During the next decade nearly 2,000 large and medium-size plants were built, many of them to make military equipment, heavy machinery, and electronic components. These were supported by other investments ranging from the Panzhihua Steel Works to research institutes (some transferred from the coast), as well as urban, energy-producing, and transport infrastructure. Li, W-Y. (1987, pp. 3–4) has suggested that 200,000 million yuan were invested in the third-line area: during the Cultural Revolution period and its aftermath (1966–76) it absorbed at least two-fifths of all state investment. In effect, the aim was to create a self-sufficient system which by the mid-1970s included almost 30,000 enterprises employing sixteen million people. Impressive though these figures are, Li (1990, p. 32) makes the point that because these enterprises 'were directly controlled by central ministries and operated in areas having weakly developed economies and poor infrastructure, their production lagged far behind that of their longer-established counterparts in the coastal zone, though their equipment and technology were much better'.

Special Economic Zones

The next major stage in the development of regional policy was the establishment of Special Economic Zones (SEZs) in 1979. These were a more sophisticated version of the concept of 'export commodity bases' that had been suggested by Zhou Enlai in 1960 and established in 1971–2 as an outward-looking policy (Chiu, 1986, p. 26). The first 'unified export commodity production base' was set up in Foshan Municipality (Guangdong Province) in 1973 and was followed by fifteen others.

The origins of the present open-door policy, however, can be traced to Hua Guofeng's 'Ten-Year Economic Programme' announced early in 1978 which specifically called for massive imports of technology from the West, especially in the form of 'turnkey' projects (Keuh, 1987, p. 446). Deng Xiaoping and his associates quickly dissociated themselves from this programme which they regarded as an unrealistically ambitious 'outward leap'. Reassessments in December 1978 and February 1979 led the Second Plenary Session of the Fifth National People's Congress in June 1979 to order cut-backs in capital construction projects: in 1979 and 1980 alone 415 large and medium-size projects and 2,510 small ones were suspended or postponed. Emphasis instead was put on agriculture and light industry, as well as on housing and other urban facilities. Indeed, the ratio of productive to non-productive investment changed from 83:17 in 1978 to 66:34 in 1980 (Lin et al., 1984, p. 294). In addition, defence establishments turned over some of their capacity to making goods like washing machines, radios, and furniture for consumption by the domestic market (Lin et al., 1984, p. 283). By the end of 1986 it was claimed (Lu, Y., 1987, p. 14) that two-thirds of the 400 military enterprises in China were producing 'competitive civilian products which account for over half of their output'.

The series of reforms initiated in 1978 (see Introduction) were a recognition of the need to make more efficient use of resources. As already noted, much of the inland investment had been wasteful while, deprived of funds, coastal infrastructure had deteriorated and industrial technology had not kept abreast of developments abroad. The Chinese leadership realized that, at least in the short-term, production and managerial know-how would have to be imported. Various schemes — including joint venture arrangements and compensation and barter trade deals — were encouraged to eke out scarce foreign exchange reserves. The goals of increasing efficiency and productivity and attracting foreign investors all pointed to the need for a greater emphasis on the coastal zone.

The problem faced by the leadership was how to manage political aspects of greater contact with the outside world. It was thought less dangerous, from this point of view, to carry out the initial experiments in a distant province rather than in Tianjin, Shanghai, or elsewhere in the country's industrial heartland. Guangdong Province had two advantages. Firstly, many of the residents of nearby Hong Kong and Macao had family connections there and it was believed that this would facilitate the flow of investment funds. Secondly, it was hoped that the development of closer economic ties would help further the political goal of reunification with Hong Kong, Macao, and even eventually with Taiwan.

On 30 January 1979 the State Council designated Shekou (in Bao'an County, Shenzhen) as an 'industrial zone' and a few weeks later the administration of Bao'an and Zhuhai Counties were

restructured to bring them under the direct control of Guangdong
Province. As Chiu (1986, p. 27) also noted, this was

an essential step in minimizing bureaucratic proceedings and increasing the
power of decision-makers . . . This new administrative arrangement also en-
abled larger and more direct budgetary allocations for infrastructure development. The Shenzhen Capital Construction Committee was formed to plan
industrial improvements in Shenzhen and to outline measures for using
capital, technology, equipment, and raw materials that could be drawn from
Hong Kong.

In August 1979, Shantou Municipality (Guangdong Province) was
declared 'a trade and investment zone', and the following month
Vice-Premier Gu Mu announced that SEZs would be established at
Shenzhen (327.5 km^2) and Zhuhai (6.8 km^2) in Guangdong Province.
It was anticipated that these places — adjoining, respectively, Hong
Kong and Macao — would be attractive to foreign entrepreneurs
(including Overseas Chinese) wanting to set up joint ventures. By the
end of the year two more SEZs (together covering 4.1 km^2), at
Shantou (Guangdong Province) and Xiamen (Fujian Province), had
been established although they were not formally proclaimed until
August 1980. They were allowed to offer preferential terms relating
to land costs, labour, and taxes. Their purpose, summarized by Zhao
Ziyang in 1983 (cited by Chiu, 1986, p. 28), was that they

are not being developed for solving the employment problem, nor should they
go solely after increases in output. Rather, they were areas demarcated for attracting enterprises of high technological and knowledge content through the
offer of preferential treatment. They are to serve as windows of advanced
production, technology and management methods of the world (*Shenzhen
Special Zone Herald*, 14 November 1983).

Initially much of the effort went into developing basic infrastructure
on what had been previously farmland.

The establishment of four SEZs in the south-east of the country,
along with their early success in attracting overseas investment and
the opportunities they provided for abuse by local bureaucrats, stimulated controversy in Beijing and resentment elsewhere, particularly in
Shanghai. These concerns, along with the continuing emphasis on
foreign investment, technology, and managerial skills, led to the dec-
laration of fourteen coastal urban areas and Hainan Island as 'open
cities' in April 1984 (Figure 1.2). The majority of these were north of
Fujian Province with particular emphasis being given to investment in
Shanghai, Tianjin, and Dalian. Early the following year, however, the

Figure 1.2 Location of the fourteen open cities and the four Special Economic Zones

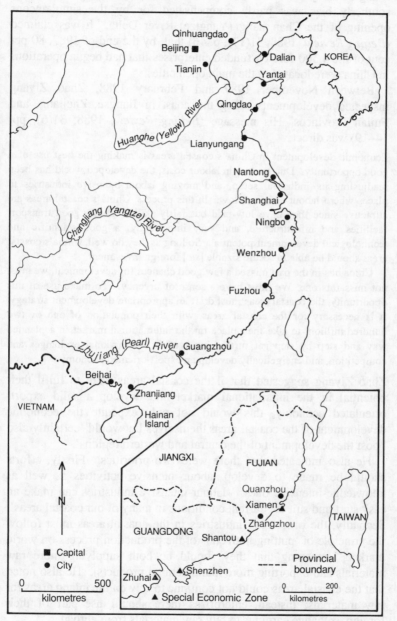

Zhujiang (Pearl) River Delta and the Xiamen-Zhangzhou-Quanzhou triangle in Fujian Province were added to the open list although this southerly bias was partly compensated for by the simultaneous opening of the Changjiang (Yangtze) River Delta. It was claimed (*Beijing Review*, 1988, 31(17), p. 46) that, by the end of 1987, 80 per cent of the 4,300 foreign-funded enterprises that had begun operations in China were located in the main open cities.

Between November 1987 and February 1988, Zhao Ziyang inspected developments along the coast in Jiangsu, Zhejiang, and Fujian Provinces. His message (*Beijing Review*, 1988, 31(6), pp. 14–19) was direct:

Economic development in China's coastal areas is making the best use of a good opportunity. Due to rises in labour costs, the developed world has been readjusting its industrial setup, and moving labour-intensive industries to places where labour costs are low. In this process, China's coastal areas are attractive since they have low-paid but fairly skilled labour, good transport facilities and infrastructure, and very importantly, a good scientific and technological development potential. So long as they do well, China's coastal areas should be able to secure sizable [*sic*] foreign investment.

China has in the past missed a few good chances for development, we must not miss this one. We must have a sense of urgency. To make use of this opportunity, the coastal areas must draft an appropriate development strategy. It is necessary for the coastal areas, with their population of one or two hundred million, to take their place on the international market in a planned way and step by step get further involved in international exchanges and competition, and energetically develop an export-oriented economy.

Zhao Ziyang suggested that if the coastal areas were to fulfil their potential in the international market and develop a solid export-orientated economy, this would not only expedite the economic development of the coastal areas themselves but would 'certainly also boost the development of the central and western regions'.

He also indicated that there were two priorities. Firstly, efforts should be made to develop labour-intensive activities as well as knowledge-intensive ones: 'labour-intensive industries can make an easy start and suit the current conditions in many of our coastal areas'. Secondly, the processing industries in the coastal areas must follow the principle of 'putting both ends of the production process on world markets' (meaning that they should be both supplying more raw materials and exporting more manufactured products). He also noted that the coastal areas could not continue to rely on the inland areas for raw materials; instead, enterprises there should use part of their foreign exchange earnings to buy raw materials from abroad.

Zhao Ziyang gave much the same message to a March 1988 conference of administrators from the coastal zone who recommended to the State Council that more coastal areas should be opened up to further promote the integration of China with the global economy. Shortly afterwards the State Council expanded the open coastal zones to 320,000 km² (Figures 1.1 and 3.4), raised the number of counties and cities included from 148 to 284, and thus increased the total population in the open zone from ninety to 160 million (40 per cent of those in the Eastern Zone). At the same time (April 1988) Hainan Island, formerly an administrative region of Guangdong Province, was raised to provincial status and proclaimed the fifth SEZ.

The emphasis on the coastal zone during the 1980s led to increasing discrepancies between the per capita income in this part of the country and the inland areas. The Chinese leadership went to some pains during visits to the interior to explain that the strategy to develop coastal areas would bring about economic growth elsewhere because of the increased demand for energy and raw materials and because funds, technology, and managerial skills would filter from the coast and spur the exploitation of resources further inland. In effect, the newly opened areas would be the conduits through which development impulses were to be transmitted to their hinterlands.

It is difficult to evaluate whether the establishment of the SEZs and the subsequent opening up of a third of the coastal zone can be described as a 'successful' strategy. There are several reasons.

Firstly, the SEZs were set up in a chaotic way with only a vague mandate to be 'windows' through which greater contact could be developed with the rest of the world. As do Rosario (1987, pp. 102–3) has noted, there were no clear guidelines about the kinds of investments or sectors of the economy that the zones should concentrate on developing. 'Left to themselves, the zones became a haven for making "quick" money in property, retail sales and other activities which Peking regards as non-productive.' A substantial proportion of total investment went into projects using scarce resources, which made little economic sense (such as airports with handling capacities of fewer than 20,000 passengers a year), or which were simply status symbols like luxury hotels and sanatoria. Because the SEZs were allowed to import and export without paying any, or only low, tariffs, they attracted not only foreign investment but also domestic enterprises which used them, in effect, as doors for entrepôt trade. Thus over the years many of Hunan's authorized exporters set up offices in Guangzhou and Shenzhen, while many of Hunan's state enterprises moved part of their factory operations there to take advantage of more generous investment concessions available in the SEZs (Cheng, 1989, p. 45). Indeed, Chan (1985) argues that, in the case of Shenzhen, the development was largely sponsored by domestic capital, manpower, and technology; that imports exceeded exports; and that more than half the output of foreign-related firms was sold on the domestic market.

Secondly, the SEZs have been subject to many changes in policy concerning both attitudes to foreign investment and wide-ranging internal economic and political reforms. For example, in 1985 the Chinese government called a halt to the *laissez-faire* prosperity that had been 'built on non-industrial, high-yield, short-term and often illicit activities' (do Rosario, 1987, p. 102), replaced some of the local politicians and bureaucrats, and insisted that the SEZs focus on activities that were export-orientated. The special privileges enjoyed by the SEZs revived ancient strains between China's always poorer interior and the coast. These came to a head in 1988 when the inland provinces brought pressure to bear on Beijing about their concerns that Guangdong Province, in particular, was using unfair tactics to increase exports at the expense of its neighbours. They claimed, as Cheng (1989, p. 45) explains, that Guangdong had been

using its easy access to foreign exchange, which it can legally swap for ren-minbi at rates almost twice the official exchange rate, to obtain "cheap" local currency. It has then used these funds to buy up and divert through its own traders goods which would otherwise be credited as exports from less-developed provinces.

Moreover, because it tried to industrialize rapidly — often at the expense of other activities — Guangdong made itself vulnerable to grain and coal-producing provinces which retaliated by charging higher prices and even, on occasion, levying duties at border crossings. In 1988, for example, Hunan Province established border patrols to prevent its farmers selling pigs at the higher prices available in its southern neighbour. Thus the central planners decided that from the beginning of 1989 the SEZs would be permitted to retain only 80 (instead of 100) per cent of their foreign exchange earnings while, at the same time, allowing provinces elsewhere to retain a higher percentage than previously.

Thirdly, the data available about such key criteria as the value of production, imports, exports, and investment are inadequate. Thus, in China investment in factory assets is regarded as output even though it has no saleable value. Or, again, sales to other parts of China may be recorded in foreign currency and hence shown as 'exports'. There is also considerable uncertainty about whether the figures for foreign investment in joint ventures represent hope rather than reality: not only are projects scaled down but shortages of energy and materials mean that many of those which have actually come to fruition can only operate at less than their full capacity.

Finally, it can be argued that the four original SEZs barely had enough time to establish themselves, and take advantage of their special status, before most of the eastern seaboard was opened up to the rest of the world. There are two conflicting views. It is argued that, on the one hand, the administrations of the SEZs were naïve and inexperienced but, on the other, they were not as politically and socially entrenched and committed to power networks as their counterparts in long-established communities like Shanghai. As against that, the southern provinces in particular were quick to learn how to ignore or circumvent directives from Beijing, their rationalization being that the special development zones needed greater freedom to experiment with reformist ways of doing things. As a Hong Kong investor explained to one of the authors, business and politics became so entangled that 'every party cadre is also a businessman'. On occasion this became so blatant that Beijing exerted its authority. Thus, in 1984–5 so many senior officials and residents in Hainan were speculatively importing motor vehicles for resale elsewhere in China that Beijing stepped in and dismissed, among others, the Governor, Lei Yu. It can be argued, however, that the Hainan officials were more businesslike and less 'corrupt' than popularly imagined. Thus, imported cars were eagerly sought by officials from Beijing ministries and — rented to foreign tourists — provided China with a net gain in overseas currency.

Whatever the reality, the apparent success of the southern SEZs — and hence of Guangdong and Hainan Island Provinces — may be turning sour for both economic and political reasons. Austerity measures taken in 1988 and 1989 to slow the rate of inflation and restrain the money supply adversely affected many of the kinds of consumer industries, like household electrical appliances, which had flourished particularly in the SEZs but also elsewhere in the Eastern Zone. For example, early in 1989 the government imposed a sales tax on television sets as well as a foreign-exchange-subsidy levy to offset the cost of imported components; in addition it introduced a monopoly distribution system which curbed price cutting and other promotional activities. These deliberate measures, along with unexpected falls in consumer purchasing power (such as those caused by price falls due to bumper harvests in some rural areas and crop failures in others), have exposed even more clearly the way in which resources have been misallocated: as a case in point, one estimate is that the 150 or so electric-fan assembly lines in China were, on average, operating in mid-1989 at only one-fifth capacity.

The political uncertainties facing the SEZs arise from the concerns of the conservative elements in Beijing about the wayward behaviour of southern provinces which they thought needed to be brought to heel. Although, as mentioned earlier, various measures to this end have been put in place since the mid-1980s, the removal from office of Hainan's Governor (Liang Xiang) in September 1989 and his replacement by party technocrat Liu Jianfeng, and the investigation for corruption of Fujian's Governor (Wang Zhaoguo) seem to signal a reassertion of authority and the imposition of a greater political and economic discipline by the new central leadership (do Rosario, 1989). This is given further credence by reports that attempts have been made to entice Guangdong's Governor (Ye Xuanping) to a senior post in Beijing (with the aim, it seems, of getting him away from his province and its restive military commanders), that the Province's leading trade official has been dismissed on corruption charges, and that a Vice-Governor is under investigation. 'If Guangdong, Hainan and Fujian are all wrested from reformist hands', suggested *The Economist* (16 September 1989, p. 23), 'the conservative triumph that began with the attack on Mr Zhao in the [northern] spring will be complete.'

At this stage it is unclear what changes will be made to China's regional development strategies. One view is that the ousting in June 1989 of Zhao Ziyang, who gave favoured treatment to the southern coastal provinces, will enable conservative elements in Beijing to re-allocate resources from the southern and coastal areas towards the north and inland. On 6 November 1989 the Xinhua News Agency (*News Bulletin*, p. 33) noted that the Minister of Light Industry (Zeng Xianlin) had announced plans to develop China's north-west areas 'which are largely populated by . . . ethnic minorities'. This aimed

to build the region into a major raw materials base for the nation's light industrial production [because of the] long considered concern of the nation's leaders over the growing gulf between the east and the west.

Zeng Xianlin regarded co-operation between west and east 'as a shortcut, if not the only way, to a fast development of light industry in

the west'. This tendency may be reinforced in any case by the
renewed emphasis on public ownership which will benefit northern
provinces like Liaoning and Heilongjiang (where there is a high
concentration of state enterprises) and adversely affect southern ones
like Jiangsu and Zhejiang (where private and collective enterprises are
relatively more important).

Another view is that the elevation of the former mayor and latterly
Party leader of Shanghai, Jiang Zemin, to the post of General-
Secretary of the Communist Party may dampen the swing back to
command-style central planning. In fact, both Jiang Zemin and the
former Mayor of Tianjin (Li Ruihuan) — appointed to the Standing
Committee of the Politburo — appear to be espousing orthodox
conservative policies that stress state ownership and control, and
traditional socialist values like frugality and self-reliance. Jiang
Zemin, the first provincial leader to congratulate Li Peng (who
succeeded Zhao Ziyang as Prime Minister late in 1987) for imposing
martial law on 20 May 1989, is said to be 'as unpopular in Shanghai
as Li is in Beijing' and has been described as an 'opportunist and
Party puppet' (Chung, 1989, p. 303). None the less, the promotion of
the mayors from two internationally important cities is, according to
Fincher (1989a, pp. 8–9), 'an acknowledgement of Zhao's
appreciation that China's present challenges and future prospects lie
mostly with urban centers'. Jiang Zemin's attitude to the further
development of the coastal area remains obscure. The *Beijing Review*
(1990, 33(2), pp. 6–7) notes that during a tour of Fujian Province in
December 1989 he urged 'China's coastal areas to speed up reform
and opening to the outside world'. Reportedly, he also said that:

to make Sino-foreign co-operation more fruitful, the two sides should keep
four principles on [sic] mind — mutual understanding, mutual trust, mutual
benefit and long-term considerations . . . Since the policy of reform and
opening to the outside world was adopted, we have stressed that efforts should
be made conscientiously to resist the influence of decadent bourgeois
ideology while learning from the advanced Western science and technology
and management expertise . . . Now we feel that it is not enough to keep the
influence at bay and remain defensive . . . We should occupy the ideological
front with Marxism.

The same kind of message was conveyed by Li Peng during an
inspection tour of the Shenzhen SEZ in February 1990, albeit with
more overt moralistic overtones:

those working in the special economic zones should adhere to the four
cardinal principles and spare no effort to foster advanced socialist ethics . . .

[They] should remain politically sober-minded while learning foreign advanced technology and management expertise and absorbing foreign funds. It is also necessary to crack down hard on all criminal activities, wipe out all corrupt phenomena and create a stable environment so that the local residents can lead peaceful and happy lives, foreign investors can feel at home and special economic zones can indeed be turned into models of a socialist culture and morals (*Beijing Review*, 1990, 33(9), p. 6).

The significance of the SEZs to the economy of China is indicated by the fact that in 1989 they contributed nearly 10 per cent to the value of its exports.

Cheng (1990, p. 38), however, has suggested that Shanghai's officials have viewed Jiang Zemin's promotion 'as an opportunity to reestablish the city as China's premier international financial and business centre'. In contrast, Guangdong and Hainan Provinces have not only 'failed to win more flexibility for their economic plans' but have been told 'to slow down'. As Cheng (1990, p. 39) concludes:

Gone for now are Guangdong's freewheeling days when the province fancied itself as being independent of Peking's control. The province is under pressure to consolidate its gains and slow its expansion plans — and step aside for Shanghai.

Moreover, resistance to the reimposition of central controls has been weakening not only because of purges of dissidents but also because the austerity measures introduced in 1988 and reinforced in 1989 have increased provincial dependence on state funding. In do Rosario's (1988) words:

Reformist leaders, liberal economists, independent factory managers and other reform-minded officials who manage to survive the current purge are too weak to go against the tide. Resistance at provincial and municipal levels against unpopular central controls has also been much weaker than anticipated by foreign observers as 12 months of austerity has dried up resources the localities could use to sidestep the centre's orders. In the present political climate, the risk of disobeying Peking is also higher.

It is important to bear in mind, however, that for rural dwellers, who still make up 60 to 70 per cent of China's population (see Appendix 1), the communist government is the legitimate one. As *The Economist* (6 January 1990, p. 23) noted:

After all, the madnesses of Mao's cultural revolution are long gone, succeeded by a whole decade of Dengist economic liberalisation that tripled peasant's incomes and gave them radios, refrigerators, and even colour televisions.

Others may see this as a somewhat optimistic assessment. The bumper harvest in 1989 forced down ex-farm free-market prices. Cuts in state funds for agricultural procurement along with new restrictions on rural industries, which now must concentrate on processing locally available raw materials and agricultural products rather than compete with large state-owned enterprises for energy or raw materials (Delfs, 1989, p. 23), may soon reduce rural living standards and quickly heighten disillusionment with the system. Thus, on 8 November 1989 the Xinhua News Agency (*News Bulletin*, pp. 23–5) reported that during the first nine months of the year

about one million rural industrial enterprises in China have been closed and several hundred thousand have stopped production or shifted to making other products . . . More than 10,000 projects being carried out by rural enterprises throughout the country have been cancelled or postponed, reducing total investment by eight billion yuan (2.16 billion US dollars). Loans allocated by the state to rural industrial enterprises during the period were eight billion yuan less than in the same period last year . . .The drive to rectify the economic order has already driven many rural enterprises to dire straits. The tightening of the money supply has caused fund shortages for some of the enterprises. Increased economic planning has made it difficult for some rural enterprises to get raw materials on the free market, which is shrinking daily. The reduction in capital construction in urban areas has driven millions of peasant construction workers back to the countryside.

Ironically, the rural 'responsibility' system introduced in the late 1970s freed up thousands of labourers from working on the land and encouraged the formation of rural firms, using self-accumulated capital and bank loans, to provide alternative employment. During 1988 these ventures, involved in manufacturing, transport and service activities, employed ninety-five million people or about a quarter of the rural workforce (*Beijing Review*, 1990, 33(4), p. 28).

From the beginning of 1989 the government encouraged rural adjustment by supporting profitable enterprises and closing inefficient ones and those which were deemed to be wasting electricity or raw materials. Vice-minister Chen Yaobang has also announced (Xinhua News Agency, *News Bulletin*, 8 November 1989, p. 25) that:

Over the next two or three years, no new rural enterprises will be allowed to set up except those that will be export-oriented; those that will process agricultural and non-staple materials which are in adequate supply; those that will help develop the energy and raw materials industries; those that will supply big industrial enterprises; those that will produce daily necessities in short supply; and those that will produce agricultural machines and tools.

Attempts have been made to absorb surplus labour in intensive farming, irrigation, and reafforestation projects but it is anticipated that 1990 will be a 'tougher year for the surplus rural labour force' (*Beijing Review*, 1990, 33(4), pp. 28–9).

China's Urban System

During the first decade after Liberation urban development (and the associated vigorous industrial development) was regarded as having a positive role in stimulating the economy, a view also espoused in the USSR where the policy was to transform 'consumptive' cities into 'productive' ones. However, greater emphasis was placed by the PRC on the rhetoric of eradicating the so-called 'contradictions' between (a) town and country, (b) agriculture and industry, and (c) mental and manual labour. As Sit (1985, p. 9) has noted:

The Chinese aimed to create a better spread of cities, a new pattern of industrial locations with centres removed from the coastal area, and, within each city, self-contained neighbourhood units for the organization of workplace and service provisions.

Then in 1957 regulations were issued to try to curb rural-urban migration (termed the 'blind exodus of the rural population'), but in fact peasants continued to flock to the cities.

By the late 1950s a clear urbanization policy had been formulated (Sit, 1985, p. 9) which aimed:

(a) to promote the growth and new construction of medium-sized cities of 200,000–400,000 residents which are still needed for socialist development;
(b) to constrain the growth of large cities by developing planned satellite towns and dispersing industries and the labour force; and
(c) to control the growth of the urban population by reducing rural-urban migration and lowering the natural birth-rate, and by sending out educated youths and technicians to rural areas.

The 1960s and 1970s saw many changes in settlement policy. Thus, the emphasis on development in the interior (reinforced by the third-line concept already discussed) led to the neglect of urban coastal infrastructure, including housing, with some cities actually losing population. Considerable short-term fluctuations occurred in urban growth rates as a result of the failure, in particular, of the *xia fang* and *shang shan xia xiang* movements of the late 1960s and early 1970s (during which professional workers, unemployed youths, and party cadres were sent to the country to 'learn from the peasants') and of the organized population controls during the 1966–76 period.

Whereas the average annual urban growth rate had been reduced to 0.28 per cent in 1965, it had risen to 4.21 per cent by 1970 (Sit, 1985, pp. 11–13). Taking the 1949–81 period as a whole it has been estimated by Sit that 82 per cent, and by K.W. Chan (pers. com.) that 50 per cent, of the total urban population growth of 81,050,000 persons resulted from natural increase. These national figures for the 1949–81 period give a misleading impression. Firstly, there was considerable variation in the rate of urbanization, with the interior being favoured — especially by the third-line policy — at the expense of the coastal areas. Secondly, the relative contributions made by natural increase and net migration differed widely between regions. In the north-west and central-south, for instance, net migration accounted for 43 and 34 per cent, respectively, of the total increase between 1949 and 1981. Thirdly, the importance in the Chinese urban system of cities with more than 500,000 inhabitants increased markedly, rising from 25 in 1953 (42 per cent of the total urban population) to 71 in 1980 (73 per cent).

This increased role of large cities is in part an outcome of the significant policy changes that occurred during and after the 1950s. During the First Five-year Plan (1953–7), thirty-eight new cities (mainly based on mining or industrial projects) were started of which, according to Chang (1976, p. 407), eighteen had no historical antecedents as county seats or rural market towns. Thereafter, for reasons of economy and efficiency, investment was largely concentrated in existing cities, especially the provincial capitals and industrial or port cities which occupied administrative or strategic transport positions. Another explanation is the changes in definition after 1957 which led to considerable tracts of rural land being included as part of the city-administered *xian*. This probably reflected a move towards a new concept of a self-sufficient 'city region' which would facilitate the planning and administration of food supplies, water storage, recreation space, and in some instances the development of satellite towns. It was also, according to K.W. Chan (pers. com.), a response to the rigidity of the 'vertical' planning system.

By the end of 1985 it was claimed (State Statistical Bureau, 1986a, pp. 73–4) that 382,440,000 people (36.6 per cent of China's population) lived in cities and towns compared with 211,540,000 at the end of 1982 (Figure 1.3). Much of this sharp increase resulted from the expansion of urban boundaries that was designed to slow the rate at which fertile land was being taken out of crop production. (The uncertainties about the definition of 'urban' in Chinese statistics

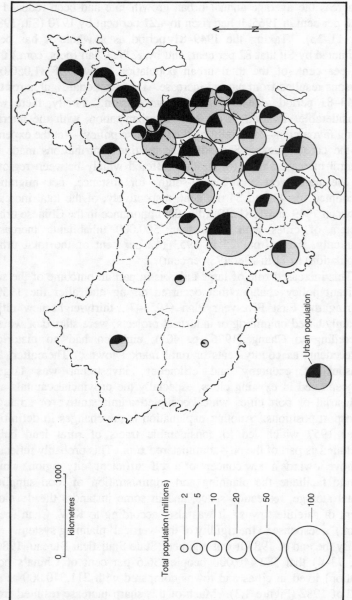

Figure 1.3 Urban and total population distribution by province, 1985

Total population (millions)

2 5 10 20 50 100

Urban population

0   1000
kilometres

Source: Population Research Centre, Academy of Social Science, Beijing (1987, pp. 407, 410).

are summarized in Appendix 1.) The basic problem is that China has
only 7 per cent of the world's total crop area but 23 per cent of its
population. In the early 1980s estimates had been made that per
capita farm size in China would decline from 0.103 ha to 0.075 ha by
the year 2000 (although, as Fincher points out in Chapter 2, there are
doubts about the accuracy of these figures). None the less, soil
erosion, loss of fertility due to over-use, and — especially —
salination, led the State Council in 1984 to require each city to prepare
development plans aimed at curbing urban sprawl. The extension of
the legal boundaries to embrace surrounding townships and rural
counties provided the opportunity for comprehensive control of urban
expansion.

China's Transport System

The inadequacies of China's transport system are proving to be a
major constraint on economic development generally and the
reorganization of its space economy in particular.

About 41 per cent of the freight task is provided by rail, 42 per cent
by inland and coastal shipping, 13 per cent by road, and less than 2
per cent by pipeline and air (Li, C., 1989, p. 30). Although
considerable investment has been made in transport infrastructure in
recent years, much of it represents an attempt to make up for earlier
neglect. Thus, only now are some of the heavily used sections of the
52,000-km railway system being electrified and double-tracked, while
about 40 per cent of the traction is still being provided by old, slow
steam locomotives. During 1989, however, China's locomotive
manufacturing industry (the largest in the world after the USSR)
turned almost exclusively to the production of diesel and electric
engines (*Beijing Review*, 1988, 31(49), pp. 8–9). Moreover, the
various modes of transport have been developed in an uncoordinated
way by separate ministries so that, among other inefficiencies, a good
deal of double handling is necessitated and the possibility of
introducing containers is reduced. These kinds of problem are
compounded by the lack of specialist freight-forwarding firms to
provide inter-modal transfer services.

Personal mobility in China remains low by international standards
but the demand is growing for additional air and long-distance bus
services. In urban areas the deliberate mixing of industrial and
residential facilities initially reduced the need for commuter rail
services on anything like the scale common in western cities. More

recently, though, the lack of an organized structure in China's large cities has made transport planning more difficult (Chapter 8).

Already the deficiencies in the railway system (the only effective link between the provinces and regions) have necessitated changes in sectoral and spatial plans. For example, China's increasing energy requirements will have to be met largely by coal, which in 1987 accounted for 73 per cent of total energy production (Gränzer, 1989, p. 9). This commodity alone, on present estimates, will make up perhaps half China's total transport task in the year 2000 when production is scheduled to reach between 1,200 and 1,400 million tonnes. Yet one major problem continues to be the inability to shift sufficient coal from the northern provinces (especially from Shanxi Province which in 1989 produced 265 million tonnes of the national total of 1,050 million tonnes) to the main industrial and population centres on the eastern seaboard and to export ports. As a result some industrial plants have been operating below capacity and some energy-starved provinces like Hunan have imported coal from overseas. To shift more coal out of Shanxi Province the railways from Beijing to Qinhuangdao, Baotou, and Taiyuan, and that from Taiyuan to Jiaozuo are being upgraded and electrified. The handling capacity of Qinhuangdao port was raised to seventy-five million tonnes with the completion in November 1989 of three new deep-water coal berths (under a project begun in 1984 using Japanese loan funds). None the less, at least four large-scale joint venture open-cast mining projects proposed in the Sixth Five-year Plan have been deferred, in part because of inadequate transport facilities which have caused Shanxi coal to be stockpiled. Instead, priority is being given to the consolidation and modernization of existing mines and new mining projects in the east (even though production costs per tonne there are greater) because the transport infrastructure is better and the ports are closer. Towards the end of 1989 the Xinhua News Agency (*News Bulletin*, 7 November 1989, p. 53) reported that feasibility studies for a 602-km pipeline to carry five million tonnes of coal slurry annually from Shanxi Province to Shandong Province had been completed and its construction (at a cost of US$232 million) would commence immediately. This will also assist China to realize its immediate ambition to boost coal exports from ten million tonnes in 1986 to twenty million tonnes in 1990.

During the 1980s China has built a series of fully mechanized container ports and deep-water berths capable of handling vessels from 30,000 to 100,000 d.w.t. By the end of 1989 there were 139 first-class ports open to overseas shipping (*Beijing Review*, 1990, 33(13), p. 30). After the Chinese Government had promulgated the 'Temporary Provisions on Preferential Treatment for Sino-Foreign Construction of Ports' in September 1985, loan agreements were made with the World Bank for four port schemes that facilitated the construction of seven container and two coal-loading projects at Shanghai, Tianjin, and Guangzhou. Despite these improvments, and the increase of China's shipping fleet to 12,000,000 d.w.t., many problems remain (see Chapter 5).

The last two decades have seen a decline in the network of navigable waterways, in part because of the apparent priority given to hydroelectric and irrigation schemes.

Road transport, which has largely remained a local government responsibility, remains another concern because most routes radiate from provincial capitals, thus forming separate networks with few interconnections between them (see Chapter 4). Even main routes, such as that between Beijing and Tianjin, are narrow and poorly surfaced, although a new freeway linking Beijing to Tanggu will soon be completed (Chapter 9). The World Bank (1985, p. 83) has pointed out that:

It is widely recognized in China that road transport should and will play a large role in the future. Yet there seems to be no strategic plan to bring this about. Indeed, during the past few years, there has been little road construction, and the situation is unlikely to improve substantially so long as roads remain almost entirely a local government responsibility.

China's Environment

Centuries of habitation have caused severe environmental problems in China. Recent policies — designed to bring the spatial structure and economy into alignment with changing economic and political strategies — have often imposed a further toll on the fragile natural environment. Despite vast energy resources, including the world's second largest accessible reserve of bituminous coal, China has long suffered from energy shortages. Non-commercial energy production in rural areas has been based on timber, thus exacerbating deforestation and land degradation. China's forest resources are small by international standards, only 12 per cent of the country being covered by forest, yet two-thirds of the timber removed annually results from illegal fellings and forest fires (Kinzelbach, 1987, p. 180).

Commercial energy production and transport deficiencies — about

20 per cent of the country's industrial capacity lies idle each year due to lack of energy (Thomson, 1988, p. 467) — have also pushed China towards exploiting alternative energy resources which will eventually have an impact on the space economy. Two nuclear power stations are under construction near Shanghai and Hong Kong respectively. China is regarded as having the largest natural hydroelectric power potential in the world (380 GW), although the best sites are in the mountainous south-west, distant from the main industrial centres (Gränzer, 1989, p. 11). China is one of the world's larger oil producers, following successful exploration programmes in the late 1950s and early 1960s. Natural gas production is concentrated largely in Sichuan Province. In recent years, however, the results of offshore exploration of oil and gas have proved disappointing.

An ambitious energy plan for the period 1989–2000 was released by the Ministry of Energy Resources in 1989 (*Beijing Review*,1989, 32(41), p. 6). The plan gives priority to the coal-producing provinces of Shanxi, Shaanxi, and Nei Mongol. Oil and gas plans focus on maintaining production levels in the east, while intensifying exploration in the west, particularly in Xinjiang. Hydroelectric power developments will be concentrated on the Huanghe, Changjiang, Hongshui, Wujiang, and Lancang Rivers, while coastal regions are encouraged to develop their own small nuclear power stations. Energy conservation and the environment are also covered in the plan.

The extensive use of coal by industry and households alike has contributed to serious air pollution in cities, particularly industrial centres such as Tianjin, Anshan, and Benxi. Extremely cold winters in the north mean that some form of home heating is required, increasing coal usage and exacerbating air pollution problems. Liquefied petroleum or natural gas, where available, has subsequently been supplied to the ten largest cities in an effort to reduce air-borne pollution (Clark et al., 1989, pp. 76–7). Programmes to reduce air pollution have, on occasion, worked extremely well. Thus, during the early 1980s Shenyang had amongst the world's highest readings of total suspended particulate (TSP) content in the air, yet by the second half of the decade the city was declared the region's first 'smog-controlled area'. Environmental problems, however, tend to be treated on a local basis. While Shenyang solved its air pollution problems, nearby Benxi's became so bad that by 1988 satellite photography could not penetrate the layer of smog that hovered over the city (Nickum and Dixon, 1989, pp. 90–1).

Water shortages and quality problems, particularly in the northern half of the country, are among the most serious of China's environmental problems. Unmet demand for water particularly affects many of China's large cities. During the summers of 1988–9 residents of both Harbin and Kunming suffered from water shortages, while in cities such as Shanghai, Changsha, and Jinan water consumption quotas were placed on industrial and residential consumers alike (*Beijing Review*, 1989, 32(35), p. 7). In an attempt to alleviate this problem, huge infrastructure projects have been undertaken. Qingdao, the chief port of Shandong Province, has diverted water from the Huanghe, while Tianjin has regularly called on water from the same river in emergencies. To supplement supplies to Tianjin, 1,000 million m³ of water has been diverted each year since 1983 from the Luanhe in the north-east, while a further proposal to divert water from the Changjiang, 1,150 km to the south-west, has also been approved (Jowett, 1986). The magnitude of these projects is significantly changing the structure of the spatial economy of the north-east by removing some of the environmental constraints on economic growth, albeit at a very high cost.

Creeping desertification across thirteen provinces and regions in North China has been tackled by the building of the 'Green Great Wall' — a forest shelterbelt being planted by peasants since the late 1970s under the auspices of the Ministry of Forestry. In the first ten years of this project 8.7 million ha were planted, and another 2.7 million ha of hillsides and deserts closed off to allow for regeneration (*China Daily*, 4 October 1988, p. 3). Salination and land subsidence has been a problem of some significance in the low-lying region around Bohai Bay, and is also being tackled through tree-planting and vegetation regeneration programmes.

While the environmental problems of China are far from insignificant, planners in recent years have generally responded directly to them. Sophisticated projects for documenting and monitoring environmental issues have been established, and results published such as in the *Atlas of Environmental Quality in Tianjin* (Environmental Science Committee, Academia Sinica and Environmental Protection Bureau, Tianjin, 1986). Active and innovative programmes have been developed for greening the cities, increasing the amount of open space in urban areas, reducing the effects of salination, conserving energy, recycling water in areas of shortages, and many more. Energy shortages are being tackled both by attempting to increase output, and by spatial restructuring measures such as improving and expanding transport capacity, relocating industries closer to energy sources, and developing power plants close to coal reserves in order to transmit 'coal by wire' and hence ease pressure on transport infrastructure (Clark et al., 1989, pp. 76–7). Yet not all China's environmental problems can or will be solved in the short term, and others are still being created. China's continuing commitment to nuclear energy is a specific case in point, while the drive towards economic growth has provided a new challenge to environmentally sustainable development.

Conclusion

The sheer size of the population, the enormous area of China, and the diversity of the country's physical environment, combine to create a very complex spatial structure. Planning to improve the space economy is further compounded by tensions within the bureaucracy. Thus, on the one hand, there is the the 'top-down' approach of the technocrats and professionals in the main ministries in Beijing which work through their local branches in particular regions while, on the other, there are the area groups, generally aligned with the Party, which assume responsibility for managing a particular region, be it a province, a city, or a township. Policies are determined by the outcome of political struggles among the actors involved in the institutions formed under the two, mutually less than compatible, organizational systems (Unger, 1987, pp. 15–20).

Nevertheless, it is clearly evident in the experience of China during the last four decades that there have been decisive shifts in the policies addressing the structure of the space economy. Not unexpectedly, there were a wide range and mixture of goals driving these strategies. For example, some had military objectives, others were politically inspired, some sought local area development, while others aimed for national economic goals such as export promotion. Although these various strategies fell short of constituting a coherent whole, their impact on the space economy of China during the 1980s has been very significant.

2 Rural Bias and the Renaissance of Coastal China

JOHN FINCHER

T H E failures of the Cultural Revolution and its aftermath from 1966 to 1976 made economic reform the guiding programme in China. Before he retired from the Chinese Communist Party Politburo in September 1987 and the Military Affairs Commission in November 1989, Deng Xiaoping spoke of the 'reforms' which he and others initiated after Mao Zedong's death in September 1976 as a 'second revolution' for China.

The political implications of that revolution became clear in mid-1989. In April and May, the successive waves of pro-democracy demonstrations that have washed over urban China since 1976 reached tidal-wave proportions. The result was a tragic hardline military crackdown in June, but, it was also new confirmation of the influence in the Party of urban leaders. The Tiananmen Incident was a crisis in China's watershed transition from a preponderantly agrarian society to one which may still join other East Asian countries in becoming essentially urban during this decade (Fincher, 1989a). The Beijing spring of 1989 showed how much the politics of reform have been a politics of hope in a country which has declared itself to be tired of poverty. For some there was too much pessimism in the Party's 1987 decision that China must live in what is called 'the primary stage' of socialism until the middle of the next century. For others, it expressed optimism about twenty-first-century China and plans for accelerating change through the 1990s. Now that Eastern Europe and the USSR have cast their lot with similar rapid changes, it has become more difficult for China's newly cautious leaders to go too slowly.

In 1984, while Premier of China's State Council, Zhao Ziyang displayed interest in the implications for China of the 'information revolution', and the possibility that compact communication and computing technology might link small, scattered Chinese enterprises into efficient production and marketing groups. The idea that Chinese socialism is still in its primary stage does not preclude the hope that during the next century China will partake in a third transformation comparable to the agricultural 'first' revolution and the industrial 'second' revolution (personal interviews, Beijing 1984, with officials who had read A. Toffler, *The Third Wave*; Brugger, 1986).

This is not merely an uneasy accommodation of Marxism and Western futurology but also of the idea that the post-modern world may take lessons in educated social discipline from Eastern Confucianism (or, at least, lessons, in a post-feudal era from the ethics and empiricism of neo-Confucianism — as opposed to the politics of imperial or late imperial Confucianism: Jiang, 1987; Nakajima, 1988). In the thought and rhetoric of China's intellectual and political leaders, visions of a twenty-first-century economy galvanized by micro-computer networks have mixed with reinterpretations of a millenium of the history of a traditional but densely developed village and urban society. Policies for the economic infrastructure are derived from historical analyses of East Asian culture.

It has been normal to express such visions in five-year plans which expound economic and social policies that guide the annual budgets of the central state. In late 1988, General Secretary Zhao Ziyang developed a Party-based 'five-year reform plan'. His initiative pre-empted for market forces some of the authority that would otherwise have been reserved for the State Council bureaucracy to exercise through the normal Five-year Plan scheduled to begin early in 1991. By mid-1989 his boldness had cost him his job as Secretary-General; however, the Central Committee has moderated the harsh criticisms issuing from hardline Army and Party leaders.

Notions of the relationship between 'the market and the plan' have been changing during Deng Xiaoping's decade of reform and the years of Gorbachev's *perestroika* in the USSR. All sides call for less detailed central planning, for more reliance on commodity and labour markets, and for integration into the world economy of an industrial establishment that had previously been orientated and, particularly through the 1960s, was sited at great cost in remote interior areas (cf. Anon., 1968; Naughton, 1988; Chapters 1 and 3).

Leaders of the USSR have come officially to agree with post-Mao Zedong Chinese reformers that communist parties are obliged by failures of post-war economic and social policies to retreat from the wartime habit of daily interference in tasks better left in peacetime to state administrators and enterprise managers. Indeed, by late 1989 Soviet leaders began to improve on the example of Chinese reformers. They know from the experience of East European reformers the dangers of exaggerated fears of inflation which help long-established state enterprises to delay changes. Fresh price and wage policies are then, after initial delays, less effective in promoting the growth of new and more efficient enterprises. China's 1989 crisis taught them new dangers of using fears of full economic reform to justify even longer delays in political reforms than in economic reforms.

The long dependence of communist parties and states on highly centralized, command economies is a legacy of 'War Communism' that goes back to the birth of 'Leninism' in the wartime conditions faced by Russia's original 1917 Bolshevik revolutionaries. Reformers in communist states have had to contend with economic enterprises whose protection and expansion was, until recently, considered essential to national defence, and also with the natural interests of economic and social constituencies of an emergent welfare state. Additionally, in China, older communist leaders could not forget how useful the issue of inflation was in winning urban constituencies away from their Nationalist Party rivals in the post-war struggles for control of the mainland. After the Japanese defeat in China in 1945, the Nationalists gradually lost much of their following in urban China because of the ravages of inflation. By 1949, this made it easier for communist armies to force them on to Taiwan. In 1989–90, mainland Chinese leaders are still afraid of the political dangers of appearing to be too much like the leaders of successful economic — and now political — reforms in Taiwan or in other prosperous and democratized East Asian societies. Too many of their Party colleagues are veterans of the late 1940s victories over the Nationalists for Chinese leaders to feel comfortable about the success of former enemies in Taiwan or Japan.

Political reforms promoted by Zhao Ziyang's predecessor as General-Secretary, Hu Yaobang, imposed five-year terms both on him and his successor as State Council Premier, Li Peng. Zhao Ziyang emphasized (Fincher, 1989a) the costs of delay in economic reforms, perhaps hoping to win another (and final) period in office by completing price and wage reforms during the remaining 1987–92 term, if not earlier.

In mid-1989 Zhao Ziyang lost office, and Premier Li Peng has been free to stress the need for 'stability' against efforts to complete major price and wage reforms by 1992. He and others, such as the elder Party economic policy specialist, Chen Yun, have invoked historic Chinese fears of inflation and of local or national dependence on outside supplies of food grains. They have won their argument that price and wage reforms should not be thoroughly implemented much before the end of the next five-year plan in 1995, if then, because of the danger of 'instability'. Li Peng may go on to win a second (and final) five-year term as State Premier by confining reform within the normal schedule of five-year plans and annual budgets which he administers through the State Council.

However, the price of victory in trying to slow economic reforms was the State Premier's alignment with conservative Army leaders in the suppression of popular demands for political reforms. Before his retirement from the Military Affairs Commission in November 1989, Deng Xiaoping arbitrated the differences between the Party and State leaders like Zhao Ziyang and Li Peng from a distance, and as an army leader. His role in politics became even less direct at the end of 1989. Even if reunification with Taiwan is delayed well into the next century, Deng Xiaoping and others know that he will be credited with the resumption of Chinese rights to Hong Kong in 1997, and with his May 1989 success in adding the normalization of Party and State relations with the USSR to his establishment of normal relations with the USA. He has become an elder statesman who has retired from his positions in the Party Politburo and the Military Affairs Commission (both State and Party), but he can still influence the handling of the problems of relations with Taiwan, the USSR, and the USA.

The 1989 May-June crisis brought a new General-Secretary, Jiang Zemin, to lead the Party. Like his new Politburo Standing Committee colleague, Li Ruihuan, he is a former Mayor. These urban leaders are from Shanghai and Tianjin respectively. The logic of political events that must be considered in following the planning process in China (Fincher, 1989c) still pits the holder of the office of Party General-Secretary against the State Premier, as in 1988 and early 1989.

During and after the 15–17 August 1988 Beidaihe meeting of the Politburo of the Central Committee chaired by Party Leader Zhao Ziyang there was talk of 'reform plans for the 1989–93 period'. In an interview with the president of Japan's Kyodo News Service, Zhao Ziyang referred to a 'five-year reform plan' (*Beijing Review*, 1988, 31(35), p. 5). After a meeting on 30 August chaired by State Premier Li Peng, State Council releases referred to a Politburo 'plan' for wage and price reforms even while suggesting that it merely had a 'target' of allowing prices of 'most goods to be regulated by the market . . . within about the next five years' (*Beijing Review*, 1988, 31(37), p. 5).

Price and wage reforms are both designed to increase enterprise efficiency, and particularly the efficiency of state-owned enterprises, most of which are urban. There has never been much public debate about wage reforms. In State Council releases in 1988 the discussion of wages was bracketed with discussions about 'key commodities', but it remains politically adventurous to theorize about policies which treat labour as a commodity. All versions of the price-wage reform plans suggest that, even if labour is considered to be a commodity, it will remain a 'key' or state controlled one through at least the next five-year plan despite the increasing use of both full-time and part-time 'contract' labour throughout the country.

Zhao Ziyang's calls for 'structural' reforms of the economy came in combination with a steady emphasis after late 1987 on what were termed 'coastal area development strategies' (*Beijing Review*, 1988, 31(6), pp. 14–19; Yue, 1988). As discussed later, Coastal China has become an important — perhaps *the* important — issue in current economic and social planning. However, it is more than a policy construct: it has long been an important entity of East Asian, Pacific, and world history, and this is what justifies the use of the word 'renaissance' to describe contemporary developments there.

Coastal China as an Historical and Developmental Region

Coastal China is marked primarily by those points and regions where important rivers approach or reach the sea. The Zhujiang (Pearl) River city of Guangzhou and the Changjiang (Yangtze) River city of Shanghai are the most important examples: these two delta areas have played a key role in Chinese history for a millenium or more, along with some coastal areas in the south-east and north-east and their hinterlands. Southern Fujian is one of the most important of these latter areas. Located about midway between the Zhujiang and Changjiang Deltas and opposite Taiwan, it had settlements of great historical importance in Tang (618–907) and Song (960–1279) times. The southern Fujian city of Quanzhou was the eastern terminus of the great sea routes which were based in the West on Venice, 'the hinge of Europe'.

For over a thousand years, Coastal China has also had a very important inland south-north trading zone along the Grand Canal — running from the Changjiang Delta cities and densely developed rural and 'sub-urban' areas south of the Changjiang north to Beijing (see Chapter 4). The trade in the Grand Canal zone was not matched along any inland north-south axis south of the Changjiang River, but there was important long-range South China trade on the overland route running through the corridor from the Changjiang River southward through the passes of Jiangxi leading to north-eastern Guangdong and on to both neighbouring southern Fujian and to central Guangdong. Moreover, despite the lesser importance in South China of inland south-north trade not far from the coast, wind patterns made coastal sea trade there more important than that in North China. Furthermore, the latter was eclipsed by South China in world trade patterns because the exploration of the oceans by early modern sailing vessels made camel caravans and the inland Eurasian Silk Road unprofitable. Smaller Arab ships could not achieve similar levels of profitability in trade along coasts and islands between Venice and Quanzhou (McNeill, 1987).

Apart from centuries of both inland and sea-borne trade in the broad south-north region of Eastern or 'Coastal China', North Pacific contacts between China and Japan continued into early modern times, before being constrained by later Ming Chinese (1368–1644) and Tokugawa Japanese (1600–1868) efforts strictly to control, if not completely eliminate, non-official commerce and contacts as part of their military strategy. These policies were to some extent the product of, and certainly were prolonged by, East Asian military competition for control of mainland North-east Asia, including Korea.

Nineteenth-century steamships from Atlantic ocean nations facilitated imperialistic incursions and related military invasions, and overcame state policies unfavourable to trade. This led to the complete opening of the North China coast around Tianjin near the mouth of the Huanghe (Yellow) River. Steamships also 'opened' coastal routes and ports around the Shandong and the Liaodong Peninsulas. The commercial operations of steamships in the south followed very old coastal routes and those leading far up the Zhujiang and Changjiang. In the north, to some extent they transferred to the coast, and partly replaced, long-standing inland patterns of economic activity. The agricultural lands on or near both north and south coasts were among the richest, the most elaborately developed, and the most highly commercialized. By the late nineteenth and early twentieth centuries, the south coast was coming to the end of a long and fairly continuous period of relatively greater development (Blunden and Elvin, 1983).

For the first millenium or more of its history, navigable rivers kept Coastal China more a part of the inland national economy than of the maritime world economy. However, the much more rapid growth of Western Europe and North America during the nineteenth century made developments in the world economy the controlling element in early twentieth-century China. In the late twentieth century, over-whelmingly rapid external economic growth has again greatly influenced the whole nation through Coastal China.

By reducing the competition from Western Europe, the First World War set off an economic boom which was prolonged for most of Coastal China by a delay in the influence of the world Depression on the Chinese economy. Particularly in the south, the boom after the First World War was extended by, among other things, the diversion of overseas capital from alternative investments in South-east Asian economies disrupted much earlier by the Depression (Lin, Z-Z., 1987). However, the South-North Civil War of 1925 to 1928 and the Central China floods of 1931 emphasized the vulnerability of the inland economy. The Sino-Japanese War (1937–45) then led to the disruption of the external as well as internal economic systems in which Coastal China participated.

The Japanese War combined with the Civil War to force both the Nationalist and Communist parties to emphasize development of inland areas. However, geography and a long history of development and redevelopment had by the mid-twentieth century left nearly all the nation's more productive enterprises in Coastal China, where they had been based in turn on the highly developed late traditional and early modern regional economy and society.

The recovery of Shanghai may have begun even before the end of the Second World War. The post-war resumption of the Civil War to some extent promoted coastal prosperity even though it did so at the cost of inland decline. The Korean War (1950–3) and the First Five-year Plan (1953–8) required the fullest use of China's existing enterprises including those left behind in the north-east by Japan — though not, of course, those of the colonized island province of Taiwan (Duus et al., 1989).

By the late 1950s, old fears of large-scale foreign threats had been fortified by nuclearization of US and USSR forces. The logic of post-1945 threats of war was further reinforced with the logic and policy of class war. These and a particular vision of the nature and role of the peasantry in China's history and future led its rulers to withhold from the coastal zone the investment capital necessary fully to regain or maintain its pre-war status (see Chapter 1). From Liberation to the late 1970s, at least three-fifths of China's investment funds were diverted away from Coastal China to inland and frontier areas under a policy which grew ever stronger (personal interview 1985 with Ma Hong — then President of the Chinese Academy of Social Science) even though most such funds were generated in the coastal zone (see also Chapters 1 and 3).

Despite the natural and historical endowments of Coastal China, Chinese policies of 'self-reliance' and economic 'autarky' turned China inwards during all but brief periods between 1949 and 1979. By the late 1970s the foreign embargo of China organized under US leadership was a thing of the past.

The Chinese policy of 'opening to the outside' adopted in December 1978 followed a decision that national defence did not require continued attempts by the State to interfere with the natural concentration of growth in Coastal China. It also ended discrimination against the extensive commercial and service enterprises located there, which were regarded by definition as 'non-productive', 'exploitative', or 'parasitical'. It was accepted that this zone has some natural and historical advantages and the enterprises or entrepreneurial population located there should not be penalized. Since 1979 every effort has been made to encourage self-sustaining growth wherever it appears: this allowed growth in the agricultural and then in commercial and service sectors. Growth in these sectors was followed by the development of unsubsidized or only partially subsidized (and generally smaller scale) 'collective' enterprises. Formerly prohibited 'individual' enterprises also revived.

Contemporary Renaissance

These policies have led to the contemporary renaissance of Coastal China — a renaissance which has taken social and political as well as economic forms. The most publicized examples have been the four Special Economic Zones (SEZs) approved in 1979 by the Party and the State Council (see Chapter 1). These SEZs (*jingji tequ*) were created and have deliberately been used as 'buffer zones' between mainland China on the one side and Hong Kong, Macao, and Taiwan on the other. They are therefore examples of positive discrimination in favour of Coastal China just as interior areas were previously the beneficiaries of discrimination for different if not, indeed, opposite political reasons. Though many enterprises have not yet become self-sustaining, by and large the overall losses of these Zones have been made up from Hong Kong and Overseas Chinese investment.

The SEZs have also served as enclaves where reforms could continue during those periods of the last decade when overall structural reform and reform in other localities has been slowed for political reasons. At such times they have provided one form of 'bird cage capitalism', as it and the dual-track pricing system (whereby the planned production quota of a commodity is subject to a fixed price while above-quota production is subject to market prices) have sometimes been termed in internal Chinese policy debates. Functioning as latter day 'base areas' of a new economic order, the SEZs have well served their internal and external political and economic functions.

When Hainan Island was opened to foreign investment in April 1984, the government also announced that a new type of technological development zone (*jishu kaifa qu*) was to be created for fourteen coastal cities to be opened up for foreign investment (Figure 1.2). By 1989 the administrative units covered by the special 'open' policy numbered 284, embraced a population of 160 million and an area of 320,000 km² (*Beijing Review*, 1988, 31(12), p. 5). Foreign investment in Coastal China is stimulated by the fact that almost all the fifty million or so people of Chinese descent who live outside the mainland come from the coastal region.

Some fifty or so science and technology centres have been proposed to service inland cities as well as the open coastal areas. There is no particular reason for national policy to discriminate against facilities which have taken root in the Far West despite the great initial costs of their 'artificial' creation as part of discrimination against coastal sites under earlier policies. In one or two cases, such as the commercialization of Far North-west military space rocket programmes, inland sites might even number among the handful of high-technology zones that mark China's participation in space satellite launches and the information revolution (Wei, 1988).

From the Thirteenth Party Congress of September 1987 into the summer of 1988, the central documents on the development of Coastal China drew on the idea of 'international large-scale circulation' which had been proposed in a paper by a young researcher in the Economic Planning Research Institute of the State Planning Commission and had figured importantly in an internal conference on development in September 1987. As publicized in the *Guangming Daily* (30 December 1987) and the *Economic Daily* (5 January 1988), the proposal called for the use of skilled labour in a coastal population of perhaps 200 million to make high-quality labour-intensive commodities for international markets. The raw materials would, it was suggested, come from inland as well as coastal areas but the development of external markets would mean that those products sold overseas would not compete so fiercely with those made near inland markets (Xu, G., 1988).

Since much of the labour force in the coastal area has been tied to the land by the household registration system, an essential part of the proposal was the wide circulation of market information as well as technology throughout the entire production area. These and similar ideas were promoted by Premier Zhao Ziyang in an article following a Politburo meeting he chaired on 6 February 1988; at a Beijing working conference on coastal development during 4–8 March; and at the second plenary session of the Party's Thirteenth Central Committee on 15 March (*Inside China Mainland*, 1988, 10(7), pp. 33–4; *Beijing Review*, 1988, 31(6), pp. 14–19; 31(12), p. 5; Geng, 1988).

The renaissance of Coastal China is apparent from the fact that the fourteen established open cities account for about 25 per cent of China's recent industrial output and 40 per cent of its exports during 1989. Productivity in them is also about two-thirds higher than the national average. Well-known successes in 'rural' counties of the coast area include Wuxi near Shanghai (Jing, 1988) and Sheyang near Nanjing (Dai, 1988b). The former is one of the lower Changjiang Delta commercial centres that flourished prior to the Second World War and before collectivization and which is now enjoying a new renaissance. There is further evidence about the contemporary success of pre-war commercial centres further south such as Dongguan, Wenzhou, and Sunan.

Urban and Rural Land Rights and Land Markets

Throughout China the most successful rural enterprises have remained those near large cities supplying goods and services to urban establishments and consumers. This is more true than ever with the tightening of the economy in late 1989 after the crisis of June 1989. Their achievement is thus limited by constraints on the development of firms in nearby cities which they supply directly, or the firms anywhere which they supply indirectly through the markets of nearby cities (*China Daily*, 6 April 1987, p. 4).

The central problems of economic reform in China lie with the state-owned firms. Almost by definition these are the larger, mainly urban, enterprises which in 1988 accounted for 57 per cent of China's industrial output value (Li, C., 1989, p. 20). Too many are 'losing' enterprises whose poor-quality goods cannot be sold. Their operation is subsidized by transfers of revenues from self-sustaining, profit-making, state-owned firms whose goods sell well. None the less, these losing firms exert a strong influence on regional administrative and political leaders who must intervene in distribution of materials and capital in short supply which state firms stockpile or hoard. Non-circulating labour and land, as well as industrial commodities in the cities in which the vast majority of state enterprises are found, are monopolized and hoarded.

Price and wage reforms are designed to assist efficient enterprises of all types, and to penalize even state-owned enterprises when they consistently fail to become self-sustaining. By the end of 1987, some seventy-two of China's 381 cities had been selected for measures penalizing state-owned enterprises that were failing (Ge, 1988). However, these constraints on general price and wage reforms direct attention to the need also for reforms affecting land use and land exchange in urban areas as well as to the reforms of the land system already undertaken in rural areas.

Late 1984 brought a critical stage in the relationship between economic reform in rural and urban China. This was the period of negotiations of the extension for fifteen years from January 1985 of the term of contracts that gave individual households the 'responsibility' for cultivating up to 95 per cent of the land within the domain of China's innumerable natural villages. These village settlements were locked in large artificial, administrative units called 'communes' before 1979. The rural reforms of 1979–84 almost exactly reversed the previous ratio which allowed only 5 per cent of arable land to be reserved for private cultivated plots and reserved 95 per cent for collectively cultivated fields.

Individual households have always had exclusive rights to, as well as responsibility for, particular private plots. However, the rights to these plots and to the land on which family houses were built were qualifications on the formal ownership by the national state of all land since the reforms of the 1948–52 Liberation period. From about 1957 to 1979 land was administered for the national state by local communes into which villages or regroupings of villages were collected as 'production brigades'. Collectivized land was cultivated by household members as participants in 'production teams' within each 'brigade'.

Most communes were in fact conterminous with what are once again called townships (xiang). Nearly 60,000 townships are now administrative centres under the authority of more than 2,000 counties with capitals in their own 'county cities' (xian cheng). Township authorities are no longer responsible for the cultivation of the land. The rural reforms which dismantled the commune system between 1978 and 1985 introduced 'production responsibility' contracts accompanied by short-term or in some cases long-term *ad hoc* or oral 'contracts' governing related household rights to the use of agricultural land. Since 1 January 1985 the production responsibilities and rights of members of individual households have been governed by formal written contracts renewable from 1 January 2000 or, in some cases, later.

In October 1984, while long-term contractual rights to cultivated land were being returned to rural households, Zhao Ziyang issued a programme for urban reforms that had been considered by the Party Central Committee a few weeks earlier. This was drawn up at the same time as the conclusion of an agreement between China and the UK for the resumption in 1997 of the sovereign rights of the People's Republic to the territory of Hong Kong.

Arguably, Hong Kong is the city which is commercially and financially most significant for the Chinese economy: it is an important industrial city and one of the financial capitals of the world. During the reversion negotiations, it became essential for the PRC to display its determination and ability to bring its own cities closer to the development standards set by Hong Kong. This was dramatized for urban planners by the 1984 visits of the principal representative of the People's Republic in Hong Kong to the one area — Kowloon's former walled city — not covered by the Treaties on which the UK based its rights in Hong Kong, Kowloon, and the New Territories. China's representative called for urban renewal of the area, which grew over a century into a single, dense, high-rise agglomeration of adroitly constructed but run-down accommodation.

Land rights are a critical issue in China's urban reforms because of problems with the reallocation of land for industrial, transport, commercial, and residential use. Industrial and transport issues were well covered in the Seventh Five-year Plan (1986–90). However, the problems of commercial and residential land use proved too hard to incorporate in that Plan and they were thus deferred for consideration in the Eighth Five-year Plan (1991–6) (personal interviews, May 1986 and April 1987, Chinese Academy of Social Science).

It has remained relatively less difficult to allocate land for job-creating industrial areas and for the short-distance urban-rural transport improvements which everyone is demanding. As long as the reallocations involve new jobs and homes for present occupants, this is true even when the land has previously been under the kind of cultivation characteristic of the Chinese version of intensive East Asian agriculture. This was particularly the case when, as was happening by 1984, a new system of long-term land-use contracts was being introduced for agricultural households, which included even those cultivating agricultural land within recognized central urban administrative districts (*shi/zhen/cheng*). The reallocation of land already in use for commercial and residential purposes is, however, an entirely different question, even where it is designated as part of rural administrative areas (*xian*).

During the Seventh Five-year Plan, the large-scale approach to land-use problems has been the domain of administrative entities such as the Central Land Planning Office which in 1986 assumed responsibility for identifying key areas or regions for comprehensive development during the rest of the century (*China Daily*, 9 January 1987). The land-use problem in both urban and rural China has been essentially a micro-economic and micro-social one, as can be appreciated from the political sensitivities involved in the postponement under the Seventh Five-year Plan of all but a few 'experiments' in establishing a 'market' for the exchange of rights to land or to land use.

Even after 1984, the principal examples of land transactions recognizing rights to residential and in some cases commercial properties have been the domain of the Overseas Chinese Commission and its provincial and local branches.

There have always been some private houses or apartments newly constructed exclusively for sale to Hong Kong or Overseas Chinese and available for use by their local relatives. Immediately after the Cultural Revolution, the policy of 'reversing verdicts' against Cultural Revolution victims included the restoration to Overseas Chinese of buildings in older residential and even mixed residential and commercial quarters. Most of this property had been seized in rural areas during land reform, and in urban areas during collectivization, invaded by squatters, or seized by local authorities during the Cultural Revolution.

Initially, the policy of restitution of real estate was implemented very slowly, but was extended as local authorities became able to provide space for displaced Cultural Revolution squatters in newly constructed residential blocks. Restitution increased as the deterioration of particular older properties required an infusion of outside capital to prevent their collapse.

More recently, Overseas Chinese resumptions of property for restoration and upgrading were followed by the popularization of proposals to grant property rights to foreign as well as Overseas or Hong Kong Chinese investors in industrial and technological development zones. By 1987 a central 'Bureau of Real Property Industry Administration' was operating in Beijing in the Ministry of Urban and Rural Construction and the Environment with responsibilities for the development of a general market in real estate (Lin, Z-Q., 1987).

State Council provisions 'for the encouragement of investment and development in Hainan Island', promulgated on 4 May 1988, indicated that 'the land-use right of all state-owned land [there] is open to paid-transfer . . . However, the maximum tenure is 70 years and is subject to extension upon approval if necessary' (*Beijing Review*, 1988 (31)36, p. 26). In other words, the provision covers up to the middle of the twenty-first century, the period specified in recent years as that for the continuation of the 'one country, two systems' policy adopted towards Hong Kong's future evolution. More recently the mid-twenty-first century has also been specified as the minimum period to be allotted to the 'primary stage of socialism' in which China now finds itself.

The announcement about Hainan Island came at almost the same time that the principal representative of Beijing in Hong Kong was explaining the introduction of fifty-year terms for land rights under current reforms. Elsewhere in Coastal China, 'property deeds' to urban houses were again accepted from their owners as security for loans extended by 'pawnshops' reopened for business for the first time since their function was discontinued during the collectivization of urban enterprises in 1957 (*Beijing Review*, 1988, 31(36), p. 28). Despite local setbacks in mid-1989, the policy of freer exchange and sale of real property and property usage rights has been reaffirmed in late 1989 and 1990.

Even during the most radical phases of collectivization, houses remained the possession of rural households which occupied them. During the Thirteenth Party Congress in September 1987, discussions were held about the possibility of allowing peasants to sell rights to land if they leave for work and residence elsewhere (*Shanghai World Economic Journal*, 27 October 1987, p. 28). Meanwhile, numerous methods have been devised for dealing in individual cases with the cultivation of land as well as the use of residences in rural areas.

There are many precedents in China for the inventive use of

opportunities for the exchange of urban land. In China, as elsewhere, urban land transactions and the use of space over and under such land have long been very complex. Population densities have made the same true for rural land. High population densities, a high level of commercialization and of the circulation of population as well as of agricultural and other commodities have characterized the history even of 'remote' inland rural areas such as central and northern Shaanxi Province (the historical complexities of property rights in real estate in coastal China are discussed in Fincher, 1978).

Housing and Constraints on Population Movements

When the 1930s Depression began to affect China, its impact was mixed with, or interrupted by, the greater impact of the Japanese invasion in 1937. The post-war period and the early years of the People's Republic afforded only sporadic opportunities for the revival of Coastal China's economy which has had to wait for the changed international and domestic climate of the post-Mao decade to begin its contemporary renaissance.

In pre-war China, the flexibility of the land system facilitated the physical rebuilding of central areas of many of the coastal cities. The post-First World War Venetian style architecture of Quanzhou in central Fujian still provides one of the most dramatic examples of such rebuilding even though the city was declining relative to other coastal cities. Today, Tianjin (notwithstanding the 1976 earthquake) and Shanghai are well known for the buildings which have survived as examples of longer lasting prosperity in pre-war Coastal China. Of the largest coastal Chinese cities, only Hong Kong has been rebuilt since the 1950s in such a way as to eradicate traces of the pre-war prosperity of Coastal China (including the special case of Kowloon's walled city). The participation of domestic and Overseas Chinese capital in the coastal boom and the related pre-war rebuilding of the mixed commercial and residential central urban structures, however, is still best observed elsewhere, such as the central streets of Guangzhou, Shantou, Xiamen, and Ningbo, and in inland cities like Jinan and Gaoyang.

There is already architectural evidence of the contemporary renaissance of Coastal China but this must be sought primarily in 'rural counties' where whole villages have recently been rebuilt, sometimes *in situ*, one house at a time and sometimes by building 'second' houses (one at a time) in an adjacent group until the old village becomes an annexe of the new one (fieldwork interviews conducted during 1987).

On China's far south-eastern coast, evidence of increased prosperity includes a major boom in residential construction in such 'rural counties' as Chao'an, Jieyang, and Tong'an. There and elsewhere along the coast the boom reflects increases in household income from the direct earnings of their members. Some of this is due to rising levels of agricultural productivity, including such services as transport of agricultural produce, and activities like stonemasonry and carpentry for which the housing boom has created a demand. There are also traditional household handicrafts, such as weaving baskets or mats from straw and making pottery. All these economic activities are usually classified as 'sidelines' to 'agricultural' activity, as is piece-work on garments for urban enterprises.

Even more of the increased household income is due, however, to the involvement of household members in 'non-agricultural' activity (see also Chapter 4). Wherever they work or live, it has become very difficult to identify China's peasants by their economic activity because so many are completely, or almost completely, occupied in tasks which make them 'peasants who are not like peasants' (*China Daily*, 18 June 1988). Many of these new opportunities for an increase in household income being spent on residential construction are accounted for in official figures by the growth of rural output. In 1986, agriculture accounted for 53 per cent of the total output value of rural China as it was then defined, industry for 32 per cent, building for 8 per cent, commerce and catering for 4 per cent, and transport for 3 per cent (*Beijing Review*, 1987, 30(42), p. 23). By 1988, non-agricultural production accounted for over half the total production of all rural areas.

In the Changjiang Delta area is the important 'rural' county connected with Wuxi City, north-west of Shanghai. Only 5.5 per cent of the 'rural' product of this county comes from agriculture or sidelines to it. Although overall agricultural product remained fairly constant during the 1978–87 period, the labour force involved declined to about one-third. Township and village-run rural industry has absorbed the remainder along with the new additions to the total labour force. By 1988, only 22 per cent of the labour force of 548,000 worked in agriculture, while four times as many were employed in the 5,000-odd county, township, and village enterprises. Agricultural output (411 million yuan) and the size of the grain crop (489,000 tonnes) remained about the same as before but the value of the county's rural industrial product increased during the decade from 478 million to 7,067 million yuan (Jing, 1988).

Unlike the pre-war experience, the recent building boom in rural counties of Coastal China is only marginally affected by direct overseas remittances. To an increasing extent, however, it involves *de facto* remittances from large cities to which, or through which, rural household members go to earn their income. The rural housing boom thus adds to the evidence that, judged by *how* Chinese use their time, the population is almost certainly already predominantly urban. The population may soon also be urban by definitions of *where* they use most of their time.

The elasticity of the concept of 'sideline' activities and production in agriculture suggests the difficulty of making economic distinctions between rural and urban China, a problem that was already familiar to scholars and officials in pre-war years. The first result of the policy of promoting rural industry during the past decade has been to legitimize many activities that were treated as examples of crime or corruption but which continued despite attacks on 'rich peasants', 'landlords', and 'bad elements' who by definition lived from such 'exploitative' activities before the post-war land reform and the post-1956 collectivization drives. The post-1957 policies in both rural and urban China stifled as much commerce and the service sector as they collectivized. However, the post-1977 changes involved the surfacing of much underground activity while also allowing its now well-recorded natural increase. Official interest in the promotion of rural industry has thus done much to clarify the realities of economic life in the Chinese countryside even before the reforms of the late 1970s. Since 1977–8 many of the cadres who formerly ran communes from their township headquarters have been responsible for encouraging what has only gradually come to be called 'rural industry' in small 'towns and "county" cities'.

Activities in the service sector are notoriously difficult to define and value in both developed and developing economies, but this problem is particularly complicated in China because it is still overcoming decades of determined efforts to minimize the importance of 'non-productive' or 'exploitative' economic activities while, at the same time, aspiring to participate in the 'information revolution'.

By the late 1980s the streets of Shanghai and other large cities of Coastal China were jammed day and night with pedestrian and vehicular traffic which is evidence of the contemporary renaissance of this zone. Many sophisticated attempts have been made to estimate the number of people not resident in Shanghai who circulate through the city while engaged in such activities, and to determine the localities from whence they come (e.g. Floating Population Research Group Fudan University, 1987; see also Appendix 1). However, the discussion of their activities still depends on high quality but very impressionistic journalism and imaginative literature. In late 1988 the Shanghai Public Security Bureau gave credence to impressionistic reports of the increase in the floating population by raising its estimate to 1.7 million, almost double previous figures.

The household registration and identity system administered by the Public Security Bureau still forces most members of the Chinese population strictly to limit the amount of time they can spend in large cities despite efforts at reform begun in 1984 (Fincher, forthcoming). The system has always done this directly by making those who do not hold local residential credentials liable to fines or even imprisonment if they 'overstay' — operating, in other words, like an internal passport system. Until the late 1970s, the system controlled population movements indirectly by its link with the rationing system.

Without the proper registration papers to which only *de jure* 'urban residents' were entitled, it was impossible to buy scarce rationed grain and other staples. It might have been possible to leave one's home and to stay elsewhere by avoiding contact with the police but it was very difficult to get enough to eat without ration coupons granted only to holders of local registration credentials. During the late 1970s, the opening of free markets and the increases in agricultural production made finding food a minor matter for any with sufficient funds to pay premium prices for grain or to buy coupons from those who did not need to buy it from state stores. Despite the decreasing effectiveness of police fines on those who overstay, the household registration system still imposes a severe indirect restraint on population movement by its effect on housing. This is because over 70 per cent of housing is controlled by work units and barely 20 per cent by local governments. Since household registration is tied to local employment, and vice versa, the codification of the registration system in 1957 confirmed the monopoly of housing supplies by urban work units (personal interview, Chinese Academy of Social Sciences, 1987).

Used in combination with efforts to develop 'small and medium cities' the internal passport system and the work unit monopoly of housing construction and allocation together explain why the efforts to distribute urbanization more evenly throughout the country have been only partially successful. However, these policies involve considerable costs. One is the overburdening of the transport system, which led by 1987 to an increase in the number of dramatic road and waterway accidents. Commercial travellers and their commodities crowd the transport system in large part because of the obstacles they face in establishing more regular means of supplying their operations. Without even the formal right to stay very long in the cities, not to speak of the difficulties in finding housing or commercial premises, they must make very frequent use of whatever vehicles are available. This is one reason for the extraordinary explosion of legal and semi-legal imports of vehicles in 1985 when 200,000 cars, minibuses, and vans were imported to meet the needs of business and taxi companies (*Beijing Review*, 1987, 30(35), p. 27) and for the expansion of China's own motor vehicle industry.

Another cost of concentrating urbanization in 'small and medium' cities is the fuelling of the rural construction industry by the huge investment there of earnings from commerce and the urban service sector. In many coastal cities of China, most regular employees even of state-owned enterprises have second jobs. Cadres operate as middlemen for 'commission' that could make them liable for prosecution for accepting bribes, but which might also be essential to the success of other enterprises; technicians accept contract consultancies on the side which can earn them several times their normal salaries but which they are allowed to continue as long as they share their earnings with their official employing enterprise; workers with local residence rights do odd jobs out of hours for other residents or become hawkers or small-scale merchants; and workers from 'rural counties' employed on a contract basis earn additional income from odd jobs and hawking even while living temporarily in makeshift shelters (*China Daily*, 31 August 1987, p. 27).

Under the present household registration system, those without urban residence rights have no place to invest their earnings except in their 'rural' home counties. At the same time, the stagnation of construction by urban work units forces increasing numbers of urban residents to rent or buy houses in 'rural' areas even if this means commuting long distances on inadequate transport systems.

Urbanization and the Rural Bias in Planning

Not least among the costs stemming from the household registration system is the distortion it introduces into data about the extent of urbanization in China. There is much impressionistic information on

the movements and activities of the country's floating population
(*liumin*) which can be supplemented by that on the extent of
residential construction in the countryside and the expansion of market
stall areas in cities. Both impressionistic and indirect evidence can
also be combined with reliable statistical evidence on more easily
measurable economic activities and residence patterns.

The three types of evidence, in combination, make it plausible to
estimate China's present urbanization rate as well over 40 per cent. At
the time of the 1982 census, the official figure for China's urban
population remained below 21 per cent (Table A1.1). Zhao Ziyang's
1984 announcement of China's new programme for urban reform was
followed by an expansion of the administrative boundaries of many
cities to include suburban counties surrounding central urban districts
(and other definitional changes discussed in Appendix 1). Mainly for
these reasons, the urban population reported by the State Statistical
Bureau for year-end 1985 exceeded 36.6 per cent and for year-end
1987 it was 46.6 per cent (Fincher, 1989b). If it were to include populations even of 'township' towns of 2,500 with a substantial number
of people who do no agricultural work, the figure could exceed 70 per
cent (*People's Daily*, 9 August 1988; Fincher, forthcoming).

China has been known through most of the twentieth century for its
peasantry and its peasant revolution; understandably, therefore, it has
not been easy for many Chinese, and some foreign observers, to accept
the predominantly urban character of the late twentieth-century
Chinese population. Along with the downward fluctuations in annual
grain production figures, and double-digit inflation, the rise in China's
urbanization rate has greatly alarmed many important political figures.
These mainly come from a group which also expressed alarm about
the strength of 'bourgeois' tendencies in the arts and ideology in the
campaigns of 1983, 1987, and 1989 against 'bourgeois tendencies'.
However, some prominent proponents of greater intellectual and
political freedom and democracy have also expressed their scepticism
about China's rapid urbanization (Selden, 1988). In China,
conservatives and liberals make a tacit alliance on issues such as the
dangers of 'over-urbanization', the evils of which have increased
pressure on China's statisticians to revise their reports of rapid
urbanization (*People's Daily*, 18 August 1988).

Current patterns of East Asian development and longer-run Chinese
history suggest, however, that the preponderantly urban character of
late twentieth-century China should not appear surprising, whether or
not it is thought to be alarming. Marco Polo identified China as the

world's most urban society in the thirteenth century. Japanese 'Marco Polos' of the 1910s, like Naito Kanan, identified early twentieth-century China as again a leader in urban development. In the post-First World War period, such developments influenced the revolutionary strategies of founders of the Chinese Communist Party like Chen Duxiu, and Comintern supporters like Karl Radek. By the standards of the People's Republic's own programme for coastal development, nearly a quarter of the Chinese population has a belated opportunity to take what the history of East Asia after the First World War suggested to be its natural place in the general development of this region. However, since the Second World War China has been lagging. Even as propounded before the mid-1989 fall from power of General-Secretary Zhao Ziyang, the proposals for 'international large-scale circulation' of commodities in Coastal China appear to remain in part a new effort to postpone, if not indefinitely prevent, the growth of large cities (*Inside China Mainland*, 1988, 10(8), pp. 9–13).

Questions arise as to whether the PRC's urban development policies have been at odds with East Asian history. Thus, it is unclear whether the large-scale movement of commodities will eventuate without the much freer circulation of the labour force in ways likely to increase the size of China's large cities: for example, the circulation of technological and market information — even through the best computer networks — dictates the rapidly increasing movement of technicians, designers, market specialists, managers, and skilled workers who need and use such information. It is also uncertain to what extent the development of international markets is incidental to the emergence of 'large-scale', concentrated domestic markets in the leading metropolises of Japan, Korea, and Taiwan, and how long China can stand apart from trends — perhaps best reflected in the history of Hong Kong — without great cost to its own development policies.

Shanghai, for example, must wait before it can plan in open fashion for the larger future with which it has already been confronted by the acknowledged *de facto* circulation of a huge population of Chinese still treated formally as outsiders. Shanghai City Proper (see Chapter 8) contained just over 6,000,000 *de jure* residents at the 1982 census, and a similar number were located in the remainder of the Municipality. Yet, without increases of *de jure* in-migration beyond the present extremely low levels, the City Proper population by the year 2000 is unlikely to increase even by 10 per cent — accepting the probability that the current fertility rate of about 1.3 will decline even further as the population ages.

Shanghai is the centre of a four-province delta that accounts for about one-third of the nation's GNP. Coastal China's development is likely, if anything, to increase the relative economic importance of the city. The floating population of people registered as residents in places other than Shanghai in 1988 was already nearly one-third the number of Shanghai's registered urban central district residents. Such floating populations are usually composed of younger, predominantly male, working-age people.

A politic approach to the problem created by Shanghai's current rural-urban immigration crisis would be to calculate the economic costs of present policies in terms of the loss of rural land to residential construction. It has been estimated that the expansion of China's urban areas between 1982 and 1984 consumed nearly 500,000 km² of rural land, nearly 90 per cent of which was used for relatively low density construction common to the towns and cities with populations from 2,500 to 250,000 (fieldwork interviews conducted during 1987). Even more land has been absorbed by village construction fuelled by 'remittances' carried back from their city activities by members of 'rural' households.

Arguably, China can well afford such losses of rural land, as long as agricultural productivity continues to rise rapidly. China might therefore do well to resign herself to the fact that it is economically more rational to concentrate on industrial crops and certain industrial products and to import more food grains. In any event, the true extent of China's 'diminishing' supply of arable land is unclear. Remote sensing (satellite) data revealed to Chinese planners nearly a decade ago that official figures for arable land had to be expanded by more than 20 per cent to correct distortions that had accumulated over two decades or more. Local productivity figures were routinely exaggerated under the commune system. This was done by minimizing the size of cultivated areas and concealing increases in the size of cultivated areas through reclamation. Figures provided to higher-level grain procurement authorities from the teams or brigades became the basis of the huge under-reporting of the cultivated area in national aggregates. In 1982 floods due to over-cultivation of land in upper Changjiang watersheds made this clear well beyond those circles of the nation's leaders who had been reading unpublished 1981 investigations of the danger by Chinese journalists.

It can also be argued that the bias in favour of dispersal of urban growth explains much of the huge trade deficit caused by the rapid expansion of imports in 1985. The imported vehicles which accounted for some of these deficits were required to cope with the very vehicle shortage that policies of resistance to large city growth had helped to create.

The social costs are no less important than the economic ones of the continuing rural bias of urban planning which distorts the social as well as economic development of a country that enjoyed an urbanization rate probably in excess of 20 per cent as early as the thirteenth century; which subsequently experienced large-scale de-urbanization of light industrial production through complicated out-putting systems that depended on the free circulation of much of the population; and which none the less went through new periods of re-urbanization. As already suggested, the experience of urbanization in the early post-First World War years may have raised urbanization back to levels of the Song Dynasty as they stood at the time of Marco Polo's visit (1271–95). Subsequent de-urbanization resulted from South-North Civil War in the 1920s; the full-scale invasion of China by Japan in the 1930s; and the anti-urban bias of defence-orientated policies of the 1957–77 period of the Great Leap Forward and Cultural Revolution. Urbanization resumed in the mid-1970s.

China's twentieth-century experiences of de-urbanization led to a revolutionary tradition which has made a vice of China's long pre-modern and modern experience of urban development. The costs as well as the victories of that tradition of peasant revolution have been very high. The forced collectivizations of Stalin's First Five-year Plan reflected an urban bias. The costs could be justified, if at all, only as a necessary prelude to creating an urban workforce in a country still suffering from an endemic labour shortage. Mao Zedong's urban and rural collectivization policies of 1957 reflected a rural bias that had evolved during the decades of civil war and national war that began in the mid-1920s. Like Stalin's urban bias, Mao Zedong's rural bias could be justified, if at all, only as having been necessary then, as previously, both for national survival and for the completion of an unfinished civil war that kept China divided.

The costs of Stalin's urban bias in formulating his First Five-year Plan no longer appear necessary to Soviet citizens, and the costs of Mao Zedong's rural bias during the formulation of his own 1956–67 development plan appear unnecessary to many Chinese. Yet this latter bias still persists. Its problems are not easy to address from the perspective of long-standing foreign traditions of urban planning which resist the growth of large cities. In their cost-benefit analyses of the possibility of major growth of China's ten or twenty largest cities,

Chinese or foreign urban planners would be mistaken not to assume that the social costs of the continuing rural bias may be fully equal to the even more readily calculated economic ones. After the popular pro-democracy demonstrations in urban China and the Tiananmen Incident of June 1989, the political costs of rural bias are at least as clear as the economic and social ones.

3 Contemporary Spatial Issues

LI WEN-YAN

SPATIAL development in the People's Republic of China (PRC), the world's largest developing country, has always been a challenging problem. It is determined by several basic features. China, covering 9.6 million km², includes not only fertile plains, basins, and river valleys favourable to agriculture but also large tracts of desert, high altitude plateaux, and precipitous mountain areas unsuitable for human settlement. Because of its 1,100 million population, the per capita arable land is only about 0.1 ha. Moreover, much of the cultivated land has poor yields. Generally, too, the productivity of China's grasslands tends to be low.

China has a wide variety of mineral resources, including considerable reserves of non-ferrous metals like antimony, tin, and zinc, but some key minerals for establishing a powerful national economy, such as iron ore, copper, and bauxite, are not abundant in proven reserves and most of the deposits are not favourable for processing because of poor quality. With more than 800,000 million tonnes of coal, 10,000 million tonnes of oil, and 370 million kW of exploitable hydroelectric power, China's energy resources are rather rich, but their distribution is very uneven. Coal deposits are mainly located in the north, particularly in Shanxi Province and its neighbouring areas; most oil deposits are in Heilongjiang Province, the Bohai Rim Area and the Xinjiang Uygur Autonomous Region; and 70 per cent of the hydroelectric power is in the south-west. Moreover, the per capita availability of some important mineral resources, land, and water is quite low.

As both consumer and producer of social materials, total population and the labour force are important factors in regional economies. The spatial distribution of China's population is unbalanced as is its inhabitable land. The most densely populated areas and most of the metropolises are situated in coastal provinces and in the Changjiang (Yangtze) Basin and North China Plain. As a result of historical circumstances and geographical conditions, the level of economic development varies greatly between different regions. Table 3.1 shows the situation in selected coastal and interior provinces.

Table 3.1 Basic data for selected provinces (autonomous regions or municipalities), 1987

Province	Population (million)	Gross value of industrial and agricultural output		Total industrial output value		National income per capita 1986 (yuan)	Average income of peasants (yuan) (sample survey)
		total (000 m. yuan)	per capita (yuan)	total (000 m. yuan)	per capita (yuan)		
COASTAL							
Shanghai	12.5	110.6	8,844	106.7	8,534	3,471	1,059
Jiangsu	63.5	197.1	3,105	159.1	2,506	1,064	626
Zhejiang	41.2	107.8	2,618	85.0	2,064	1,042	725
Guangdong	64.5	128.6	1,995	89.6	1,390	897	645
Liaoning	37.8	121.3	3,213	104.4	2,765	1,299	599
INTERIOR							
Sichuan	104.5	111.4	1,066	72.5	694	515	369
Guizhou	30.7	21.9	713	12.7	413	406	342
Shaanxi	30.9	36.2	1,171	25.8	837	531	324
Gansu	21.2	22.5	1,056	16.0	756	570	296
Xinjiang	14.2	19.8	1,383	11.6	814	740	453

Source: State Statistical Bureau (1988a).

The most developed and richest areas with the densest populations are the Changjiang Delta; the Zhujiang (Pearl) River Delta; the Beijing-Tianjin-Tangshan area; the Liaodong Peninsula; the Shandong Peninsula; the Jianghan Plain (Middle Changjiang and Lower Hanjiang Plain); the Sichuan Basin; and the Guanzhong Plain (central part of Shaanxi Province). With the development of export-orientated horticulture, township enterprises, foreign trade, and services the annual per capita income of the rural population can be as much as 2,000 to 3,000 yuan (more than triple the national average) in, for instance, the rural area of the Zhujiang Delta. In contrast, according to a preliminary survey by Jiang (1988) there are six types of poor area, covering 664 counties, mostly in remote hilly areas or loess plateaux (Figure 3.1). These had an aggregate population of 210 million in 1985 of which 92 million earned less than 200 yuan per capita annually, or less than one-tenth of those living in the richest areas. The difference in per capita income between these two categories is much more pronounced than the average between the thirty provinces.

Basic Challenging Problems

Since the founding of the People's Republic in 1949, great achievements in economic development have been made, and obvious changes can be seen in most of the formerly poor rural areas. Even in the vast periphery, several industrial cities have emerged. However, because of the above-mentioned basic geographic features and the long evolution of self-sufficient economies in various areas, differences in development levels between provinces and regions cannot be expected to decrease overnight. In fact, despite the significant improvements that have occurred in the peripheral areas, the gap between the rich and poor provinces has been widening, particularly in recent years.

From the macro-economic point of view, China has been facing four major challenges with respect to spatial development.

How to handle properly the relationship between national economic growth rate and more balanced regional economic development

During the 1950s, due to the weak basis of the economy, its isolation from the international environment, and the reliance on the assistance from and experiences of the USSR, the Chinese government concentrated its limited material and financial resources on 156 major

Figure 3.1 Poverty patterns in China

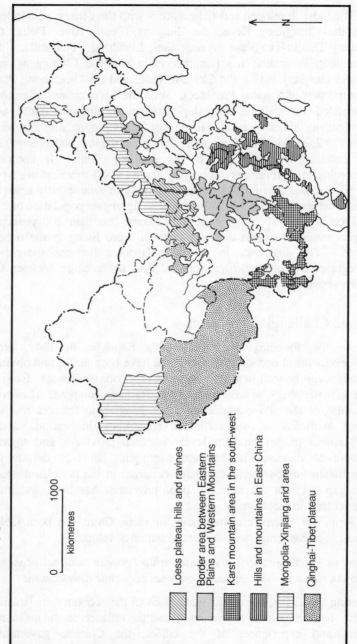

```
                                                    N →

              0        1000
              └─────────┘
              kilometres
```

☒ Loess plateau hills and ravines

☒ Border area between Eastern
  Plains and Western Mountains

☒ Karst mountain area in the south-west

☒ Hills and mountains in East China

☒ Mongolia-Xinjiang arid area

☒ Qinghai-Tibet plateau

Source: Compiled by Jiang, D. (1988), based on 1985 data.

(mainly industrial) projects located predominantly along the Harbin-Dalian railway (with Anshan, Shenyang, Changchun, Jilin, and Harbin being the most important centres); the Beijing-Wuhan railway; and the three westward railways from Beijing to Baotou, Shijiazhuang to Taiyuan, and Zhengzhou to Lanzhou. In south-eastern China and coastal cities elsewhere, economic development was mainly achieved through restructuring the ownership and management system, a strategy that has proved successful.

Between the late 1950s and the early 1970s, however, two strategic decisions made by Chairman Mao Zedong — the Great Leap Forward in 1958–60 and the Third-line Construction from 1964 through the early 1970s (Figure 1.1) — had serious negative effects despite some positive results. Thus the Great Smelting Iron and Steel programme, to be attained by setting up thousands of backyard furnaces, proved to be a complete failure. Neither nationwide high growth rates nor a more even spatial distribution of heavy industry was realized. The Third-line Construction programme did to some extent promote the economic development of the inland provinces but the result was not as large as expected and was gained at the expense of nationwide economic growth.

During the 1980s the same problem remained: maximizing the growth of the national economy and balancing the development of thirty provinces could not be realized simultaneously. Over-emphasis on state assistance to underdeveloped areas to try to help them catch up with the developed ones (as was done during the Third and Fourth Five-year Plans 1965–75) only led to an overall fall in the growth rate of the whole country. It thus seems that during the 1990s much of the national investment should go to the existing core areas with national or subnational significance. In a relatively short period, of course, the gap between advantaged and disadvantaged areas in the level of economic development may to some extent widen but, in the long-term, an accelerating national economic growth rate will create the possibility of narrowing inter-regional differences.

How to handle properly the relationship between the coastal areas and the interior

Soon after the founding of the PRC, under the political and military circumstances which then existed, the coastal areas became the frontline of national defence and the interior was regarded as the strategic hinterland. During the early 1960s, the coastal regions and the northern and western border zones were regarded as 'first-line' areas, and hence heavy industry was not located there. In contrast, priority was given to the interior regions — or 'third-line' areas — which were perceived as being the safest despite their inaccessibility and backward local economies (see Figure 1.1). This decision created hundreds of important industrial enterprises and some strong nodal points in the interior at the expense of the development of coastal provinces.

The interior, as a whole, has abundant mineral resources (especially energy and non-ferrous metals) and also a wealth of agricultural produce such as cotton, tobacco, grain, and animal products. Since the coastal areas lack these it was appropriate to allocate some key projects, including iron and steel works, coal-mines, engineering, and non-ferrous metal works, to Shanxi, Henan, Hubei, and Hunan Provinces. Unfortunately, in the early 1960s, the industrial construction emphasis was shifted westwards which meant that such major industrial centres as Wuhan, Taiyuan, Luoyang, Zhengzhou, and Chang-Zhu-Tan (the Changsha-Zhuzhou-Xiangtan area in Hunan Province) were unable to get enough investment funding from the state to realize a relatively strong industrial system focusing in the long-term on certain specialized sectors.

According to Lu, D. (1987), the gravity line of the national capital investment in 1952 was 530 km inland, as compared with 760 km during the First Five-year Plan (1953–57) and 925 km during the Third and Fourth Five-year Plans (1965–75).

During three decades of construction the interior's share of total industrial output increased from about 30 per cent in the early 1950s to 40 per cent in the mid-1980s, but over-emphasizing the investment share in the interior could not yield corresponding results. Even though during the 1952–78 period, 62 per cent of total capital construction investment was channelled into the interior, the ratio of the per capita gross value of industrial and agricultural output of the interior compared with the coastal area declined from 1:1.5 to 1:1.9.

How to handle the proper relationship between specialization of the regional economy and its comprehensive development

With the development of modern industry and the realization of a complete industrial structure, every region should have leading industries playing a specialized role in the national or subnational economy as well as more or less diversified industrial sectors acting as support or supplementary activities. Generally, the central government pays greater attention to the development in every region of nationally significant specialized sectors while local governments are more concerned with those serving regional development and basic local needs.

When energy or raw material production are the specialized sectors, there are usually contradictions in the orientation of the regional industrial structure, as well as restricted investment opportunities to expand output and shortages of water and power. Questions arise as to whether more efforts and resources should go to the specialized sectors and, if so, what means can be used to get more regional revenue and thus better meet the basic needs of the local people. Sometimes the disputes which occurred between the central ministries and local governments have been so fierce and time-consuming that, in the end, compromises had to be decided by the State Council.

For example, Shanxi Province was asked to produce more coal and electricity for the whole country and North China respectively, but it did not greatly benefit the provincial economy because the price of coal was set very low, most profits gained from power generation and supply went to the state, and many problems relating to coal shipment, water supply, and environmental pollution were created. The provincial government had to spend more to improve the infrastructure for major specialized industries but this frustrated its efforts to develop light industries that could earn it much greater profits and tax revenue. Therefore, as a compromise, the central government decided in the early 1980s to subsidize every tonne of coal shipped out of the province and authorized the provincial government to sell the above-quota coal to clients at free-market prices. This income could be used to equip the local coal-mines, build roads, or develop other industries and services. Even so, the industrial structure of Shanxi Province has not improved as much as expected.

How to deal properly with the relationship between urban and rural areas

According to State Statistical Bureau figures (see Appendix 1), at the end of 1987 about 55 per cent of China's population was living in rural areas. The population of the 381 designated cities was 262 million in 1987 of whom 129 million were non-agricultural. As most secondary and tertiary industry is located in these cities, the urban areas are more developed and the population there leads a better life.

These 381 cities with 12 per cent of China's population, produced 730,000 million yuan-worth of industrial output in 1987, or about 62 per cent of the national total (after excluding the 340,000 million yuan

Figure 3.2 Distribution of industrial centres, 1987

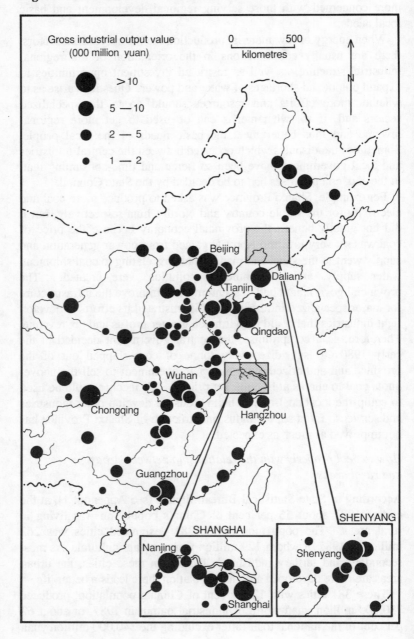

Table 3.2 Shares (per cent) of different size cities in the industry of China, 1987

Item	Total of 381 cities	Cities with urban population of (m.)				
		>2.0	1.0–2.0	0.5–1.0	0.2–0.5	<0.2
Number of cities	381	2.0	4.5	7.9	27.0	58.6
Non-agricultural population (m.)	130	23.6	17.1	16.6	24.1	18.6
Number of industrial enterprises (000)	177	16.6	13.0	12.4	25.4	32.6
Total industry output value (000 m. yuan)	730	28.0	17.0	15.8	23.6	15.6
contributed by:						
large enterprises	267	32.9	20.0	17.8	21.3	8.0
medium enterprises	164	28.8	17.8	16.3	25.1	12.0
small enterprises	299	23.3	13.9	13.6	24.7	24.4
Profits and taxes (m. yuan)	143	30.7	18.0	17.1	21.2	13.0
Number of industrial enterprise workers (m.)	42	22.8	17.5	17.9	25.8	16.0

Source: State Statistical Bureau (1988c).

produced by village-run enterprises) (Figure 3.2). Of this, three-fifths came from large cities with urban populations exceeding 500,000 (Table 3.2). In addition, employment in commerce, government agencies, scientific institutes, and educational and cultural institutions are also mainly concentrated in the cities. In contrast, most of the rural population engaged in agriculture earns a much lower income than urban residents. Thus, in 1987, a sample survey of urban employees' families showed an average annual per capita income of 916 yuan: the equivalent for farmers' families was 463 yuan (*Beijing Review*, 31(10), p. vii). The problem of overcoming the imbalance in living standards between urban and rural areas has always faced China's government.

With the economic reform starting in rural areas after Liberation, both agriculture and industry have witnessed a rapid growth during the past three decades. In particular, township enterprises have developed very rapidly in recent years. Though mostly small in size, these produced an aggregate value of output amounting to as much as 240,000 million yuan. During the 1950–85 period an estimated 79 million peasants moved to the cities and towns to become non-agricultural population (Wang, 1988).

As a result, as many as 50,000 market towns (including 7,500 designated towns) have flourished and expanded. Since town development is fundamentally spontaneous it has brought about many problems, such as environmental pollution and the spread of built-up areas across fertile cultivated land. In contrast, rural areas located far from towns remain economically stagnant and educationally backward because of weak transport links or harsh physical conditions. They lack modern industry.

Regional Development Strategy and Related Problems

After the late 1970s, leaders of the Chinese Communist Party and the central government began to show much concern about the development strategy of the country as a whole and different regions as well. Zhao Ziyang first pointed out that the vast territory of China can be delineated into three zones: the Eastern, the Middle, and the Western (Shao, 1987). This classification reflects the major spatial disparities in social and economic development and constitutes the framework for the strategic allocation of national construction. There are different suggestions and opinions about the exact demarcation of these zones (Wu, C-J., 1986).

Figure 3.3 The three major economic zones as defined by (a) the author, (b) the State Planning Commission, and (c) C-J. Wu

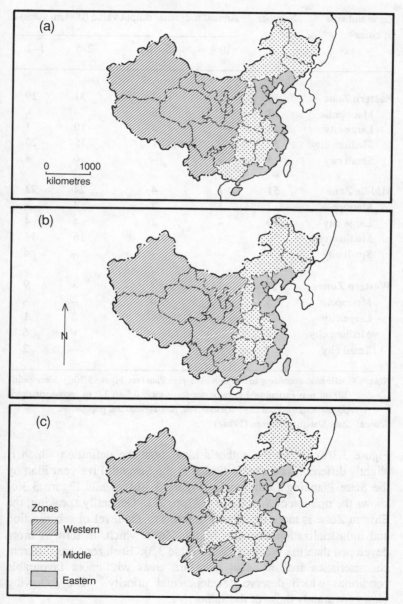

Table 3.3 Distribution of the leading industrial centres between economic zones, 1987

Zone and size of cities[a]	Number	Annual industrial output value (000 m. yuan)			
		>10	5–10	2–5	1–2
Eastern Zone	79	7	12	31	29
Metropolis	13	7	6	–	–
Large city	16	–	5	10	1
Medium city	36	–	1	15	20
Small city	14	–	–	6	8
Middle Zone	51	1	4	24	22
Metropolis	7	1	2	4	–
Large city	10	–	2	4	4
Medium city	30	–	–	16	14
Small city	4	–	–	–	4
Western Zone	17	1	4	3	9
Metropolis	5	1	4	–	–
Large city	3	–	–	2	1
Medium city	7	–	–	1	6
Small city	2	–	–	–	2

Note: [a]Definition according to Seventh Five-year Plan (see Figure 3.3(b)). Metropolis: 1.0 m. non-agricultural population; large city: 0.5 to 1.0 m. non-agricultural population; medium city: 0.2 to 0.5 m. non-agricultural population.

Source: State Statistical Bureau (1988c).

Figure 3.3(a) shows the author's idea about the definition which is slightly different from that indicated in the Seventh Five-year Plan by the State Planning Commission (Figure 3.3(b)), while Figure 3.3(c) shows the opinion of Wu, C-J. (1987, p. 22). Generally speaking, the Eastern Zone is more developed in terms of the level of urbanization and industrialization than the Middle Zone which, in turn, is more developed than the Western Zone (Table 3.3). Each zone has different characteristics and, in each, there are areas with more favourable conditions which deserve developmental priority.   The following views are mainly those of the author.

The Eastern Zone

The origins and implementation of the open-door policy since the late 1970s have been described in Chapter 1. By 1988 the open areas along the coast totalled 320,000 km^2, or about 31 per cent of the Eastern Zone (Figure 3.4).

The foremost task for the coastal region, as the central government has stressed, is to develop greatly the export-orientated economy. With its plentiful labour force, convenient communications, and better economic infrastructure, the coast has greater opportunities to further develop industries such as textiles, machinery, electrical appliances, electronics, and foodstuffs so as to meet the demands of the domestic and export markets. However, one model cannot suit all cities and areas. Certain industrial sectors and products have to be chosen as the leading or pilot ones according to the particular set of geographical circumstances, natural resources, development history, economic foundation, and scientific and technological conditions. Thus, in some areas it is still necessary and appropriate to expand the production of iron, steel, and petrochemicals and build more coal-fired power plants, although the coastal zone as a whole is short of energy, water, and other resources.

Within the coastal zone, there are five relatively developed areas: Central and Southern Liaoning, the Beijing-Tianjin-Tangshan Area, the Shandong Peninsula, the Changjiang Delta, and the Zhujiang Delta. In the first two of these, it seems that there is still scope for the expansion of such resource-intensive industries as iron and steel, petrochemicals, basic chemicals, and construction materials, because they have a vast hinterland endowed with abundant mineral resources and adjacent energy sources. Given the existing concentration of scientific and technical personnel there, engineering, electronics, textiles, and light industry can be further developed by renewing equipment and upgrading products. The main problems challenging development are that several cities are short of water and lack adequate infrastructure, and that much of the equipment in major industrial enterprises needs to be updated. The question also arises as to how to manage thousands of industrial enterprises in a planned way while, at the same time, giving them initiative and vigour.

From a long-term strategic point of view, for the purpose of playing a core role in forming the complete spatial economic system in China, and acting as part of the newly industrialized chain in the West Pacific region in the future, three economic belts may be extremely important.

Figure 3.4 Main features of the Eastern Zone, 1987

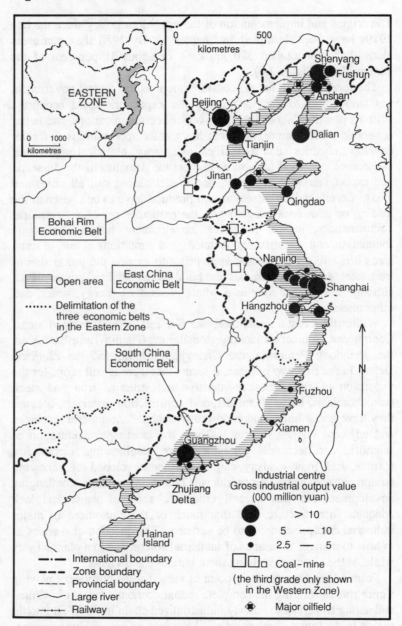

Bohai Rim Economic Belt

This area consists of the Provinces of Liaoning (see Appendix 2), Hebei, and Shandong and the municipalities of Beijing and Tianjin; it covers 500,000 km^2 and has a population of 191 million. In 1987 its annual industrial output value was 356,000 million yuan, or a quarter of China's total. With abundant iron ore, coking coal, oil, and a variety of other non-metallic resources, the author predicts that the Bohai Rim will attract several iron and steel centres; oil, petrochemical, and chemical works based on marine resources; enterprises building ocean-going ships, motor vehicles, and equipment for heavy industry; specialized cotton and fruit processing centres; and places making electronic and other products. In addition, a strong integrated transport system will be formed focusing on Beijing and around the Bohai Sea. With the further development of the export-orientated economy, various kinds of manufacturing have good prospects. The urban system of this area has eight leading central cities (Shenyang, Fushun, Anshan, Dalian, Tianjin, Beijing, Qingdao, and Jinan). The rapid growth of local, particularly township, enterprises encouraged the rapid growth of medium and small-size cities (defined in Table 3.3). Given its several advantages, this area could become a major industrialized megalopolis not unlike the manufacturing belt in the eastern part of the United States.

The most challenging problem in the Bohai Rim Area is to organize a rational water supply and utilize it economically and effectively. Both the large number of cities and the vast rural areas need an enormous volume of water, a resource that North China, on the whole, lacks. In this regard, inter-regional diversion of water (such as from the Changjiang River to the north) is badly needed. Abundant energy resources exist within and beyond the Bohai Rim Area, an advantage which does not exist in other coastal areas. However, as this is the main outlet for some 150 million tonnes of coal from Shanxi and Nei Mongol (mainly to other parts of China), the coal trade has been, and will continue to place, a heavy burden on the transport system.

East China Economic Belt

This area focuses on the Changjiang Delta and includes Jiangsu, Zhejiang, and Anhui Provinces with Shanghai as the core. The Changjiang Delta is the most developed manufacturing base in China, and there is considerable raw material production within the Delta and in Jiangsu and Anhui. Manufacturing has recently developed rapidly in all these provinces. Township enterprises have been flourishing in Jiangsu and Zhejiang. Moreover, intensive agriculture in East China provides considerable quantities of grain, cotton, silkworm, and aquatic products. Therefore in 1987 the whole belt contributed 26 per cent of the gross value of industrial and agricultural output in China.

With the widening of economic reform and further opening to the outside, Shanghai can become a world city in terms of production and foreign trade and the whole belt a comprehensively developed area. Shanghai, situated in the middle of China's long coastline and at the mouth of the Changjiang River, has long been the nation's leading commercial centre and light industrial base. After 1949 it became the most important comprehensively developed industrial area and, with the recent implementation of the open policy, its industrial production and foreign trade have greatly expanded. The port of Shanghai, the largest in China, handles about 130 million tonnes annually, linking foreign countries on the one hand and the Changjiang Valley on the other (see Chapter 5).

Taking into account the spatial relationship between Shanghai, the Changjiang Delta, and the middle and lower stretches of the Changjiang Basin, this region could bear comparison with the West European manufacturing belt. It seems similar in size and functions if the following relationships are compared: Rotterdam and Shanghai; the Benelux countries and the Changjiang Delta; the Ruhr and the Lianghuai-Nanjing area; and the Rhine and the Changjiang Rivers. The main issues in this major belt can be briefly summarized.

Energy supply

Lacking any energy resources, this developed industrial area depends mainly on the major coal and oil-producing provinces like Shanxi, •Shandong, and Anhui. As the ever-increasing demand for energy is large and urgent, coal and oil have long been a heavy burden to both railway and marine transport: thus it is necessary to expand the handling capacities of the railways and of the ports concerned.

Export-orientated economy

With its sound economic basis and advanced technology, this area has so far been acting as the most important industrial and commercial base to absorb raw material resources from, and sell various manufactured goods to, the vast interior. None the less, even though the value of its exports has increased remarkably it still has a great potential. Considering its advantageous geographical position and economic strengths, there should be an increase in the rate at which foreign investment and technology is absorbed. The most important prerequisite is to improve conditions available to overseas investors.

Allocation of industry

Existing industries are concentrated in Shanghai, the Suzhou-Wuxi-Changzhou area, and in Nanjing, so that some adjustments are needed in their spatial organization. For example, the manufacturing of low-grade products should be transferred to other parts of Jiangsu and Zhejiang Provinces, and to Anhui, Jiangxi, and other inland provinces; the production of middle-grade or even high-grade goods should be shifted to other medium and small-size cities (provided the latter have similar production conditions); and some industries should be moved away from the railways to the coast so as to reduce the density of railway traffic (Zhang et al., 1987, p. 122).

South China Economic Belt

With the Zhujiang Delta as the core, the South China Economic Area covers Guangdong Province, the newly established Hainan Province and most of Guangxi and Fujian Provinces. This area has several favourable conditions for development, including its proximity to Hong Kong and its subtropical climate, so that both its urban and rural economies have been booming in recent years with the implementation of the open-door policy. For example, previously the gross value of industrial and agricultural output of Guangdong Province was equivalent to only two-thirds that of Shanghai, but in 1987 it exceeded the latter, amounting to 129,000 million yuan. Almost every year since 1980 it has recorded a growth rate of more than 10 per cent. Even the forty-seven mountainous counties have experienced a rapid economic growth, some as much as 30 per cent in the past few years. Among China's Provinces, Guandong ranked third in 1985 in terms of national income, whereas in 1980 it ranked sixth.

The Zhujiang Delta, covering an area of 39,000 km² (although various authors suggest different definitions) and having a population of twenty million (18 and 25 per cent, respectively, of the Guangdong Province total), accounted for 67 per cent of Guangdong's gross value of industrial and agricultural output. As the development model in the Delta began to alter from 'heavy industry–light industry–agriculture' to 'foreign trade–industry–agriculture' and fully opened to the outside world, the industrial structure and allocation also greatly changed.

Taking textiles, electronics, plastics, domestic electrical appliances, and foodstuffs industries as the 'pillars', the industrial structure of the Delta is now characterized by the coexistence of technology-intensive, capital-intensive, and labour-intensive activities. A series of export-orientated agricultural and related production bases and thousands of processing industries which manufacture goods mainly for the world market, particularly through co-operation with Hong Kong enterprises, have mushroomed throughout the Delta.

As a result, more and more rural workers have been transferring to non-agricultural jobs and migrating to cities and towns (see Chapter 7). In 1985, the registered non-agricultural inhabitants (exclusive of agricultural population engaged in non-agricultural activities) made up 36 per cent of the total regional population. Many small cities and rural towns emerged with township enterprises as the backbone.

Guangzhou, the capital of Guangdong, and Shenzhen, one of the four Special Economic Zones (SEZs) in China, are playing the leading roles in South China. Since these two cities have most of the scientific and technological institutes and a large share of state investment, and are endowed with more decision-making power, many key industrial projects have been located here. In addition, other SEZs and open cities, such as Shantou in eastern Guangdong and Xiamen and Fuzhou in Fujian, have also developed rapidly in recent years.

Facing the South China Sea and connecting closely with South-east and South Asia, the South China economic belt could become an integral part of the booming Pacific Basin economic region. In many respects it can be likened to the flourishing Mediterranean countries.

South China has some serious disadvantages. It is very short of energy except for the relatively abundant hydroelectric power in the mountainous areas and thus relies mainly on long-distance coal and oil shipments from North China. Hence people have high hopes about the possible exploitation of oil and gas in the South China Sea, but so far only some small oilfields and a moderately large gasfield have been discovered. Because of this, construction of large-scale hydroelectric power stations in Guangxi is badly needed, and even the possibility of constructing nuclear power plants in Guangdong should be considered.

The Middle Zone

This zone, covering 18 per cent of China's territory and including one-third of its population (Figure 3.5), has plentiful mineral and energy resources and is rich in agricultural, livestock, and forest products.

Figure 3.5 Main features of the Middle Zone, 1987

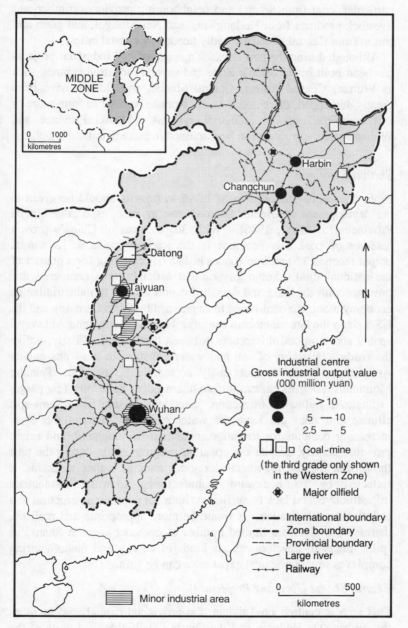

Raw materials can be easily transported to the coastal areas: in particular, coal from Shanxi and neighbouring provinces, timber and livestock products from Heilongjiang and Nei Mongol, and grain and cotton from Central China are badly needed by coastal cities.

Although during the past decades a series of key industrial projects has been built in the Middle Zone and several industrial centres, such as Wuhan, Central Hunan, Central Shanxi, and Baotou have been greatly developed, there is still much work to be done to form more or less complete regional industrial systems. Shanxi Province and Wuhan and its surrounds can be discussed in more detail.

Shanxi Province

From the macro-economic point of view, priority should be given to the development of Greater Shanxi's energy base, especially Shanxi Province (Li, W-Y., 1986). With 30 per cent of China's proven reserves of coal, this province is the leading producer: its annual output reached 230 million tonnes in 1987, accounting for a quarter of the national total. Some government officials have compared this province with the Ruhr and Appalachia and wanted to industrialize its economy along the coal-based lines pursued by West Germany and the USA since the late nineteenth century. However, they ignored several spatial and temporal differences between these cases. Firstly, unlike the ready availability of rail and water transport in the Ruhr and in Appalachia, Shanxi is not easily accessible because the Taihang Mountains along its eastern and southern edges have very few passes to facilitate railway construction. Secondly, Shanxi has a semi-arid climate and does not have the water resources to meet the ever-increasing demand for irrigation, industrial development, and urban growth. Thirdly, despite the apparent progress made during the past three decades, the provincial economy remains rather weak, as is reflected by its backward manufacturing industry, inadequate infrastructure, and lack of sufficient funds for capital construction and technical transformation. It would be more appropriate and realistic, therefore, to choose a limited number of compact areas in Shanxi as 'pilot' areas to develop various kinds of energy and manufacturing complexes so that practical experience can be gained.

Central Shanxi (Jinzhong Prefecture)

This area is centred on Taiyuan, the provincial capital, and includes the Xishan, the Hedong, and the Qinshui coalfields, and parts of the

Huoxi coalfield, where the proven reserves total 80,000 million tonnes. Thanks to the many varieties of coal available and a relatively sound economy, both energy and raw material and engineering industries have been well developed. Taiyuan is an important centre for heavy industry with coal, steel, chemicals, and machinery as its leading sectors. The most challenging problems are, on the one hand, the limited water supply (with the Fenhe River being the major source for industrial, urban, and agricultural use) and, on the other, the water and air pollution which is worse than in most other cities. Provided these two problems can be reduced by measures designed to save water and manage environmental pollution, the steel and chemical industries could be further developed. The coal and iron ore deposits are near each other but the beneficiation of the ore is restricted by the extreme difficulty of dressing the ore because of the fineness of the mineral particles, so that until now most of the ore smelted in Taiyuan Iron and Steel Works has been brought in from outside the region. Judging from the sectoral structure of the regional industry, this industrial base can be regarded as a comprehensively developed manufacturing-mining area.

North Shanxi (Yanbei Prefecture)

This area has the basic advantage of abundant deposits of good quality coal which is particularly suitable for steam-raising and coal-gas generation, and which is shipped to every province in China and traded on world markets. The Datong underground coal-mine, being the most accessible and important energy supplier for the Beijing-Tianjin area, has, since the late 1970s, become the largest operation in China, producing more than thirty million tonnes in 1987. Furthermore, small locally run coal-pits have mushroomed around Datong City in recent years, and a major US-Chinese joint venture (fifteen million tonnes annually) began operations in 1987 at the Antaibao opencast mine of the Pingshuo coalfield, some 300 km south of Datong. All these developments strengthen North Shanxi's position in both domestic and world markets.

Three large power-generating plants have been set up in Datong and Pingshuo and a 500-kV transmission line linked to Beijing has been completed. However, lack of water will limit the development of large water-consuming manufacturing industries. Taking into account the abundant non-metallic minerals adjacent to coal-mines, North Shanxi will play an important role as a coal-power and construction-materials base in North China.

South-east Shanxi–North-west Henan

This includes Changzhi, Jincheng, and Jiaozuo municipalities and their surrounding counties. It occupies the major part of Qinshui coalfield, the second largest in China, and is endowed with more than 40,000 million tonnes of proven coal reserves, mainly superior quality anthracite. Compared with North and Central Shanxi, this area is relatively rich in water resources, both surface and underground. Particularly in Jiaozuo, located downstream on the Qinshui River, there is plenty of water. The excessive volume of shaft water in the Jiaozuo coal-mine, which creates production difficulties, can be utilized as the water source for power generation and other water consumers. However, as the southern outlet for coal shipments from Shanxi Province and the transport hub in North-west Henan, Jiaozuo is the most convenient place to collect together coal, bauxite, and other minerals from this area and surrounding prefectures. Therefore there is every advantage to form an energy and manufacturing complex in Jiaozuo with power generation and aluminium production being the leading sectors of the regional economy. A major project producing power, aluminium, and cement is planned.

Wuhan and its Environs

Wuhan, the provincial capital of Hubei, is situated in China's midland and on the middle reaches of the Changjiang. As the Beijing-Guangzhou railway crosses that river here, Wuhan is well known as a 'thoroughfare to nine provinces' and has long been an important commercial centre. During the past thirty years, the framework of an integrated industrial system has formed in Wuhan and its surrounding area — the Jianghan Plain. With favourable transport conditions and abundant resources, especially iron ore and agricultural produce, metallurgical, machinery, chemicals, textiles, and foodstuffs industries are now the pillars of the regional economy. Moreover, 400 km north-west of Wuhan is located the Second Automotive Plant, headquarters of the Dongfeng Automotive Enterprise Group, the largest such group in China (Li, W-Y., 1990, pp. 27–30). More importantly, there are 468 research institutes and 143,000 researchers devoted to the natural sciences, ranking third in China only after Beijing and Shanghai, as well as thirty-five colleges and ninety-two information institutes. This will promote the development of high-technology industry and the technological transformation of the existing enterprises.

However, during the past ten years characterized by the implementation of the open-door policy, Wuhan has been disadvantaged compared with the coastal cities. Previously, Wuhan's gross value of industrial and agricultural output was almost the same as that of Guangzhou, but in 1987 the gap between them was 2,300 million yuan. The foreign trade volume of Wuhan is only 0.25 per cent of the national total, equivalent to one of the four economically leading counties in the more open Zhujiang Delta.

Even worse, Wuhan ceased to be the focus for its vast hinterland, the neighbouring Province of Hubei. Hunan Province is tending to co-operate more closely with Guangdong; Jiangxi Province has joined the Shanghai Economic Region; and Henan Province, the main supplier of energy and agricultural produce, is more interested in getting an outlet at Lianyungang, the most important seaport east of Henan. Wuhan's problems have drawn much attention from government officials and scholars who are wondering whether Wuhan should open its door as the coastal cities did, or concentrate its main efforts on developing the vast interior markets with its competitive products. Perhaps both are needed. However, the most important thing is not just waiting for and requiring the central government to endow more authority and a more relaxed economic policy, but to take practical steps to promote more R. & D. business in major industrial sectors and to strengthen Wuhan's function as an information centre for the interior.

The Western Zone

The Western Zone covers 70 per cent of China's land area and has 28 per cent of the total population (Figure 3.6). If Sichuan and Shaanxi Provinces (which could be called 'Near West' or could even fall into the category of the Middle Zone according to some scholars) are excluded, this zone has only 16 per cent of the national population (Li, W-Y., 1988, p. 96).

The basic characteristics of this zone are its vast land area (6,780,000 km^2) and sparse population; its great mineral and energy resource potential; its large pastoral area and considerable quantities of livestock products; its inaccessibility; and its poorly developed economic base. However, considering its weak geopolitical position, the state has invested heavily there during the past three decades. Several industrial centres have taken shape and industrial projects have been built in the so-called third-line region and in the capitals of the autonomous regions and provinces.

Figure 3.6   Main features of the Western Zone, 1987

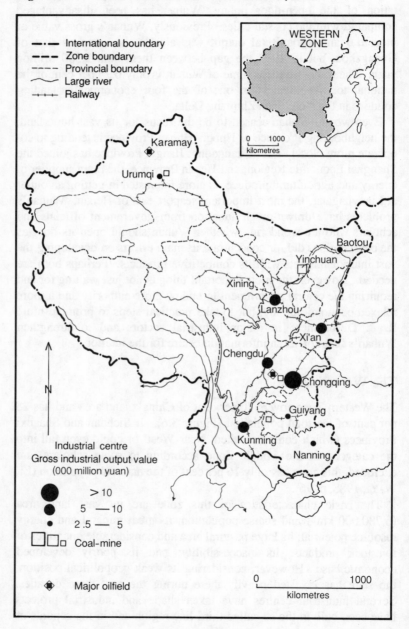

However, 'most of the projects do not have close links with the regional economy apart from ore and energy supplies' (Li, W-Y., 1988, p. 105), and 'most key projects, particularly those in small and medium-size cities, have to set up various infrastructural and service trades . . . with their funds . . .' (Li, W-Y.,1988, p. 106), thus giving rise to 'plant run communities'.

The main problems facing the industrial development of the Western Zone, using Xinjiang Province as an example, are as follows.

Firstly, long-distance freight costs make locally produced raw materials and manufactured goods less competitive on the domestic market. For instance, though with enormous potential resources, Xinjiang coal can only be offered at competitive prices as far as Wuwei – the eastern city of the neighbouring Hexi Corridor or, again, despite its higher quality and much lower refining costs, Xinjiang beet sugar cannot compete with Guangdong-produced cane sugar even in Xi'an (Li, W-Y., 1988, p. 106).

Secondly, harsh physical conditions and remoteness greatly increase the investment needed to extract and transport mineral products. Oil is a good example: situated in the Junggar and Tarim Basins, the Xinjiang oilfield has very large potential resources. However, the extremely arid climate, the vast Gobi Desert, the sparsely populated area, and the very long pipeline needed (at least 3,000 km) would make the investment per tonne of oil capacity almost as high as that of offshore oilfields.

Thirdly, backward technology and inefficient management mean that most industrial firms — locally run ones in particular — suffer from low productivity and high costs. They can seldom compete with the Shanghai or Tianjin-made goods in the local market in terms of price and quality. Implementation of the policy of 'enlivening the domestic economy' raised the enthusiasm of counties and townships to run more small factories, such as woollen and cotton mills, but these could only sell their products locally. In the meantime, the large modern textile mills in the coastal cities and even Urumqi, the capital of Xinjiang, cannot obtain sufficient supplies of raw materials. Contradictions thus often occur between different levels of government. The essential problem is whether to give priority to efficiency and economic results or to balanced allocation and assistance to backward areas, or how to compromise between these aims.

The development of the Greater North-west, for instance, must rely on the close co-ordination between different sectors and on economic and technological co-operation between north-western and coastal provinces. Three scenarios, that is, a centralized large industrial belt, moderate-size regional industrial centres, and local industrial points, should harmonize with each other (Li, W-Y., 1988, p. 107). The former, of course, will play leading roles and are expected to have diversified industrial structures. Main economic belts in the Western Zone could include the Upper Huanghe (Yellow) River industrial belt, the core area of North Xinjiang, the Guanzhong Plain, the Chengdu-Chongqing area, and the Central Guizhou area.

It is unrealistic to expect the vast periphery to catch up with the developed coastal provinces quickly but, from a long-term planning viewpoint, it is necessary to work out an ambitious strategic plan for this zone, particularly for the major promising areas.

Although the Western Zone has so far benefited much less from the national open-door policy than the Eastern Zone, possibilities exist to develop the westward links with the USSR, Central Asia, and Islamic countries, thus promoting the development of the Greater North-west, particularly the Xinjiang Uygur Autonomous Region.

Conclusion

Given China's complicated physical, social, economic, and political circumstances, its spatial development seems to have more complex problems than in many other countries. The current regional differences in development levels are so obvious and sharp that the rich/poor gap among the thirty-one provinces and hundreds of prefectures and cities and between urban and rural areas cannot be narrowed quickly. Certainly, the increasing disparity between the underdeveloped interior and the rapidly growing coastal areas is a long-term problem to be faced in the process of modernization.

Apparently any strategic consideration about spatial development in China has to combine the unique characteristics of every given region with the overall national territorial planning. The past three decades of socialist construction show that the strategies of rigidly obeying one model of economic development or even a universal political slogan, and of persisting in a one-sided approach to local interests at the expense of the national unified allocation of resources, are irrational and hence harmful to the future of China's modernization.

4 Passenger and Freight Patterns and Transport Development

R. J. NAIRN

CHINA'S economy is transport-intensive, using an exceptionally large amount of freight transport by world standards. More than three tonne/km are required per dollar of GNP, compared to well under two tonne/km in India, Brazil, and the USA. Of the larger countries only the USSR is more freight-intensive than China, generating over four tonne/km per dollar of GNP (World Bank, 1985, p. 82). Freight intensity is determined by such factors as country size, the relative locations of natural resources, industry, and population (Yenny, 1986, p. 20). In China about 38 per cent of the population and 55 per cent of industrial production are located in the Eastern Zone while mineral resources — especially coal — need to be transported from the Middle and Western Zones. This chapter examines the implications for China's development of freight and passenger movements and transport issues at three different geographical levels: inter-provincial, the urban-hinterland relationship, and intra-urban level.

Inter-provincial Transport

Railways

Although railways dominate transport in China, the railway system has expanded only slowly since the Great Leap Forward period (1958–60). Railways handled 41 per cent of the tonne/km of freight moved in 1989, compared to 84 per cent in 1975, and 72 per cent in 1979. Coal was by far the largest tonnage carried, accounting for 39.5 per cent in 1982. During 1989 over 51 per cent of total passenger/km of travel occurred on the railways. Given the scale of the railway operations, the rapidly growing demand on the system and the current congestion, Chinese planners recognize that railway investment must be vigorously pursued. Overall, railway freight density is very high but the rail network and the inventory of railway equipment is relatively small for the task being undertaken: thus the emphasis recently has been on introducing new technology to facilitate intensified track use, as much as on the construction of new track. However, in view of the experiences of other countries, where road freight has grown in importance due to economic rationalization, the need for a shift in the inter-modal balance is well recognized.

None the less, China's railways operate efficiently under difficult conditions. Freight densities average fifteen million tonnes per route-km — double that of the USA and three times that of India. These figures are even more impressive when it is recognized that 40 per cent of the locomotives in China are steam-driven and these generally haul only small loads of 3,000 tonnes or less (Yenny, 1986, p. 21).

Coastal Ports and Inland Waterways

The development of coastal ports was given little priority before 1972, but the subsequent growth of foreign trade led to an increase in the total cargo-handling capacity from 120 million tonnes in 1972 to 217 million tonnes in 1980, and 312 million tonnes in 1985 (see Chapter 5). China's modern waterway fleet has increased rapidly since the 1950s, and in 1985 had a total capacity of twenty-nine million tonnes.

In 1989, China's waterways accounted for 4.5 per cent of freight tonne/km and 3.2 per cent of the passenger/km of traffic. Inland waterways handle much of the east-west freight traffic. Three main waterway systems are based on the Changjiang (Yangtze) River in central and east China, the Zhujiang (Pearl) River in the south, and the Heilongjiang (Amur) River in the north-east. The Huanghe (Yellow) River, which drains the North China Plain, is plagued by heavy silting which considerably reduces its navigational use. The Grand Canal, completed in 1293, still provides an important north-south corridor between Beijing and Hangzhou, 1,750 km to the south. The various segments have, however, quite different navigational conditions. Some reaches — such as those between Beijing and Tianjin and between Linqing and the Huanghe — are suitable only for small country boats; others like that between Xuzhou and Yangzhou have been upgraded to accommodate vessels up to 2,000 d.w.t.

In 1984 the navigable waterways (defined as those more than 0.3 m deep) totalled 109,300 km of which, however, 52,600 km have a depth of less than 1.0 m and can only be used by vessels of between 10 and 80 d.w.t., and a further 36,700 km can be used for only part of the year because of droughts or floods, or because — as in the case of the Heilongjiang system — they are frozen for several months each winter. In short, only about 20,000 km are regularly maintained to

ensure a year-round depth of at least 1.0 m, while fewer than 5,000 km
are wide and deep enough to accommodate vessels over 1,000 d.w.t.
Much of China's water-borne traffic thus consists of many tiny craft
operating along a vast network of small rivers and carrying traffic that
elsewhere would be shifted by road. During the 1980s there has been
a reappraisal of the role of inland waterways in the overall transport
task. After the formation of the People's Republic in 1949 the length
of navigable waterways was increased from 73,600 km to a peak of
170,000 km in 1960. By 1979, however, the length had declined to
about 108,000 km partly because insufficient funds were made
available to maintain existing navigable channels but mainly because
of the construction of irrigation and power dams (though some of the
affected stretches were carrying only small volumes of freight).

Roads

In 1979 China's entire 875,000-km road network included seventy
national trunk highways (110,000 km). While the highways are the
principal means of transport in the Far West, elsewhere they are
mainly used for short-haul work because of the absence of an
integrated network suitable for long-distance freight movements. In
addition, roads sometimes end at provincial boundaries due to a lack
of interjurisdictional co-ordination. In 1979 fewer than half China's
villages were linked with motor roads, while many were more than ten
kilometres from *any* kind of road. By 1985 the 920,000 km of roads
linked 93 per cent of the townships and 64 per cent of the rural
villages (Wang, D., 1985). The annual growth of road traffic is very
high at 15.5 per cent, increasing road's share of tonne/km freight
traffic from 9.6 per cent in 1979 to 13 per cent in 1989, despite an
annual growth rate of 9.7 per cent in the freight task undertaken by all
modes. Road passenger traffic has grown at an annual average rate of
15.4 per cent, increasing the share of passenger/km carried by road
from 26.1 per cent in 1980 to 36.8 per cent in 1985 and 42.5 per cent
in 1989. However, Wang, D. (1985) noted that 'most of the motor
vehicles in use are time-worn, low in carrying capacity and slow [with
an] average working speed [of] only 30 km per hour'.

Air Services

In 1980 China had 159 domestic air routes totalling 110,000 km, and
another twenty-one international and regional routes covering 80,000

km. The network is based on Beijing, with other main nodes at Shanghai and Guangzhou. The annual growth of air freight is very high, but from a low base. Passenger and freight traffic increased rapidly at 20 per cent per annum between 1949 and 1980.

Industry and Freight

Although the inter-provincial freight task mainly involves rail and water transport the emphasis has been placed on improving inter-modal transfer facilities and container traffic. Chinese planners recognize that there must be an improvement in inter-modal co-operation, particularly for container transport, that economic rationale and transport pricing policies must be stressed in adjusting modal shares of the transport task, and that efficiency must be improved through equipment modernization and management training. Although rail transport in 1985 still absorbed the largest share of the capital investment, the outlays on the development of airways, waterways, and highways were proportionately higher than their shares of the overall transport task (Table 4.1).

Table 4.1 Transport and communications capital investment, 1985 (m. yuan)

Sector	Total
Railways	7,716
Waterways	3,666
Highways	2,314
Airways	2,061
Telecommunications	695
Post/telegraph services	377
Pipelines	145
Postal services	95
Loading facilities	1
Total	17,095

Source: State Statistical Bureau (1986a, p. 316).

For many years emphasis was given in the Chinese spatial economy to local self-sufficiency so that almost all provinces continue to produce not only basic foodstuffs and building materials but also industrial goods ranging from iron and steel to consumer durables which in most countries are geographically concentrated to take advantage of scale economies. While there are concentrations of manufacturing activity in the coastal region and of coal-mining in the north-west, economic activity is spread widely and fairly evenly throughout the provinces. Thus, 52 per cent of the provinces have 78 per cent of the population, 80 per cent of the freight moved, and 81 per cent of the value of both agricultural and industrial production.

Figure 4.1 demonstrates trends in domestic freight movements, together with growth rates in some industries which typically generate significant freight movements. Growth in domestic freight slowed in the late 1970s and early 1980s, confirming the view that it was not keeping up with industrial growth. However, between 1980 and 1989 freight tonne/km increased by an annual average of 9.3 per cent while passenger/km growth averaged 11.2 per cent.

Figure 4.1 Freight and production growth, 1950–85 (1980 = 100)

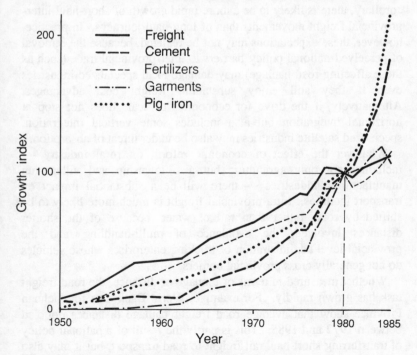

Source: State Statistical Bureau (1986a, pp. 246–8, 323).

The rationalization of production now occurring will mean more regional specialization and greater demands for transporting raw materials and consumer products. The current pressure on all modes of transport throughout China is recognized as a major constraint on the fulfilment of these policies and an obstacle to economic growth.

Intra-provincial and Urban-hinterland Transport

Intra-provincial Freight

If economic reform is leading to industrial specialization between provinces, it should be even more apparent on the intra-provincial scale since freight costs are lower, and any parochial elements carry greater weight. Rapid growth might be expected, therefore, in specialized satellite industries in provinces containing key growth industries (such as mining enterprises supplying steelworks). Geographically, these are especially concentrated in smaller provincial cities or in the major urban areas and their rural hinterlands. As a corollary, there is likely to be a more rapid growth of short-haul inter-provincial freight movements than of long-haul journeys. In practice, however, these expectations may not be realized, because the removal of perceived national policy barriers to inter-provincial trade (such as those affecting road haulage) may damage local specialized industries even if they still enjoy substantial freight cost advantages. Alternatively, if the drive for economies of scale does not stop at horizontal integration but also includes some vertical integration, specialized satellite industries may also be under threat of absorption.

Whatever the effect of economic reform on rural industry — including not only agriculture but also township and village-run manufacturing industries — there will be a substantial impact on transport facilities. Intra-provincial freight is much more likely to be shifted by road, rather than rail or water, because of the shorter distances involved, the avoidance of multi-handling, and the provincial-level administration of trucking enterprises whose vehicles do not generally cross provincial borders.

Whether measured in terms of tonnage or distance, the road freight task has grown rapidly. For example, World Bank data for Sichuan Province show that average road freight haulage distances doubled between 1972 and 1985. This is partly the result of a national policy of transferring short-haul rail freight to road transport, but it may also be partly due to the expansion of rural industry and/or intra-provincial trade and the local pre-processing of raw materials. Although the significance of these factors needs further investigation, changes in road freight movements may, none the less, serve as an adequate — if incomplete — indicator of the spatial shifts in industrial development.

Aspects of intra-provincial transport can be demonstrated by considering Liaoning Province (see also Appendix 2). Liaoning is a major industrial province containing several larger centres and key industries. It has its own major port (Dalian) and good rail connections to Beijing as well as Jilin and Heilongjiang Provinces to the north. A major highway from Harbin to Dalian is under construction and will bisect the province. Sections of this highway have already been opened.

Shenyang is the centre of road freight in the province, with agricultural produce important in the road freight to the port at Dalian. With Anshan an important centre for iron and steel production, and Fushun for coal, the movement of construction materials forms a large part of the road transport task. Road freight data for Liaoning Province show that in 1986 commodities such as raw and construction materials and agricultural produce, which are unlikely to be sensitive in the short-term to changes in economic policy, accounted for 67 per cent of all movements. Another 2 per cent was made up of fertilizers, pesticides, fuel, and oil. Thus, less than one-third consisted of consumer and other items that might be more readily affected by shifts in economic policy.

Urban-hinterland Transport

The pattern of development in the hinterlands of major industrial cities in China has reflected an approach whereby minor industry has been integrated into the development of community centres in farming areas, thus providing a wider range of job opportunities and a buffer against seasonal unemployment. Some of the highest-income households earn their living in these areas, enjoying buoyant nearby urban markets for their produce and a stable market for their 'sideline' activities like transport and house building. While, new urban residential permits are not easily available, this pattern of development has probably reduced the pressure for urban drift, particularly among young people. However, if extensive horizontal or vertical integration of industrial production takes place through displacement or relocation, the rural hinterland development pattern will change and pressures for urban commuting and/or urban drift will intensify.

Intra-urban Transport

The concentration of economic activity in the main cities (Table 3.2), has led to increased attention being given to their traffic and transport problems, both by local planners and international development agencies. This discussion draws on studies of traffic and transport in Shanghai (Maunsell & Partners Pty. Ltd. et al., 1986b), and three large cities in Liaoning Province (Pak Poy & Kneebone Pty. Ltd. et al., 1987) — Shenyang, which had a total population (city excluding the urban counties) of 4.2 million in 1985, Anshan (1.3 million), and Fushun (1.2 million) (State Statistical Bureau, 1987, p. 218).

Personal travel in Chinese cities is dominated by the bicycle and suffers from serious congestion and high accident rates. This traffic severely interferes with bus services which are slowed to such an extent that they usually cannot compete with the bicycle. Even so, shortages of funds make it difficult for local authorities to obtain sufficient buses to provide comfortable services and reduce overcrowding. Improvements have concentrated on separating bicycle and other street traffic and controlling congestion at intersections so as to improve the speed and competitiveness of buses. In addition, methods of improving bus-body manufacture have been investigated.

Several cities, such as Beijing and Shenyang, have appreciable investment in elevated road crossing structures with sufficient flexibility to separate present and estimated future bicycle and vehicular traffic. Network connectivity is usually poor and current investment is often focused on the missing links in the urban fabric. In general, however, the presence of freight traffic and privately owned vehicles such as motorcycles is not yet a dominating influence in most urban areas, although planning to cope with the growth of motorized traffic is becoming of critical importance.

Few cities have off-street transit systems, such as the underground railways in Beijing and Tianjin or the light-rail systems in Anshan and Dalian. Indeed, light-rail systems have been removed from several cities, including Shanghai and — more recently — Harbin. With the exception of the Beijing underground, these off-street systems use old rolling stock and need extensive updating and renewal. Shanghai recently started to construct an underground system which is due to come into full operation in 1995 (see Chapter 8). Recent investigations have revealed that commuting patterns in Shanghai differ greatly from those in Western countries like Australia. The spatial organization of residential and workplace locations in Shanghai was almost the reverse of that found in, say, Sydney. In the latter, employment tends to be concentrated in and around the CBD and at several suburban centres, with the residential areas being widely dispersed, particularly in the periphery of the urban area. By contrast, very high population densities occur in the older part of Shanghai and, while the Huangpu waterfront provides many jobs, there are large concentrations of industrial employment in the outer fringe areas (Figure. 8.1). This means that the peak-morning journey-to-work pattern does not concentrate in converging radial patterns as it does in many Western cities but is much more widely dispersed. Such a pattern is more difficult to service economically with mass-transit systems.

Detailed household surveys conducted in 1985 and 1987 in Shanghai and the three Liaoning Province cities provide useful data about travel behaviour which are especially interesting when compared with similar information for Australian cities (Table 4.2a). While there are only small differences between the Chinese cities as to why people travelled, those surveyed in Sydney and Canberra travelled more often and had more diverse reasons for their journeys.

In contrast, choice of travel mode varied considerably between the Chinese cities surveyed. The use of bicycles, buses, and rail services in Fushun and Shanghai contrasts with the usage in Shenyang and Anshan (see Table 4.2b). Fushun has intra-urban commuter rail services and Anshan has light rail services but Shenyang has neither — although many people commute from its hinterland to the centre of the city by rail. Part of the explanation is that Fushun is a linear city which makes it easier to provide efficient public transport services. In addition, employment in Anshan is dominated and unbalanced by the Anshan Iron and Steel Works, into which there is poor access for public transport and considerable congestion at the entry points. Shenyang, a large and more diverse city has an unbalanced employment distribution and a very overloaded bus system.

The Shanghai and Liaoning studies did not focus on the direct effects of urban congestion on industrial productivity, about which little is known. Undoubtedly, though, the excessive travel times (approximately twice those in comparable Australian cities) combined with the daily physical effort of cycling or the discomfort of bus travel must affect work practices and productivity. Peak-hour congestion is much more severe in the three Liaoning Province cities than in Sydney or Canberra. A potential solution is to reduce such congestion by spreading work starting and finishing times in co-operation with industry and business.

Table 4.2 Travel behaviour in Chinese and Australian cities

	Shenyang	Anshan	Fushun	Shanghai	Sydney	Canberra
(a) TRAVEL PURPOSE						
Home	49.2	48.3	48.5	49.0	38.0	40.7
Work	37.8	34.1	32.7	36.0	32.7	22.4
School	6.4	8.1	7.8	2.0	6.6	13.5
Shop	4.6	3.9	6.0	7.0	12.4	14.0
Other	2.0	5.6	5.0	6.0	10.3	9.4
Total (%)	100.0	100.0	100.0	100.0	100.0	100.0
(b) TRAVEL MODE						
Walk	33.4	33.1	40.4	44.0	11.5	12.8
Bicycle	55.3	53.5	24.6	13.0	1.0	3.2
Bus	9.3	10.2	25.7	36.0	17.0	8.7
Rail/ Other	0.3	2.5	8.7	7.0	13.2	a
Motor Vehicle	1.8	0.6	0.6	n.a.	57.3	75.3
Total (%)	100.0	100.0	100.0	100.0	100.0	100.0

Note:　　a No intra-city rail service operating.
Sources:　Maunsell & Partners Pty. Ltd. et al. (1986b); Nairn & Partners Pty. Ltd. (1987); Pak Poy & Kneebone Pty. Ltd. et al. (1987).

China's major urban areas are also the main foci for the inter-modal transfer of freight. Shanghai, for instance, handles over 43 per cent of all multi-modal freight passing through Chinese ports, while the collection and distribution of rail freight by road contributes significantly to urban traffic. However, freight vehicles comprise only a small proportion of the traffic on the most congested urban roads and its presence at peak periods can be regulated. None the less, growing congestion must add to urban freight costs. While traffic management solutions are being proposed to ameliorate this problem, there are other potential solutions — one of which is for urban industries to become more vertically integrated so as to reduce the amount of freight moving between different sites. Restructuring industrial enterprises to reduce freight costs may also provide strategic planning opportunities to reduce personal commuting costs and overall congestion. It will be interesting to observe whether, as these pressures increase, policy initiatives of this kind gain acceptance in China.

Conclusions

It is readily apparent that transport remains one of the key challenges in the development of China's contemporary spatial economy. The location and structure of industrial production have begun to change as a result of the economic reform programme. This, in turn, has influenced the pattern of demand for freight and passenger services from one province to another, between urban areas and their hinterlands, and within the larger cities.

The high rate of increase of road traffic, servicing both passenger movements and short-haul freight, has not reduced the need for further expansion of the capacity of the railway network. At the same time, it has underlined the need for improved inter-modal co-ordination if an integrated transport system is to be developed. Within the larger cities, the dominant role played by bicycles, the paucity of privately owned motor vehicles, and the distinctive land-use and travel-demand patterns which characterize most Chinese cities pose major problems for planners. The mechanisms by which transport planning, investment, and operations can be adapted to play their parts in the economic reform programme still need further clarification and understanding.

5   Development and Problems of China's Seaports

SINCE the middle of the nineteenth century China has lagged far behind Western countries in foreign trade and marine transport as a result of the closed-door policy pursued by the Qing Dynasty and the political instability and economic stagnancy during the first half of this century. Even in the 1950s and 1960s, after the founding of the People's Republic of China (PRC), the development of sea transport and port facilities was still limited by political and military circumstances. It was not until the late 1970s, when the government adopted a policy to invigorate the domestic economy and open it up to the outside world, that foreign trade and international economic and technological co-operation developed rapidly. As a result, the need to modernize and extend seaports along with the development of coastal areas was recognized as being essential to the development of the national economy. During the 1980s the rapid development of the Special Economic Zones (SEZs) and other coastal cities and counties after they were opened to foreign investment (see Chapter 1) placed considerable pressure on their associated port facilities and reinforced the need for them to be enlarged and modernized.

The Chinese Port System

In 1949 there were only six major coastal ports in the whole of China, with a total of 119 berths, sixty of which were deep-water ones able to handle vessels of more than 10,000 d.w.t. (Ding, 1987). Seaport development since then can be divided into three stages.

(a) The first, 1949 to 1972, was marked mainly by the reclamation, full utilization, and technical transformation of some existing facilities. On average only 1.3 deep-water berths were added each year.

(b) The 1973–80 period saw a rapid expansion of foreign trade, especially after 1978. The main seaports thus became clogged so that construction was accelerated. Fifty deep-water berths were built and total handling capacity was increased by 100 million tonnes. Those at Dalian and Qingdao, which were capable of handling bulk oil carriers of up to 100,000 d.w.t., were the largest yet seen in China.

(c) The third stage after 1981 emphasized even more the inadequacy of China's port facilities because of the additional freight task generated by the open-door policy. Thus, the Sixth Five-year Plan (1981–5) laid further stress on harbour construction: in addition to the enlargement and redevelopment of existing ports, several deep-water berths were re-established or newly built including others for seagoing vessels at Nanjing, Zhenjiang, Zhangjiagang, and Nantong along the lower reaches of the Changjiang (Yangtze) River. During this five-year period work commenced on 132 deep-water berths of 10,000 d.w.t. or more: fifty-four of these were completed and thus another 100 million tonnes were added to the nation's total seaport cargo-handling capacity. By the end of 1988 there were 212 deep-water berths capable of taking ships of 10,000 d.w.t. (Li, N., 1989, p. 30).

Expansion of Ports and Facilities

A general survey of China's ports in 1985 counted 1,947 ports capable of handling more than 10,000 tonnes of cargo annually; of these 195 were situated along the coast. The overall length of all the sea-berths totalled 179 km. During the 1949–85 period the number of deep-water berths (for vessels of 10,000 d.w.t. and over) in seaports increased from sixty to 217, while medium-class (3,000 to 10,000 d.w.t.) and small-class (less than 3,000 d.w.t.) coastal berths increased from 119 to 3,017 (State Statistical Bureau, 1988b). By 1987 the twenty-three main seaports had a total of 587 berths with a throughput of 394 million tonnes in 1987 (Table 5.1). In addition, the sixteen deep-water berths established along the lower reaches of the Changjiang have helped to relieve the congestion at Shanghai Port.

Port construction during the 1980s, reflecting the ever-increasing demand for coal and container transport, has provided a solid base for the implementation of the open-door policy and the development of foreign trade which by 1985 made up 35 per cent of the total through-put of China's seaports (State Statistical Bureau, 1988b, p. 126). Coal and oil — the main bulk cargoes — accounted in 1987 for 30 and 20 per cent, respectively, of the 406 million-tonne throughput of the seaports that handled more than 10,000 tonnes a year (Table 5.2). The Ministry of Transportation has estimated that the number of seaport berths may reach 2,000 during the next thirty to fifty years, of which 1,200 will be deep-water ones (*Economic Daily*, 28 February 1989).

Table 5.1 Throughput and berths at seaports handling more than one million tonnes in 1987

Port	Throughput (m. tonnes)			Berths (no.)	
	total	outwards	inwards	total	of 10,000 d.w.t. class
Dalian	46.1	35.9	10.2	52	25
Yingkou	1.2	0.8	0.4	10	1
Qinhuangdao	53.8	50.8	3.0	18	16
Tianjin	17.3	6.7	10.6	46	24
Longkou	3.1	1.5	1.6	8	–
Yantai	7.0	3.4	3.6	16	3
Weihai	1.2	0.8	0.4	5	–
Qingdao	30.3	23.5	6.8	31	16
Shijiu	4.2	4.2	–	3	3
Lianyungang	8.9	5.5	3.4	16	11
Shanghai	128.3	39.5	88.8	102	47
Ningbo	19.4	7.6	11.8	28	8
Haimen	3.9	0.6	3.3	7	–
Wenzhou	3.3	0.9	2.4	11	–
Fuzhou	4.3	1.7	2.6	25	2
Xiamen	4.3	1.5	2.8	37	4
Shantou	2.5	0.8	1.7	11	–
Shekou/ Shenzhen	1.5	0.4	1.1	12	2
Huangpu	26.2	8.5	17.7	30	21
Guangzhou	6.9	3.2	3.7	87	–
Zhanjiang	14.2	4.6	9.6	18	13
Haikou	2.0	0.6	1.4	9	–
Basuo	4.0	3.8	0.2	5	3
Total (23 ports)	393.9	206.8	187.1	587	199

Source: State Statistical Bureau (1988b, p. 351).

Spatial Distribution of Ports

The geographical distribution of ports has been improved (Figure 5.1). Some of the older ones have been expanded, and several modern deepwater berths have been constructed, including those at Shijiu (Shandong Province), Lanshan (south of Shijiu, Shandong Province),

Zhenjiang, Shenzhen, and Fangcheng, and at Zhangjiagang on the Changjiang River. New deep-water areas have been opened up in the existing seaports, such as Dalian, Yingkou, Qingdao, Lianyungang, Qinhuangdao, Yantai, Shanghai, Ningbo, Fuzhou, Xiamen, and Huangpu, and at the river ports of Zhenjiang, Nantong, and Nanjing.

Table 5.2 Cargoes shifted by seaports handling more than 10,000 tonnes during 1987

Cargo	Total throughput		Outwards		Inwards	
	tonnes (m.)	per cent	tonnes (m.)	per cent	tonnes (m.)	per cent
Coal	121	29.8	73	34.5	48	24.8
Oil	82	20.3	56	26.7	26	13.3
(of which crude oil)	(62)	(15.4)	(44)	(20.8)	(18)	(9.5)
Metal minerals	27	6.6	10	4.9	17	8.5
Iron and steel	22	5.6	6	2.8	16	8.5
Mineral construction materials	24	5.9	8	3.6	16	8.5
Cement	3	0.7	1	0.4	2	1.1
Timber	10	2.4	3	1.3	7	3.5
Non-metallic minerals	10	2.4	6	2.8	4	2.1
Fertilizers and farm chemicals	18	4.4	5	2.6	13	6.4
Grain	33	8.1	12	5.7	21	10.6
Salt	8	2.1	4	2.1	4	2.0
Other	48	11.7	27	12.6	21	10.7
Total	406	100.0	211	100.0	195	100.0

Source: State Statistical Bureau (1988a, p. 353).

Bulk-handling Facilities

Several oil, coal, and mineral deep-water berths able to handle vessels of 50,000 to 100,000 d.w.t. have been completed at Beilun (Ningbo Port), Dalian, Qinhuangdao, and Shijiu. The large-scale bulk-handling berths built during the 1980s are equipped with advanced loading and unloading equipment and so are more efficient. A good example is the Beilun ore-transfer terminal in Ningbo Harbour which came into operation at the end of 1982. This has one 100,000-tonne ore

Figure 5.1 Distribution of seaports in China

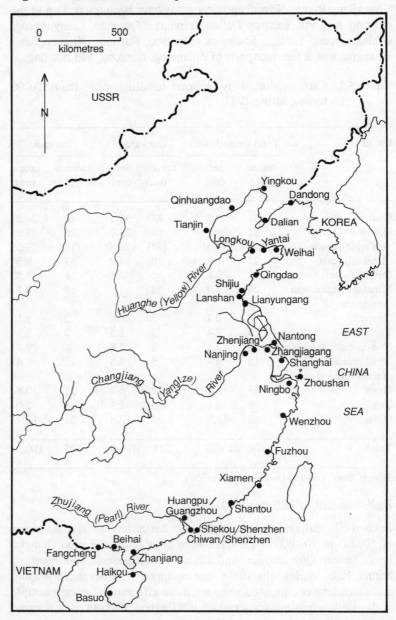

discharging berth, two 25,000-tonne ore loading berths, and a stockpile capable of holding 500,000 tonnes. Others are Qinhuangdao Harbour and Shijiu Harbour which, respectively, can handle thirty-eight and fifteen million tonnes of coal annually. At Qinhuangdao a major expansion scheme has been underway since the mid-1980s. Construction of three coal berths, beginning in April 1984 and completed five years later, increased the harbour's annual export capacity by thirty million tonnes. Of its 1987 throughput (fifty-four million tonnes), 70 per cent was coal (*Beijing Review*, 1988, 31(27), p. 31). It is proposed that by the end of the century Qinhuangdao will have forty-two berths with a handling capacity of 125 million tonnes: if this is achieved it would be one of the ten largest harbours in the world and the leading exporter of coal.

Container facilities

The construction of container berths has been an important innovation during the 1980s: previously this type of freight had accounted for only about 20 per cent of the throughput handled for foreign trade. During the 1980s, however, the use of containers has expanded rapidly. Eight berths have been constructed at Tianjin, Shanghai, and Huangpu (four of them being in operation by 1985), thus making these three ports major centres of seaborne container traffic.

Meanwhile, several old wharves at Shanghai, Dalian, Qingdao, and Xiamen have been reconstructed and converted into semi-container terminals or multi-purpose wharves. By 1985 the total installed capacity amounted to 800,000 twenty-foot equivalent units (TEUs) (Yang, 1987). The first full deep-water container terminal in China came into operation in 1981 at Xingang (Tianjin Port), and by early 1988 it had seven berths for special purposes and an annual capacity of 400,000 TEUs (Zhang, 1988). The container wharf at No. 4 Basin, Tianjin, with three berths totalling 895 m, can simultaneously accommodate one ship with a capacity of 1,000 TEUs (23,000 d.w.t.) and two others with 1,800 TEUs (35,000 d.w.t.). The water in front of the berth has been dredged to 12 m, and the storage yard has a capacity of 14,918 TEUs (Yang, 1987). Two berths at the Duntouji container terminal in Huangpu Port, Guangzhou, came into service in April 1983: one can accommodate second-generation container ships. The two berths in No. 9 District of Shanghai Port, put into use in 1983, can also accommodate second-generation ships and have an annual capacity of 200,000 TEUs. By the end of 1987 China had twenty-three ports (sixteen being seaports) for international container shipping: during that year the total international trade throughput amounted to 689,000 TEUs (State Statistical Bureau, 1988b, p. 168).

Regional Impacts

The open-door policies and the upgrading of harbour facilities have had considerable impact on the hinterlands of the ports. Chen (1984) estimated that 70 to 80 per cent of the volume of cargo handled by Tianjin and Shanghai in the early 1980s originated from within a radius of 500 km. In most instances port-related activities form the most important industrial base and this strengthens the links with the hinterland (Hoyle and Pinder, 1981; Hoyle and Hilling, 1984).

Of the eight seaports listed in Table 5.1 that each handled more than 10 million tonnes in 1987, only two (Qinhuangdao and Zhanjiang) have limited hinterlands and are used mainly for the export trade in coal, oil, and other minerals. In contrast, the others (Shanghai, Tianjin, Huangpu/Guangzhou, Dalian, Qingdao, and Ningbo) all have vast hinterlands and are also the leading industrial centres. Consequently, these cities, each of which had more than one million inhabitants in 1987, have multiple functions. For the same reason, Fuzhou and Xiamen rank seventh and eighth in terms of industrial output value which is higher than their ranks in terms of port development (Table 5.3).

The role of seaports in the SEZs has greatly changed. For example, the industrial output value of Shenzhen, Zhuhai, Shantou, and Xiamen increased, respectively, 96.4, 11.7, 2.3, and 2.5 times during the 1980–7 period. The high growth rates for Shenzhen and Zhuhai are a reflection of their proximity to Hong Kong and Macao. During this same period, the number of deep-water berths rose from none to five, including Shekou and Chiwan, and the throughput handled by all the berths in Shenzhen alone increased from 300,000 to 3,540,000 tonnes. The previously small frontier town of Shenzhen with only 84,000 people became a medium-size city of 287,000 inhabitants.

Problems Facing China's Seaports

Despite great efforts, the growth in the handling capacity of China's seaports has failed to keep pace with demand. The volume of sea transport expanded after 1978: thus the cargo handled at the twenty-three seaports listed in Table 5.1 increased from fourteen million tonnes in 1952 to 193 million tonnes in 1978 (Xue, 1984, p. 105) and

394 million tonnes in 1987. During the Sixth Five-year Plan Period (1981–5), the throughput of seaports that handled more than 100,000 tonnes a year increased by an average of 8.4 per cent annually (State Statistical Bureau, 1988b, p. 126). As a result, serious delays are commonplace but it seems that there will be no quick solution.

Table 5.3 Rank order and scale of some seaports, 1987

Port	Throughput		Gross industrial output value		Population	
	rank	tonnes (m.)	rank	yuan (000 m.)	rank	m.
Shanghai	1	> 30	1	> 10	1	7.21
Qinhuangdao	2	> 30	14	< 2	14	0.46
Dalian	3	> 30	4	> 10	4	2.27
Qingdao	4	> 30	5	5–10	5	1.29
Huangpu	5	5–30	3	> 10	3	3.41[a]
Ningbo	6	5–30	6	5–10	7	1.04
Tianjin	7	5–30	2	> 10	2	5.54
Zhanjiang	8	5–30	13	< 2	8	0.96
Lianyungang	9	5–30	12	< 2	13	0.48
Yantai	10	5–30	9	2–5	10	0.75
Xiamen	11	1–5	8	2–5	11	0.56
Fuzhou	12	1–5	7	2–5	6	1.23
Wenzhou	13	1–5	11	< 2	12	0.54
Shantou	14	1–5	10	2–5	9	0.78

Note: *a* Guangzhou.

Sources: State Statistical Bureau (1988a, p. 351; 1988b, pp. 23–31, 95–103).

Spatial Maldistribution

The distribution of seaports along China's 18,000-km coastline is far from ideal, with most of the larger ones being located north of Shanghai (Figure 5.1). The average distance between ports capable of handling more than 50,000 tonnes annually is about 500 km and there are only eleven deep-water berths able to handle ships over 10,000 d.w.t. for every 1,000 km of coastline. Furthermore, of the deep-water berths, ninety-nine are located from Lianyungang northwards and 146 from Shanghai northwards (see Table 5.1): together the latter handle 77 per cent of China's total volume of cargo. Shanghai alone accounted for 33 per cent of the cargo that passed through the twenty-three main seaports in 1987, thus necessitating the wasteful transfer of large tonnages. Moreover, little attempt has been made to develop harbours on the 6,500 or so coastal islands, many of which have no such facilities. Even Hainan Island and the Zhoushan Islands have only a few berths capable of handling vessels of 10,000 d.w.t.

Shortage of Specialized Ports and Berths

There are very few large-scale specialized berths for cargoes like coal, oil, ores, cement, timber, and containers. For example, north of the Changjiang River mouth there are only ten 10,000-tonne coal handling berths (at Qinhuangdao, Qingdao, and Lianyungang), and three special coal berths (at Bayuquan, Yingkou, and Sijiu); to the south, only Shanghai, Ningbo, Mawei, and Huangpu have special coal unloading berths. The lack of such facilities is yet another obstacle preventing sufficient quantities of coal from Shanxi Province, in particular, reaching the densely populated industrial centres along the east coast.

Disharmony Between Port and Other Types of Development

Whereas major seaports, like Dalian, Tianjin, and Shanghai, are short of berths and lack adequate handling capacity, several local ports – especially in South China – are under-utilized. At many ports land along the waterfront has been used for other purposes, thus limiting the area available for warehousing and bulk storage. For all China's ports warehousing averages 117 m^2 per metre of waterfront, and in Qingdao (China's fourth busiest port) the figure is only 48.1 m^2.

With the exception of Shanghai and Huangpu where several transport modes are available to handle freight to and from the port, most have to rely very largely on railway facilities. For example, some 80 to 90 per cent of the freight handled at Qinhuangdao and Dalian, the second and third busiest ports, arrives or leaves by rail.

In some coastal cities, the growth of industry and population has been so rapid that the construction of port facilities has lagged behind. At Dalian and Qingdao, for instance, shortages of fresh water, electricity, and inner city transport have created problems for the smooth running of the port. In contrast, at places like Shijiu, Beilun, Beihai, and Fangcheng, the construction of residential accommodation and other urban infrastructure has lagged behind harbour construction, thus weakening the local economies.

An overall difficulty is that much more attention has been paid to the construction of individual ports than to the rational development of port *systems*. As a result, wasteful duplication has occurred: in the Zhujiang (Pearl) River Delta, for example, even though Huangpu port already existed and Shekou and Chiwan Harbours have been built at Shenzhen, other new facilities are under construction or are planned.

Conditions for the Development of China's Seaports

China has a continental coastline of 18,000 km and an island coastline of 14,000 km. There are more than 100 excellent harbours and gulfs from Dalian, Liaodong Bay, and Bohai Bay in the north to Beibu Bay in the south, and thirty-three deep-water sites suitable for constructing berths to handle vessels of 50,000 to 100,000 d.w.t. (Anon., 1985). Basically, then, the development of China's deep-water berthing facilities has been far from adequate. For example, with more than half the oil production, one-third of the steel output, and one-seventh of the national output value in 1987, north-east China (with 2,100 km of coastline) has only twenty-six deep-water berths capable of handling vessels of 10,000 d.w.t.. Mainly located in Dalian, these can barely handle 90 per cent of the region's foreign trade.

Inland Rivers

The Changjiang and Zhujiang systems are by far the most important: in 1984 the former transported 220 million tonnes of freight (67 per cent of all inland waterway traffic) and the latter carried 54 million tonnes (16 per cent). On the Changjiang, ocean-going vessels of up to 10,000 d.w.t. can, on high tide, reach Nanjing, 350 km upstream, while vessels of up to 5,000 d.w.t. are able to travel a further 700 km to Wuhan. Although Nanjing is China's busiest inland port with a throughput of thirty-six million tonnes a year, three-fifths of this consists of crude oil which is ferried across the river from the terminus of the Shengli pipeline to the refinery on the southern shore. The 98-km port area has thirty-nine docks which can berth seventy-five 2,000 to 25,000 d.w.t. vessels simultaneously. In 1987 Nanjing began a container shipping operation with a US partner (Dai, 1988a, p. 15).

Port Development Strategies

The future development of seaports should take account of the need to establish a system to make rational use of waterfront areas and thus ensure the efficient handling of minerals and raw materials as well as import and export cargoes. Consideration should be given not only to the layout of the harbour areas in a particular city but also to the regional and national distribution of such facilities. Seaports should be 'grouped' with overlapping hinterlands and functions so as to create greater flexibility. There are three major east coast port groupings.

(a) The Bohai Rim Area which includes (i) the central hub port of Dalian with its 'wing' ports such as Dandong, Yingkou, and Huludao; (ii) the central ports of Qinhuangdao and Tianjin; and (iii) the Shandong Peninsula group which includes Yantai and Qingdao.

(b) The South Shandong, North Jiangsu, and Changjiang Delta group which includes (i) the South Shandong/North Jiangsu ports centred on Lianyungang and Shijiu; (ii) the Changjiang Delta ports centred on Shanghai but including also the river ports of Nanjing, Zhenjiang, Zhanjiagang, and Nantong; and (iii) those south of Hangzhou Bay centred on Ningbo and Hangzhou including Zhoushan.

(c) The southern group includes the 'second-class' ports of Wenzhou, North Fujian, South Fujian, the Zhujiang Delta, Zhanjiang, Hainan Island, and Beihai-Fangcheng.

An appropriate structure of port groupings can form a sound basis for both the technical transformation of old ports and harbours and the sensible selection of new ones. In practice some port groups are being formed and this has led to the dispersal of cargo handling from overtaxed old ports to under-used medium and small ones.

One example is Dalian port, located at the southern end of Liaodong Peninsula (see Figure A2.1). This has an excellent seagulf and a strategic location as its hinterland includes the whole of north-eastern China: this explains why it ranks highly in the import-export trade. However, it lacks the capacity to handle the available traffic so that additional deep-water berths have been constructed at Zhanyuwan and Dayaowan; cargo has been dispersed to ports like Dandong, Yingkou, and Huludao; and Bayuquan Harbour (Yingkou) and Dadong Harbour (Dandong) are being built up. All these rearrangements will enable this group of ports to operate as a system.

Another example is the group of ports along the central part of the coast from Lianyungang to Hangzhou Bay. These occupy an extremely important strategic position with a very large hinterland, and therefore they should be given development priority. This is particularly the case with the Changjiang Delta group of ports centred on Shanghai. This latter port, which includes twenty provinces in its hinterland and has sea links with 150 countries and regions, is the largest multi-functional port in China and the hub of a network of river, ocean, and land transport connections. This port is grossly over-burdened and there is little potential for more development along its waterfront. Moreover, as the Changjiang is only 7.5 to 9.5 m deep at its mouth it is navigable only to vessels of less than 25,000 d.w.t. (Huang, 1987). However, ports like Nantong and Zhanjiagang to the north and Ningbo and Zhoushan to the south could be tapped as conditions there are favourable for the construction of large-scale deep-water container berths.   Already a port combination with Shanghai as its centre has been organized to redistribute cargoes to these other ports, and it is hoped that in future it will be possible to disperse cargo even further afield. In addition, an outer port with con-tainer handling facilities has been established at Shanghai.

A basic national strategy is to emphasize coastal development now as the basis for accelerating the economic growth of inland areas later. The extension of port facilities, however, must be synchronized with the construction of the necessary urban infrastructure: in short, invest-ments in port and urban development must go hand in hand (Zheng and Gu, 1987).   Early in 1990 the China Ocean Shipping Company began a container shuttle service connecting the ports of Shanghai, Xingang (Tianjin), Dalian, and Qingdao aimed at assisting vessels on scheduled international sailings to collect and distribute cargoes.

Most investment during the remainder of this century will be concentrated in four core areas: Central and Southern Liaoning Province, the Beijing-Tianjin-Tangshan area, and the Changjiang and Zhujiang Deltas. Thus, it is likely that an overall port-city system will be formed with the Bohai Rim Economic Belt, the Changjiang Delta, and the South China Economic Belt as the three main sub-systems. Dalian, Tianjin, Qingdao, Shanghai, and Guangzhou will be the main centres.   More reform of the port and city management systems is required, especially because of the open-door policy. For more than thirty years, fifteen of the important seaports were controlled by the Ministry of Communications independently of the relevant provincial and municipal governments so that many contradictions occurred. In addition, foreign trade, railways, and large enterprises have been managed separately so that co-ordinated overall planning was very difficult.

During 1984 and 1985, the ports of Tianjin, Shanghai, and Dalian began to implement systems of 'joint leadership by ministry and municipality' with the latter as the top organ, and port offices were given more financial authority. From 1987 all the seaports had changed their management system and began to be run by the cities in which they were located. It is necessary for port-cities to have greater control over the overall management of their enterprises, transport facilities, urban construction, urban economy, and the development of foreign trade.

6 Spatial Aspects of the Natural Increase of China's Population

T. H. HULL

MOST discussions of population change in the People's Republic of China (PRC) begin with the statement that it has the largest number of inhabitants in the world and then move on to discuss the rate of growth and government policies to control it. Such approaches correctly highlight the problems of the size and velocity of change, since these dimensions have global implications in an age of fears about the impact of population on the environment, and consequent questions of climatological change, carrying capacity, and prospects for the cessation of population growth. Consideration of the magnitude and rate of growth alone is, however, inadequate to provide an understanding of the demographic challenge facing the PRC. Of equal importance is the geographical distribution of the population and the spatial differentials of the components of changes in natural increase: fertility and mortality. This chapter considers some of these spatial issues in an attempt to understand China's recent experience in controlling the rate of growth of its large population.

Immediately after Liberation, China's new government had little idea about the size or rate of growth of the population. Due to many years of social disruption the country had not had a modern census, and thus one of the first priorities was to hold a head count. This was carried out in 1953 and produced an estimate of 568 million. This figure was surprisingly large, and supported the argument that the rate of population growth should be curtailed. A family-planning programme was instituted in 1956 but had little impact on fertility during its first few years. The available methods of contraception were relatively difficult to use, and the clinic-based approach taken by the programme reached only a small portion of the population. Moreover, despite its general expressions of commitment, the leadership did not give birth control a high priority in the turbulent political agenda of the time. The total fertility rate (TFR) of the mid-1950s was about 5.5 births per woman (Coale and Chen, 1987, p. 25), a reflection of the return to family stability after the war-torn 1940s.

At the end of the 1950s the Great Leap Forward was proclaimed and all energies were turned to attempting a major transformation of the economy. Total fertility climbed above six births per woman in 1957, but between 1959 and 1961 it fell sharply during a drought-induced famine which devastated the country for more than two years. In a vain search for food, millions of people left their homes and wandered in the countryside or went to towns and cities. Families were separated for long periods and the fertility rate plummeted to 3.3 per woman. By 1963 the economic situation had returned to normal, and fertility rebounded to unprecedented levels as family life resumed (Kane, 1987: Peng, 1987).

Following the peak in post-Liberation fertility in 1963, the registered TFR steadily declined from a national level of 7.5 to about 2.5 children per woman in 1982 (Coale and Chen, 1987, p. 25). In some provinces and cities by 1984 the TFR had fallen to or below the long-term level of fertility consonant with simple population replacement. Shanghai, a municipality with over twelve million people, had a TFR of only 1.1 in 1984, indicating that on average each couple was having only one child — the family size being promoted by the national family-planning programme. Nationally the TFR in 1986 had declined to 2.4. A general picture of recent trends in total fertility rates is presented in Figure 6.1.

Similar declines are displayed in Table 6.1 for all the provinces, municipalities, and autonomous regions included in the 1982 'One in One Thousand Survey' analysed by Coale and Chen (1987). In line with previous analyses, this Table shows the very wide variation of fertility rates in 1970. Only Shanghai had a TFR below 3, and at 2.3 it was approaching the level of replacement fertility whereby each couple produce two surviving children on average. Most provinces had TFRs over five and a few averaged six or seven surviving children. By 1982 there were major declines: five provinces had fewer than two surviving children; five others had between two and two and a half; and only three now had above four. Throughout China the decline was fairly uniform between 40 and 60 per cent, with only five high-fertility provinces registering declines of less than 40 per cent. Even so, these had TFRs in 1982 which only twelve years previously would have been regarded as moderate by national standards, thus indicating how widespread were the factors encouraging fertility decline. Even though the Eastern, Middle, and Western Zones have enormous economic and social differences, their fertility declines are remarkably similar (Freedman et al., 1988).

Figure 6.1 Total fertility rates, 1970–85

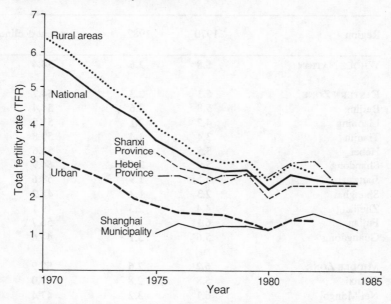

Sources: Chen (1983); State Statistical Bureau (1986b); and, for rural population, State
Statistical Bureau (1986a, p. 123).

The experience of some provinces has been remarkable. Jilin went
from high fertility to below replacement in little over a decade, and
many provinces with traditions of large family size have made a transition to small families in virtually one step. The rapidity of this fertility decline is breathtaking, and in terms of scale and initial social
background, is unprecedented in world demographic history. Since
most provinces in China are on a par with moderate-size or large
nations, the importance of this fertility decline becomes even clearer.
In terms of its global impact, China's experience is in the nature of
truly *continental* change. One measure of the effect came in early
1987 when, following a few years of apparent decline in the world
birth rate, the Population Reference Bureau (an independent monitor
of world population trends based in Washington) issued a press release
stating that world births were up largely due to small registered
increases in China's birth rate. The Bureau indicated that if China
continued to ease up on its population policy 'it will shatter current
assumptions about a continuing slowdown in the global population's
growth rate' (*Canberra Times*, 15 April 1987).

Table 6.1 Provincial trends in total fertility rates, 1970–82

Region	1970	1982	Per cent decline
WHOLE NATION	**5.8**	**2.6**	**54.4**
EASTERN ZONE	**5.1**	**2.3**	**54.7**
Beijing	5.8	2.6	54.4
Liaoning	4.2	2.1	51.5
Tianjin	3.4	1.4	59.8
Hebei	5.5	2.7	51.6
Shandong	5.9	2.1	64.9
Jiangsu	4.5	1.9	58.6
Shanghai	2.3	1.3	41.2
Zhejiang	4.4	2.3	49.1
Fujian	6.1	2.6	56.7
Guangdong	5.6	3.1	44.6
MIDDLE ZONE	**6.2**	**2.6**	**57.9**
Shanxi	5.8	2.8	51.0
Nei Mongol	6.1	3.2	47.4
Jilin	6.2	2.0	68.6
Heilongjiang	5.6	2.7	52.5
Anhui	6.4	2.4	63.0
Jiangxi	7.0	2.9	58.8
Henan	6.4	2.4	62.4
Hubei	6.0	2.2	63.0
Hunan	6.1	3.2	47.0
GREATER NORTH-WEST ZONE	**6.1**	**3.0**	**49.9**
Ningxia	6.1	3.8	36.5
Shaanxi	5.5	2.5	53.9
Gansu	6.8	2.7	60.2
Qinghai	6.2	4.4	28.1
Xinjiang	6.3	4.0	35.8
GREATER SOUTH-WEST ZONE	**6.3**	**3.3**	**48.5**
Guangxi	5.8	3.8	34.9
Guizhou	7.0	4.5	35.7
Yunnan	6.0	3.8	36.6
Sichuan	6.4	2.5	60.7
Xizang (Tibet)	n.a.	n.a.	n.a.

Source: Coale and Chen (1987, pp. 25–185).

Figure 6.2 Trends in the mean age at first marriage of women by urban and rural residence, 1949–86

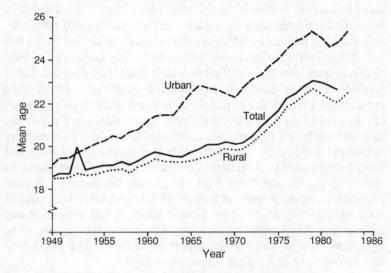

Sources: 1949 to 1981: Zhao and Yu (1983); 1982 to 1986: Li, R. (1987).

There are three immediate causes for this major decline in fertility. Firstly, the average age of marriage for women rose from about nineteen in the 1950s to about twenty-three in the early 1980s (Zhao and Yu, 1983). Most of this increase took place in the 1970s (Figure 6.2), when a campaign to promote late marriage encouraged women to wait until about twenty-five and men to about thirty years of age. These 'ideal' ages were strongly promoted, with variations between provinces, but were unrelated to the legal minimum marriage age of eighteen for women and twenty for men embodied in the 1950 Marriage Law. When the law was changed in 1981 to set a new minimum of twenty for women and twenty-two for men, the campaign for later marriage lost much of its force and the average age of marriage fell slightly giving rise to some upward pressure on fertility.

Secondly, there has been a systematic increase in the availability and use of contraceptive methods throughout the country so that current use rates in China during the 1980s were at a level more typical of a developed country than one of the poorer nations of the world (Table 6.2). There is some concern about the consistency of published estimates by the State Family Planning Commission (SFPC) because they are based on a complex system of reporting which is not unrelated to the targets used by the programme, but the general picture is clear. Three-quarters of the married women of reproductive age (or about half all the women in the age range) are currently recorded to be protected from pregnancy by modern, efficient methods of birth control, the most popular of which are the intra-uterine device (IUD) and female sterilization. Male sterilization, while only one-third the level of female sterilization, is still more widely used than the pill. Other methods, such as condoms, rhythm, and diaphragm, which have experienced a resurgence of popularity in some Western countries, are of only minor importance in the Chinese family planning programme. Regional variations in registered contraceptive use in 1981 were very substantial (Table 6.3). Generally there was greater use of IUDs and female sterilization in the Eastern Zone, and relatively high reliance on the pill in the Greater North-west and Greater South-west. Sichuan Province, however, stands out because of the remarkably high rates of male sterilization, an effective method which is less expensive and troublesome than female sterilization. Condom usage appears to be significant only in major urban complexes in the Greater North-west and, surprisingly, in Xinjiang Autonomous Region.

Table 6.2 Reported trends in contraceptive use: proportion of women of reproductive age, 1983–5

Year			Sterilization		
	IUD	Pill	female	male	Condom
1983	28.4	3.5	25.9	8.9	1.5
1984	26.6	3.5	25.4	8.4	1.6
1985	27.5	4.4	25.9	8.4	2.3

Source: Poston and Gu (1987, p. 537).

Thirdly, the increase in the availability and use of abortion services has meant that fertility can be effectively controlled, even after failure of conventional contraceptives. It is difficult to obtain current data on abortion in China, especially because of sensitivity arising out of the US withdrawal of support from the United Nations Fund for Population Activities as a result of allegations of coercion and promotion of abortion as a method of family planning. The Chinese government has consistently denied that coercion is condoned in the promotion of contraception, and has argued that in China, as in the USA, abortion is

Table 6.3 Regional variations in reported contraceptive use: per cent of married fecund women, 1981

Region	IUD	Pill	Sterilization female	Sterilization male	Condom
WHOLE NATION	**38.1**	**9.3**	**20.8**	**4.7**	**3.2**
EASTERN ZONE					
Beijing	20.8	29.5	11.3	1.4	14.3
Liaoning	42.9	5.6	30.4	1.0	5.6
Tianjin	29.4	21.4	10.6	2.1	13.9
Hebei	56.9	7.6	8.5	1.9	3.5
Shandong	40.5	2.4	23.1	15.5	1.4
Jiangsu	43.1	9.2	25.9	5.2	0.9
Shanghai	24.0	23.1	22.7	3.8	7.9
Zhejiang	27.8	11.4	31.4	3.0	1.8
Fujian	41.5	1.3	25.9	9.9	1.7
Guangdong	41.4	2.6	20.2	8.0	1.7
MIDDLE ZONE					
Shanxi	52.3	7.1	17.3	0.4	2.7
Nei Mongol	30.8	16.7	21.4	0.5	3.1
Jilin	51.2	4.1	25.4	0.4	3.3
Heilongjiang	48.8	3.4	30.7	1.1	3.3
Anhui	46.1	7.6	18.8	7.1	1.3
Jiangxi	41.8	2.8	31.1	1.3	0.7
Henan	42.1	1.9	27.5	7.4	1.6
Hubei	43.7	6.5	22.6	5.3	1.4
Hunan	28.4	2.9	34.1	9.7	1.5
GREATER NORTH-WEST ZONE					
Ningxia	18.4	23.1	33.6	0.2	1.7
Shaanxi	60.1	5.1	11.8	1.2	2.4
Gansu	41.1	3.3	34.4	0.6	1.6
Qinghai	21.5	20.4	7.8	0.1	1.7
Xinjiang	15.9	23.7	24.0	0.7	6.2
GREATER SOUTH-WEST ZONE					
Guangxi	39.1	8.4	5.1	1.5	1.5
Guizhou	45.4	1.8	8.8	8.4	1.0
Yunnan	35.5	4.8	9.4	4.2	1.8
Sichuan	35.4	3.0	9.0	30.7	1.6
Xizang (Tibet)	n.a.	n.a.	n.a.	n.a.	n.a.

Source: Poston and Gu (1987, p. 537).

sanctioned as a back-up against contraceptive failure, but is not advocated as a primary method of birth control. There is no doubt that abortion is a widespread practice, largely undertaken voluntarily by women who have been unable to obtain adequate contraceptive supplies. Most women experience at least one abortion in their reproductive careers as is clear from unpublished tabulations of the State Statistical Bureau's 'Three Province Survey' shown to the author in Beijing. Interviews he conducted in urban and rural areas of Shaanxi and Guangdong Provinces early in 1987 confirm Greenhalgh's (1986, p. 506) conclusion that abortion is discouraged by government workers and hospital staff, at least in part because it is an expensive procedure. The difficulty is that the IUD commonly used in China, the steel spring-ring, has a relatively high failure rate (Short, 1986, p. 76), and large numbers of married women are not using contraceptives even though they do not want to become pregnant. Thus, the demand for abortion services, at least for the time being, remains substantial (Table 6.4).

The fact of widespread fertility decline in China is not now in dispute nor is the means of achieving that decline, that is, radical change in behaviour with regard to marriage, contraception, and abortion (Coale, 1984). Less clearly understood are the causal mechanisms underlying these changes. Government has played a major role in promoting lower fertility and providing the technology to achieve this but it is unclear how these changes are formulated and executed, and what roles are played by the various levels of government in the fertility control policy. Beyond the direct influences of the family-planning programme there have been many other social and economic changes influencing people's desires for a specific number of children. Most of the fertility decline since 1963 occurred before the formalization of the national 'one-child per family' policy in 1979, and well before the 1982–3 period of local bureaucratic abuses which gave rise to reports of coercion in family planning (Greenhalgh, 1986, p. 491).

Governmental Changes

Underlying the fertility decline, and forming the framework of all fertility decision making, there have been major changes in the style and effectiveness of government in China since 1963. During the early years of this period, government — in line with society in general — was recovering from the 'bitter years' of famine and dislocation. In part the famine had been induced by poor economic management in 1959–60. When crops first began to fail as a result

Table 6.4 Ratios of abortions to live births, 1970–87

Year	Estimated No. of Live Births (B) (millions)	Estimated No. of Abortions (A) (millions)	Ratio A/B
1970	30.3	n.a.	n.a.
1971	26.1	3.9	0.2
1972	26.0	4.8	0.2
1973	24.9	5.1	0.2
1974	22.6	5.0	0.2
1975	21.3	5.1	0.2
1976	18.7	4.7[a]	0.4
1977	20.0	5.2	0.3
1978	20.0	5.4	0.3
1979	21.0	7.9	0.4
1980	17.7	9.5	0.5
1981	20.8	8.7	0.4
1982	21.3	12.4	0.6
1983	19.0	14.4	0.8
1984	18.1	8.9	0.5
1985	18.6	n.a.	n.a.
1986	22.0	11.6	0.5
1987	23.2	n.a.	n.a.

Note: [a] Reported in Zhang (1981, p. 113) as 6,570,000.
Sources: Hardee-Cleaveland and Banister (1988, p. 276); to 1984 based on Ministry of
Public Health (1985); see also Duan (1986).

of the drought, administrators at successive layers of government
inflated crop production reports to impress their superiors and live up
to grossly unrealistic targets set as part of the Great Leap Forward. It
thus took a long time for the true dimensions of the agricultural
disaster to be recognized and for remedial and palliative actions to be
taken. As the PRC worked its way out of the difficulties, the Party and
the government improved administrative lines of communication, and
stressed the importance of accurate information being sent from local
governmental units to the centre (Liu and Wu, 1986, pp. 271 *et seq.*).
These changes clearly had a spatial dimension, with much of the
improvement depending on the expansion of transport and communication systems that were run-down or non-existent.

The Cultural Revolution and its aftermath (1966–76) caused great dislocation throughout China, and brought hardship to millions of students, officials, and professionals. The impact on the actual structure of administration is hard to evaluate: certainly, routine activities were interrupted and many inefficient practices promoted. At the same time, an entire generation was systematically indoctrinated with Maoist thought, anti-individualism, and group discipline. This experience left its mark on the society, and altered the relationship between the individual, families, work units, and the state. The impact of these changes on patterns of family formation in different regions has not been well addressed.

In the late 1970s the Party and the government undertook a series of reforms which substantially altered the production systems of the Chinese economy. Peasants were allowed to cultivate plots of land on a 'production responsibility' basis, which required them to return a portion of the harvest to the collective, but allowed them to keep the remainder of the crop for their own use or sale. Free markets were set up in competition with state-run stores and farmers were allowed to sell their own produce in nearby towns and cities. Industry was encouraged through the establishment of Special Economic Zones and a system of township enterprises. Arguably, much of the energy behind the reforms of the late 1970s arose as a reaction to the excesses of the Cultural Revolution. The enthusiasm with which peasants took up the cultivation of individual plots and participated in free markets in the cities was matched by the growing interest of government and intellectuals in a wide range of cultural and social endeavours. The movement that started in 1978 sought to bring about 'Four Modernizations' in agriculture, industry, science and technology, and national defence. But as the events of late 1986 and early 1987 attest, this was not to be accomplished by an importation of 'bourgeois liberalization'. Any change, according to Zhao Ziyang, must proceed in accordance with the 'Four Cardinal Principles' of adherence to the socialist road, the people's democratic dictatorship, leadership of the Communist Party, and Marxism-Leninism and Mao Zedong thought. It was this concern that sparked major leadership changes in January 1987 and led to a campaign to rid the country of bourgeois liberalism, defined as opposition to the leadership of the Party. One unfortunate, but predictable, side-effect of the campaign was the report that people who did not use family planning, or for that matter participate in the reafforestation campaign, were being accused by over-zealous local functionaries of being 'bourgeois liberals': the central government was quick to brand this as nonsense and call on the officials to avoid such politically charged rhetoric.

Thus, the image of the 1953–88 period is of large waves of national change carried forward by many small regional and locally based experiments, reforms, and reactions. The picture is immensely complex, but not all the changes to, or reiterations of, the governmental and Party administrations are important to an understanding of the changes in fertility behaviour. The three aspects of most direct relevance are the place of population planning in the economic planning system, the initiatives of government in birth control programmes, and the influence of broad socio-economic changes on fertility.

Population in a System of Centralized Planning

In a socialist economy and a Communist state the issue of control is crucial. The various units of the economy are not fully self-regulating even under the reforms introduced in the PRC since 1978, and the price system does not always serve the function of setting market-clearing terms of exchange. Instead, producers and distributors rely on information from central authorities to help them set the levels of production. If that advice is incorrect the market is put under stress, with either over- or under-production indicating an inefficient exploitation of resources. Efficiency thus rests on the quality of information received and disseminated, and the fulfilment of production plans by individual units. Government is responsible for monitoring this process and ensuring that individual producers conform to the expectations of the economic plan.

To achieve these goals, the government of China — in common with governments everywhere — has developed a large battery of control instruments including the principles and policies to guide decision making, routine procedures for collecting and forwarding information, and the system of sanctions which enforce compliance with government orders. Economic planning is a continuous process within a regular cycle of five-year plans set at all levels of government. The plans are drawn up on the basis of suggestions generated at lower levels of government, and reviewed, revised, and compiled at higher levels. Planning involves both horizontal and vertical consultations, with the planning agency at each level conferring with other departments at the same level before passing on suggestions or decisions to different levels. In the rhetoric of the planning process stress is placed on carefully examining the 'concrete realities' and seeking 'truth from facts' in developing targets. In the final analysis the plan should, ideally, represent a complex consensus among the various components of the government and the Party.

Population plans are conceived as a specialized component of the total planning process, with the SFPC responsible for setting 'production targets' at all the levels of the system, down to the neighbourhood units. As with all economic plans, officials are admonished to pay attention to the realities of their local situations and told to be responsive to the concerns of the people under their responsibility.

Because of the way population concerns are integrated into the process of planning, targets are not set as rigid, immutable goals but are open to variation, either through redefinition or reinterpretation as the situation changes, or as difficulties are discovered. At the local level the discussions of plans involve a basically 'common-sense' approach by people who have firsthand experience of the problems of implementation and, in time, their experiences and concerns are reflected through the government structure to high levels of decision making. One way of depicting this process is in terms of a 'precipitation-evaporation' cycle, where policy pronouncements come down in a deluge, and reactions from implementation units rise up more slowly, yet effectively, to build up pressure for another downpour.

Although it is obvious to people in China, Westerners need to understand that planning processes are regarded as being an integral part of the current economic reforms, rather than something being replaced by the structures of the reforms (Liu and Wu, 1986). Planners regard the current developments as the natural culmination of the socialist economy in China, which had only been interrupted in the past by the foolishness of the Great Leap Forward and the Cultural Revolution — both of which were basically harmful to the planning process they were seeking to build. The Tiananmen Incident in June 1989, and mass arrests thereafter, have sent shockwaves through the planning system, but it is too early to determine how the events will affect the birth control programme.

Government Initiatives in Family Planning Policy

The development of fertility control policies and plans has seen a series of 'campaigns' in China.
(a) *First* campaign, 1956–9. (Relied on clinics and was interrupted by the failure of the Great Leap Forward.)
(b) *Second* campaign, 1962–6. (A refurbished programme interrupted by the Cultural Revolution.)

(c) *Third* campaign, 1971–9. (This was named *wan*, *xi*, and *shao* [later marriage, sparser child-spacing, and fewer children] to reflect the core messages of the campaign.)

(d) *Fourth* campaign, 1979–84. (One child per couple.)

(e) *Fifth* campaign, 1984–present. (Reflected in Document 7 of 1984 and Document 13 of 1986 which modified the one-child policy.)

Each had its own particular character reflecting the period when it was formulated. They were not *stages* in the development of the family-planning programme so much as different styles of family planning based on the emergence of various governmental structures. This distinction is important as it helps to explain the fragility of family-planning policy in the face of administrative and socio-economic changes. It also serves to shift attention away from the rhetoric of family planning policy *per se* to the question of how that policy is formulated and, by extension, how it might be altered.

The first campaign was a product of the Great Leap Forward, the second was an attempt to rekindle the effort to reduce fertility but was cut short by the Cultural Revolution, and the third was a conventional attempt to promote a programme of voluntary fertility control. The fourth campaign is the most puzzling because, although it came about at the formation of a period of new openness in the PRC, it represented an unprecedented attempt at government control in family decision making. It must be distinguished from the fifth campaign because the reforms begun in 1984 and consolidated in 1988 have created an entirely new approach to family planning and, by extension, population planning. The fourth campaign was essentially an aberration out of context with regard to the post-1978 reform period: the fifth campaign thus represents a correction of that deviation.

The major forms of national family-planning policy are contained in documents of the Central Committee of the Communist Party, the Five-year Plans, and the directives of the SFPC. The structure and function of the programme are also affected by the decisions of the Ministry of Health, the Ministry of Communications, and other agencies charged with service and logistic responsibilities for family planning. The central policies are expressed in terms of general principles and long-term numerical targets. On their own they do not constitute a blueprint for action and, in fact, the generality of expression leaves a fairly wide margin for interpretation by those lower government levels responsible for actual implementation and planning.

A typical scenario for the development of policy is illustrated by the 'one child per couple' campaign (1979–84). The first hints of this came in 1977 and 1978 as lower governmental levels, grappling with the demands of the third campaign, sought to ensure equitable compliance with the goals of drastically reducing the rate of population growth. Local policy innovations of setting a maximum family size were suggested and tested, and these were reported to higher levels of government and disseminated through the mass media. Demographers presented projections which indicated potential populations of 1,400, 1,200, and 1,100 million people if there were, respectively, average family sizes of three, two, or one offspring per couple.

During the Second Session of the Fifth National People's Congress in June 1979, Premier Hua Guofeng called for measures to reward one-child families and provide old-age security to childless people. This marks the start of the official campaign for one child per couple. Some members of the national leadership acknowledged that the 'one child' slogan was essentially an ideal, and early statements showed that they anticipated at least 30 per cent of couples would have more than one baby. This would have been possible within the target of holding population at 1,200 million by the year 2000, but the simplified rhetoric of the campaign, overly enthusiastic calls from the leadership, and misunderstandings by local cadres, led to the impression that *no* couple could have more than one child. The government admitted that there were grave problems with the policy when in 1984 the Central Committee indicated that the rigid notion of a one-child limit had created a 'big hole' because it was so obviously unenforceable on a large scale. Thus they called for the opening of a 'small hole', by allowing some exceptions to the one-child limit, but only on the agreement that there be no third or higher parity births allowed.

What had been an inadvertently rigid policy now became flexible. Reactions varied around the nation, but in many regions it was reported that the use of contraception dropped substantially, and the range of 'exceptional' cases skyrocketed. In Guangdong, the provincial and local family-planning officials instituted a *de facto* two-child policy, ostensibly in recognition of the economic needs of farming families, but also because of pressure from the returned Overseas Chinese community which forms an important and outspoken minority section of the population. In Shaanxi Province the government tried to hold the line on exceptions but the pressure was great, especially among the prosperous farmers in the peri-urban regions around Xi'an because one of the things they wanted as part of their new prosperity was a second child, particularly if their first was a girl. In response to these kinds of local pressures the Party issued a new directive in 1986 calling for a greater effort to reduce the range of exceptions (Greenhalgh, 1986), but officials were still able to rationalize their implementation plans in terms of 'local concrete realities' and the Party call largely went unheeded.

At a national conference on family planning in December 1986, Premier Zhao Ziyang reiterated the great concerns of the leadership about the rate of population growth, and the consequences of exceeding a population of about 1,200 million in the year 2000. He declared that population planning policy was vital and should not be changed in the near future. At the same time, the policy he described, of a one-child 'ideal' but with a second child allowed 'in a planned way' for couples who have 'real practical difficulties', left room for substantial manoeuvring by parents and local officials. Thus, as large posters went up around the country calling for support of population planning as a basic state policy, officials in several provinces were turning their attention from the prevention of second births in rural areas to the prevention of third and higher orders of parity. Though Zhao Ziyang fell from grace in 1989, this part of his reform policy has been retained and reiterated.

Continuity and Change in the Socio-cultural Setting of Fertility Behaviour

While government planning and fertility policies became more flexible and responsive during the 1980s, several socio-economic changes have also gradually altered the context within which parents are considering their family-building decisions.

Housing

For years the shortage of residential accommodation in cities has made life very difficult for families of any size, but more specifically for families with many children or extra-nuclear family members. The situation is improving, but as apartments gradually become more spacious the expectations of urban dwellers are rising. Now the problem is not only where to find room for the children, but also the refrigerator, sewing machine, washing machine, television set, and other appliances.

Education

With the rehabilitation of the education system and the reintroduction of examinations, as well as the stress on education to achieve the 'four modernizations', urban parents are increasingly concerned about their children's schooling. Coaching schools are appearing in the major centres to give the single child an edge over classmates. Both the government and the parents seem agreed that high levels of investment of time and resources are necessary to rapidly raise the 'quality' of Chinese children, and this makes reductions in numbers of children quite sensible. Whyte and Gu (1987, p. 485) have documented that 'high aspirations for children, particularly high educational aspirations, are associated with stating a preference for a small family, and even for the approved single-child family', but they warn that this process may have reached hard financial limits, with parental hopes pegged much higher than the capacity of the government to provide schools and jobs. In such a situation Whyte and Gu worry that parents may decide that larger family sizes are more secure economic guarantees than small families facing limited opportunities for higher education and prestigious employment.

Health guarantees

In urban areas reported infant mortality rates under 20 per 1000 live births are only marginally higher than those prevailing in developed countries, while in the countryside there have been substantial declines of mortality in recent years. While by no means offsetting the large reductions of family size resulting from fertility control, this control of mortality has given parents in some regions confidence to think that, even if they restrict the number of offspring they bear, those children are likely to be healthy survivors. Nevertheless, in 1981 the infant mortality rate in Xinjiang Province was more than 100 per 1000, and five other Western Zone provinces had rates exceeding 50 per 1000. Conventional wisdom would have it that such rates are incompatible with long-term maintenance of very low fertility rates.

Dual career families

Overall 70 per cent of women aged fifteen and over are in the work-force, and the proportion for those aged from twenty to thirty-four is about 90 per cent. As in developed countries, this pattern of dual-occupation families means that housework and child care must be either obtained commercially or carried out in what might otherwise be recreation or study time. Young urban parents seem convinced that family life under such conditions is better with fewer children. In rural areas the rapid expansion of employment related to the township enterprise system and specialized household production activities (such as private plots, small manufacturing and transport businesses, and processing activities) has meant that rural families are increasingly faced with urban-industrial style pressures. While women's labour-force participation is high, they still carry the major share of household tasks, and for them this dual burden makes the problems of fertility even more immediate.

Cost of children and rising aspirations

There is a growing image in cartoons and photographs of the 'little emperor or empress', a single child surrounded by adults all trying to amuse him or her. Shops are filled with expensive clothes, toys, furnishings, and books, all of which represent substantial outlays, even though salaries are rising. For the urbanite and the successful rural family the cost of keeping a child in a modern style of life is rising much faster that the general cost of living (Whyte and Gu, 1987).

Guarantees of support in old age

In response to the call made by Hu Yaobang in 1979 most county governments have made efforts to provide housing and other assistance to old people who have no surviving children. In some parts of Guangdong Province some discussion began in the mid-1980s of giving a special pension to parents who are sterilized after having two daughters, to discourage them from trying to have a desired son. Throughout China local governments are experimenting with various old-age support schemes, in an attempt to remove one of the more salient perceived benefits of child-bearing. Perhaps the most important initiative might be one of the simplest, and this is the expansion of institutions — such as banks and post offices — to make personal savings more convenient and secure.

Child labour

Under conditions of rapid development the expansion of formal employment and schooling opportunities has undoubtedly displaced children from many informal sector opportunities. Certainly young children are still seen around cities and on farms doing some work, but the impression is that these are increasingly rare cases. Some local officials report a tendency for children to leave school directly on finishing their primary education to take jobs in the rapidly expanding township enterprises. One township in Shaanxi Province addressed this problem by refusing to hire any under-age workers, and offering financial incentives to children who stayed on at school and received good grades. These contradictory trends need more intensive study, both with regard to the actual behaviour of children and the attitudes of parents in relation to the economic and other values of child-bearing in these rapidly changing times. Most important at the moment appears to be the fact that pressures to allow exceptions to the one-child policy centre on the need for children to be available as part of the family labour force in rural agricultural families, especially those in mountainous and isolated regions. It is thus quite likely that the reforms reducing the power of co-operatives in favour of family production systems will exacerbate this motivation for larger families (Hull and Yang, 1987).

Property as an institution

The expanding range of personal property which is permitted and feasible contributes to the reordering of priorities for personal invest-ment and consumption decisions. This is dramatically seen in any of the peri-urban areas around major cities where apartment blocks and personal housing are springing up, and where small enterprises have been established very rapidly. There was great optimism in the 1980–9 period, and the drive to improve personal economic conditions seemed to be boundless. Some of the new entrepreneurs were very fluent during fieldwork interviews in ascribing their success to the economic reforms and their agreement with the population policy, both of which are seen as parts of the seamless web of government involvement in shaping their control over property and family.

Implications

Fertility decline in China has been the product of a total social and economic change which has transformed the country since Liberation. The decision-making framework within which marriage and child-bearing decisions take place has been irrevocably altered. An elabo-rate network of incentives and sanctions has been set in place at the local government level to encourage people to modify their fertility behaviour and conform to a 'one-child per couple' norm. Major factors in this transformation are the activist role of the central gov-ernment in setting population and fertility goals at both the national and the family levels, and the efficiency with which the government has acted to provide contraceptive and abortion information, educa-tion, and services to the entire population, thus making radical fertility control technologically feasible.

The post-1978 economic reforms have substantially altered the way government operates at the local level, and tended to reduce the coercive power of local officials over their constituents. Access to land, jobs, food, housing, and consumer goods was being increasingly left to the market, and this took power away from local officials who, in a command economy, could easily require people to conform to family-planning guidelines under threat of direct or indirect economic sanctions. This change obviously has implications for the family-planning programme and the motivation for child-bearing, and is at least part of the explanation for the changes of policy between 1984 and 1989.

The demonstrations in Beijing during December 1986, and the leadership changes which followed, have signalled a modification, or at least a redefinition, of the economic reforms. To a considerable extent they were a reaction to the need to adapt centralized policies to regional needs and realities. These were largely recognitions of the pressures of poverty in isolated rural communities where agriculture remains the mainstay of economic welfare. In contrast, much of the country in the Eastern and Middle Zones have experienced rapid economic growth and diversification. In February 1987, Party leaders urged the masses in these areas to work selflessly for the development of the country and to concentrate on saving rather than ostentatious spending. Prior to this announcement the symbols of the reforms had been the large houses being built by newly rich peasants, and the consumer durables being purchased at a fast rate by urban workers. The implications of these events for the family planning programme are not clear. They might signal the start of a new era of discipline, and a more rigorous implementation of fertility and population targets. If so, it may be possible to restrain the predicted baby boom of the late 1980s and early 1990s, but they may reflect a continuing power dialogue at high government levels which will have little impact on the actual implementation of the family-planning programme.

The government is committed to a family-planning policy which retains some elements of the one-child campaign, but allows various exceptions to relieve social pressure and discontent among people whose level of socio-economic development attaches high economic value to offspring. These people are most heavily concentrated in the Western and some Middle Zone provinces. Greenhalgh (1986, p. 508) believes that this policy will be maintained for the rest of the century, implying, in effect, a series of spatially defined fertility control policies. The decision to maintain the general policy is not a demographic issue so much as a political question turning on the total development of governmental power and the economic reforms in China. If the past is a guide to the future, there is unlikely to be an easy or settled answer to these problems, either nationally, or among the enormously diverse regions of this huge country. Meanwhile, it is imperative to closely monitor the changing spatial patterns of fertility behaviour in China so as to gain insights into the future population of the world.

7 Economic Reforms and Rural to Urban Migration

CHUNG-TONG WU AND XU XUEQIANG

ECONOMIC reforms during the 1980s, especially in the rural areas, led to significant changes in the Chinese economy through the re-orientation of spatial development policies and the relaxation of many regulations governing internal migration. The reorganization of production, the distribution of land to households, and the promotion of more diversified economic activities led to accelerated rural occupational changes, particularly in the more prosperous areas (Wu, C-T., 1987a). The results, such as the release of rural labour, have had direct and indirect impact on the rest of China. Many peasants moved from less to more prosperous rural areas or to small and medium-size towns and large cities. This chapter examines this phenomenon, beginning with the reservoir of surplus rural labour, the policies which directly or indirectly influenced these population shifts, and the impact of this migration on the cities. It then presents the results of a survey conducted in Guangzhou Municipality — a rapidly growing city.

Surplus Rural Labour

Between 60 and 75 per cent of China's population, depending on the definition used (see Appendix 1) resides in the rural areas which also have most of the nation's total labour force. Some 98 per cent of the agricultural labour force is engaged in cultivation, as distinct from forestry, fishing, and animal husbandry (Yu, 1987). In 1986 it was estimated that 484 million people would still be engaged in agriculture in 1990 and 534 million by the year 2000 of which perhaps 200 million will be surplus to rural needs (Li, Q., 1986; Zhang, 1987a).

These estimates are based on the experience of the 1980s during which between 46 million people (Han, 1987) and 52 million (Yu, 1987) transferred out of agriculture, and especially out of cultivation activities. Han estimated that some 64 per cent shifted into rural industries located in villages and small towns, 19 per cent into building and construction, 5 per cent into transport activities, and close

to 8 per cent into services and commerce.   There is increasing
recognition, however, that villages and small towns cannot cope with
the expected large influx of labour (Ding, 1988). From the beginning
of 1978 until the end of 1985, perhaps as many as 38.9 million people
were absorbed into the labour force of cities and towns: even then,
there were still 2.4 million urban residents seeking employment at the
end of 1985 (Chen, 1988, p. 24). Chen considered that 30 to 40 per
cent of the agricultural workers (which — according to Wu, C-T.,
1987a — made up 48 per cent of the rural labour force) was surplus.

These national figures can be supplemented by more specific
information about several coastal regions. In a ten-village study in
Zhejiang Province it was shown that between 1984 and 1986 the
distribution of village labour force by sector changed significantly.
The proportion engaged in cultivation dropped by 21 per cent. Of
those who left cultivation, just under 47 per cent were absorbed by
forestry, fishery, and animal husbandry activities, and 53 per cent by
the secondary and service sectors (Zhejiangsheng, 1988). In the
Wenzhou district of Zhejiang Province about half the 2.6 million rural
labour force shifted from cultivation to the industrial and service
sectors largely through engaging in rural enterprises and transport
activities. Agriculture's share of the labour force dropped from 89 per
cent in 1978 to 49 per cent in 1986 (Li, D., et al., 1988). Jiang (1986)
has calculated that in 1985 about 22 per cent (1.9 million) of the rural
labour force in Fujian Province could be considered surplus. During
1985 rural enterprises absorbed just over two million, or almost 24 per
cent, of the province's rural workforce. With continued economic
reforms the future of rural enterprise is considered to be bright, but
there is recognition that its capacity to provide employment is not
unlimited: at best such activities might absorb 25 to 35 per cent of the
surplus rural labour force. In the Shanghai Metropolitan Area, (which
includes twelve urban districts and nine counties) from the beginning
of 1980 until the end of 1985, 648,000 people shifted out of
agricultural activities. The net change, however, was only 425,000
since surplus workers from other areas moved in to take their place
(Xia and Li, 1988).

The shift out of agricultural work and the stimulation of migration
of rural labour from less prosperous regions are two important features
of the present migration pattern. Moreover, out-migrants are often
highly educated. A study of the rural labour force in Hangzhou
Municipality, Zhejiang Province, in 1984 indicated that two-thirds of
those who finished high school and one-third of those who finished

middle school had migrated, whereas nine-tenths of those who are illiterate or semi-literate remained (Zhang, 1987a).

The Policy Context

Migration is prompted by several complex factors, including the desire to seek new and better opportunities (du Guerny, 1978; Portes, 1988). However, in China, which until 1979 had a tightly controlled and centrally planned economy, a series of policy changes had to be implemented to make it possible for opportunities to emerge and for individuals to take advantage of them.

The policies that have significantly influenced the flow of migrants from rural to urban areas (Wu, C-T., 1987a) are summarized in Figure 7.1. Since reviews of these policies are readily available elsewhere (Walker, 1984; Yeh, 1984; Chai and Leung, 1987) only a brief summary, highlighting the most important ones, is included here. Within the general context of system reforms that have been taking place in China during the late 1970s and early 1980s, rural reforms have been fundamental to the relative prosperity now being enjoyed in many rural areas of China, particularly in the coastal zones, and have stimulated significant shifts of labour from agricultural to non-agricultural occupations.

Rural Reform

As pointed out by Fincher in Chapter 2, the most fundamental reforms that swept China during the 1980s were those in the rural areas: these included the implementation of the 'responsibility system', the lease of land to households, and the push for economic diversification, including in particular the encouragement of rural enterprises.

The responsibility system was a break from past practice when the income of members of work-teams and brigades was based on the average income generated by the entire brigade or commune. Consequently, the more productive teams and team members had their hard-earned gains diluted by the less productive ones. Under this system the more energetic and successful teams and individuals are able to reap the benefits of their labour by retaining the income or the surplus produced. It was first implemented within the strictures of the commune system, but it developed into the 'household responsibility system' which was quickly followed by the arrangement whereby the fields or agricultural production units being worked on were

Figure 7.1 Rural-urban linkages and urbanization

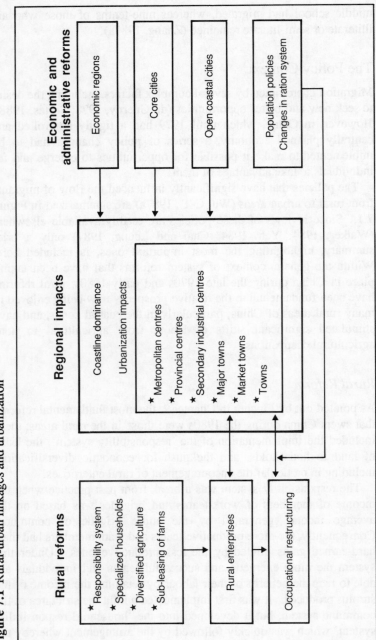

contracted to individual households to farm or manage. Peasants could also contract to run agricultural production units such as duck farms, fish ponds, or orchards. Initially, peasant households were assigned fields for five years, but (as discussed in Chapter 2) this was subsequently changed to between fifteen and fifty years and the households made entirely responsible for production. There was no uniform method for assigning fields, each locality making its own decisions. The commune or the state contracted with the household to produce a stipulated amount of staple such as rice or wheat, the surplus being at the disposal of the household which could sell it to the state procurement bureau, at the markets or elsewhere, or even on a contract basis to enterprises like hotels.

Households were free to band together and farm their combined fields. Those who preferred to engage in non-agricultural activities were allowed to sublease their plots to be worked by others; such arrangements often included a guarantee to supply the original lessee with rice or wheat at government-set prices, thus enabling the original lease holder to pursue non-agricultural activities with the certainty that low-price staples would be available. By implementing the household responsibility system and assigning fields to households, the government spelled the end of the commune system which was finally abolished in 1984. However, it was also realized that, while the responsibility system greatly enhanced agricultural productivity, it was also necessary to diversify the rural economy to promote growth and to provide employment opportunities for the vast rural labour force.

The drive towards rural economic diversification not only involved the encouragement of the other branches of agriculture — fisheries, forestry, and husbandry — but also the formation of rural enterprises to stimulate development and provide employment opportunities for those displaced from growing crops. These enterprises — undertaking manufacturing, commercial, and service activities — flourished in prosperous rural areas or near large urban centres which provided ready markets. The promotion of such enterprises also reinforced the policy of 'containing' the rural population, especially the surplus rural labour force, within the rural areas and small towns — the so-called *litu bu lixiang* (leaving the land without leaving the villages) policy. This sought to combine a spatial policy of population containment with the diversification of the rural economy which would expand the industrial capacity of the rural towns and villages to facilitate the processing of local produce or to expedite the decentralization of urban industries. During the early 1980s, urban industries were encouraged to establish branches and workshops to produce complete lines or components through direct investment or joint ventures with village or town workshops. The restructuring of the rural economy was thus accompanied by rapid occupational changes.

Residential Regulations

With early spectacular production increases in agriculture, the rapid diversification of the rural economy and the meteoric growth of rural enterprises during the mid-1980s, the government began in 1988 to relax the strict controls over residential change. Those peasants who could provide their own staples and who could prove that they had the resources to establish an enterprise, could gain permission to move to the towns. As a result, many individuals shifted to towns and cities to start up individual enterprises (*getihu*). The organized recruitment of workers from the villages by enterprises located in the urban areas was also condoned. As opportunities to purchase staples in the open market became more common and as the state rationing system became less important as a channel of supply to the individual, it became possible for rural residents to move to any urban area in which they had relatives or friends who could provide shelter. Increasingly, however, many moved to urban places even where they had few or no contacts and little knowledge of what they might encounter.

Coastal Development

When priority was given to rapid economic growth, the government after 1978 pursued a policy of encouraging the growth of the coastal region (see Chapter 1). The unmistakable message to the rest of the country was that development priority was being placed on the coastal zones. This became an important determinant of the economic and social context for recent population movements. The restructuring of the rural economy led to occupational shifts in the countryside which, in part, were also responses to initiatives aimed at promoting economic opportunities in coastal regions. However, while there is no doubt that rural reforms made it possible for many to move from agriculture, the serious problem of surplus rural labour is largely the product of a long history of urban bias — a view, however, which is contrary to that expressed by Fincher in Chapter 2. Han (1987) argues that policy-makers in China have focused on urban employment problems to the exclusion of those in the rural areas.

Considerable debate continues about the efficacy of the policy of 'leaving the land without leaving the villages' (Chen, 1987). While Chen (1988) argues that it is ineffectual and instead advocates the idea of *litu yu lixiang* (leaving the land and the villages), Xia and Li (1988) assert that these policies emphasize the extremes and not the possibilities of further integration between rural and urban sectors. Still others, such as Chao and Gao (1987), favour organized labour transfers from both the backward and the developed rural areas to the largely undeveloped north-west, while Chan (1988) contends that it is preferable to encourage migration towards selected areas, such as existing towns with development potential.

Some scholars, such as Wang, H. (1987), suggest that the solution of China's agricultural problems requires the permanent transfer of arable land away from those who have left agriculture. Major changes to the policies of grain allocation are also required to make more individuals independent from agriculture. Wang maintains that the agricultural sector is often regarded by individuals and policy-makers as a social safety net, an attitude, he argues, which must be altered if changes to the agricultural sector are to be implemented and the occupational restructuring of the rural population accelerated. Other scholars, such as Liu (1987), assert that the appropriate spatial policy would be to direct surplus labour towards medium and large cities where it could be absorbed more readily: if such an idea were adopted, the flow of rural population to the cities could become a flood.

Migration Streams

During the 1980s vast and increasing numbers of people have moved, and are continuing to move, from rural to urban areas. The pattern, however, is not simply direct rural to urban migration. At least three main streams of migration can be identified: from rural areas to other rural areas; from rural areas to small towns; and from rural areas and small towns to large cities.

Rural to Rural Migration

This first type largely consists of peasants who shift from less prosperous or backward rural areas to more prosperous ones. Chen (1987) estimated that by the mid-1980s some six million peasants each year were leaving less prosperous regions to work temporarily elsewhere, and that up to 1987 in some backward villages close to 20 per cent of the labour force had departed. Some till land subleased to them by people who are no longer interested in cultivation, or work for peasants as rural labourers. One example is the movement of peasants from the Huiyang district of Guangdong Province to the rural counties of Shenzhen (Wu, C-T., 1989). In Bao'an, the rural county of Shenzhen Municipality, almost all the able-bodied working-age peasants have taken up non-agricultural work in the Shenzhen Special Economic Zone. The fields they left are being farmed by people moving into Bao'an County: officials there reported that by April 1986 the number of temporary workers in Bao'an had reached 140,000 — equal to 60 per cent of the resident population. This figure only includes people who had been reported by their work unit or had themselves reported to the authorities, but undoubtably many others, particularly those engaged in agriculture, would not have been noted.

Rural to Small Town Migration

The second type of migration may be highly organized or can simply involve individuals making a deliberate choice. Examples of the former are the systematic recruitment of labour by enterprises located in small towns and the contracting out of teams of construction workers by village administrations (Li, S-M., 1988). Many of those who migrate on their own tend to set up urban-based commerce or service-orientated enterprises (Zhou and Li, 1987). Others have taken advantage of the 1988 decree permitting those who can provide their own staples (rice or wheat) to move to the towns to carry on individual businesses or find employment. Xu and Zhang (1984) reported that in four counties of Guangdong Province, most migrants went to towns in general, county seats, and then district government centres.

Such migration patterns can be observed in the more prosperous rural regions of China and are often due to the establishment of industries with foreign investment. Li, S-M. (1988) reported on the migration stimulated by foreign investment which has filtered through to many small towns in Guangdong Province, a region that experienced rapid economic growth during the 1980s. There it is mainly the enterprises with foreign capital that have systematically recruited workers from the surrounding regions, though some come from further afield. Both Li, S-M. (1988) and Sit (1988) have noted the predominance of young females among the migrant workers and their concentration in labour-intensive industries.

In other prosperous areas, such as the Suzhou-Wuxi region of

Jiangsu Province, the rural population moving into the towns often constitutes a significant proportion of the original residents. For example, from November 1984 to June 1985, one town there had an in-migrant population equivalent to about 60 per cent of the number of original inhabitants. Shen (1987, p. 68) concluded that towns in the Suzhou-Wuxi region have only a limited capacity to absorb more residents. The majority (68 per cent) of the rural migrants to the towns tended to be engaged in industrial activities, with commerce a distant second at 13 per cent (Zhou and Li, 1987). Three types of peasants moving to the towns and cities were identified by Ma (1984): those who had to stay to finish selling their produce; craftsmen making repairs for urban households; and construction workers. However, in parts of China where industrialization in the small towns is not widespread, most peasants who moved into the towns were involved in transport and sales activities: in Shanxi Province, for instance, some 54,000 peasants were reportedly engaged in these sectors in 1986 (He, 1987; Ma and Wang, 1988). These peasants add to the flow of non-residents who frequent the towns and county seats.

Rural and Small Town to Large City Migration

The third group of migrants — those that move from rural areas and small towns to large cities — form the main focus of this chapter. In all cities in China, particularly the large ones along the eastern seaboard, there are now many so-called 'floating' or temporary residents. While some of these are *bona fide* tourists or people on business and official missions, increasing numbers have moved in to seek better opportunities. The scale of this phenomenon is substantial.

In the cities of Shandong Province, as elsewhere, many of the migrants are members of construction teams. Most are young males in their twenties who are working temporarily under a variety of contractual arrangements. Lu and Wang (1984) assert that these people pose very little demand on the cities in which they work, but also seem to assume that they will return to the rural areas after completing the projects or move on to other construction jobs. Evidence from other cities would seem to contradict such a sanguine interpretation.

In 1985 the daily population of temporary or floating residents in Beijing was estimated to be about 890,000. Yu (1987) further estimates that 23 per cent of these were members of construction teams; 24 per cent had been sent by their units located outside the capital to seek information and contacts; and a further 5 per cent were nannies or housemaids. Thus, 500,000 to 750,000 of the people in Beijing are temporary residents looking for jobs or working (see Appendix 1). These people are not recognized as legal residents because, under the resident registration system, they do not necessarily have formal permission to transfer their registered abode to Beijing. Other researchers have estimated the annual in-migration to Beijing to be in the order of 620,000 from all around the country and particularly from the surrounding rural counties into the central city (Xu, B., 1988). Although the accuracy of these estimates is uncertain, there is little doubt that there are many unregistered residents in the capital. Another example is the tourist city of Hangzhou which reportedly requires about 140,000 workers each year from the rural areas (Zhang, 1987b). Many of these have been recruited by enterprises in the city and have secure employment. Such reports, taken together, point to the large numbers who have been attracted to the cities from towns and villages. Some have pre-arranged jobs but most have moved to seek better employment or education opportunities or merely to find out what city life is all about. These motivations have been identified by the results of a pilot study carried out in Guangzhou.

Migrants in Guangzhou

Early in 1988 the authors carried out a pilot study in Guangzhou Municipality as a preliminary investigation of the phenomenon of the mobile population or, more specifically, those who had moved to the city on their own initiative. Interviews with 295 individuals (76.5 per cent males) were conducted at several locations in Guangzhou known to be the haunts of the mobile people, such as near railway stations, various overhead highway interchanges, and wharves, and in certain enterprises. While there is no claim that the sample is statistically representative, it was based on the best local knowledge about the likely concentrations of the mobile population; the results, moreover, tend to be supported by other observations (Li, S-M., 1988; Sit, 1988).

Origins

The survey respondents were largely male, in contrast to the data available on the people recruited to work in towns (Li, S-M., 1988; Sit, 1988). As might have been expected, most were single and young, with 37 per cent aged sixteen to twenty and 36 per cent aged twenty-one to twenty-five. Since the study focused on those who had come to the city on their own initiative, most were expected to have had rural origins. In fact the vast majority (89 per cent) had been engaged in agriculture prior to moving to Guangzhou and close to 95 per cent had a registered place of abode (*hukou*) outside this municipality. Indeed, 59 per cent originated from elsewhere in Guangdong or from other provinces (31 per cent). Of the latter group, 51 per cent came from Hunan, 14 per cent from Sichuan, and 13 per cent from Guangxi.

Educational Ability

As a group, the migrants were well educated: 61 per cent had completed high and/or middle school and another 19 per cent had completed primary school. This supports Zhang's (1987a) report on the rural areas in Zhejiang Province which has already been noted.

Employment

The prospect of finding employment and/or better and more suitable work were the main reasons for migrating given by 61 per cent of the respondents. Others, like 'family' and better living conditions were important but were each cited as the key reason by only 14 per cent. Nearly 59 per cent had temporary jobs and 31 per cent were under contract, but less than 2 per cent had permanent employment. Thus, the expectations of finding secure employment had not been fulfilled.

Of those with jobs, 32 per cent were employed in industrial activities followed, in order of importance, by work in construction, commerce, agriculture, and transport. Those in construction were often day labourers without any security of employment. Many of the others were employed in small enterprises undertaking such menial tasks as shoe or bicycle repairing.

The majority indicated that they had little or no awareness of employment (67 per cent), housing (60 per cent), or economic conditions (64 per cent) prior to their arrival in Guangzhou. Just over half (53 per cent) had found jobs through friends and relatives; in a society where family and kinship ties are significant, and where other avenues of finding employment are not yet fully developed, this is not surprising. Whereas for others recruitment services and individual initiatives were equally important (19 and 17 per cent, respectively), many who found work through their own initiatives had little choice but to start up as petty traders providing services such as shoe, bicycle, and tyre repairing. Most had difficulties finding any employment: 48

per cent had to wait for six months or more to find work. However, 28 per cent obtained jobs almost immediately and 20 per cent within a month of their arrival.

Female and male migrants had different experiences, possibly because of the channels by which they seek work. One third of the females but less than a quarter of the males found work immediately; 53 per cent of the males but only 40 per cent of the females had to wait more than six months. Nearly two-thirds of the females but only half the males found jobs through introductions by relatives. Indeed, female respondents, half of them between the ages of sixteen and twenty, tended to be more reliant on relatives in the cities: 60 per cent of them (as against only 27 per cent of the males) stayed with relatives when they first arrived. Female respondents, overwhelmingly working in industries (62 per cent), also tended to have quarters provided by their employers (48 per cent).

Adjusting to the City

This brief outline provides a partial view of the background and circumstances of the migrants to large cities. Although the details are for Guangzhou Municipality, migrants to other coastal cities are likely to have similar characteristics and problems (no study on similar groups is available which would enable comparisons to be made). While obtaining employment is an obvious problem, the difficulty of finding affordable and adequate housing, or indeed accommodation of any kind, is a reflection of the inadequacies of the housing situation in China where overcrowding is endemic.

Just over one-third of the migrants had found shelter in hostels provided by their work unit. These were often very small, cramped, and in poor condition, sometimes being merely temporary structures on building sites. Another one-third of the respondents were renting accommodation (though most considered that the cost was too high), while 15 per cent were boarding with families. The problem group was the 11 per cent who reported that they provided their own housing: some of these were in fact living under bridges or overhead highways, on the pavement, near railway stations, and even in squatter huts on the fringe of the city. The situation is too recent to enable any systematic information to be obtained, but a serious problem is undoubtedly emerging.

Another less quantifiable but equally serious problem was the complaint of many respondents that they were looked down upon and even exploited by the residents of Guangzhou. They reported instances of employers reneging on the agreed wages at the time of payment or were asked to undertake tasks which were not part of the agreement. Most complaints of this kind were by people coming from other provinces, and were exacerbated by the differences in dialect. Certainly, strong feelings were expressed by some people that the local residents had treated them as second-class citizens in terms of jobs, employment conditions, and housing.

A Typology of Migration

Vast numbers of rural residents are on the move in China. Various forms of migration can be discerned but the three main types identified here are organized recruitment, transfers by units, and self-initiated. If these main forms of migration are considered along with the flows identified earlier, the relationships between the types of migrants and their likely destinations can be hypothesized (Table 7.1).

Table 7.1 Proposed typology of migration

Migration	Organized recruitment	Transfers by units	Self-initiated
Rural to rural	–	–	x
Rural to towns	x	–	x
Rural/towns to cities	x	x	x

Rural to rural migration is largely self-motivated and mainly involves those who leave backward rural areas for the economically more developed parts of the country. The flow from rural areas to towns is likely to include those who are recruited to work in establishments located in these urban places, as well as others who move there to establish their own small enterprises. Finally, the migrants to the cities involve both these groups, but also include a substantial number who are transferred by their work units to related ones or to joint ventures. This type of movement is common for those units with branches or joint ventures in the Special Economic Zones.

Organized recruitment is especially significant in the small towns in the coastal regions where foreign investments and locally funded enterprises have flourished, and it may also be important in areas, such as the Suzhou-Wuxi region, where there is significant industrial decentralization. These are all prosperous rural regions. While the total of transferred personnel may be large in particular locations, relative to other forms of migration it is not numerically significant. The bulk of the migrants are self-motivated and are attracted to the large cities, especially those in the coastal regions. Like the migrants interviewed in Guangzhou Municipality, they are also likely to face difficulties with employment, housing, and access to other opportunities and services.

Conclusions

Several conclusions can be drawn from this brief review. Firstly, China is experiencing rapid urbanization fuelled both by the continuing occupational restructuring now occurring in the countryside and by the huge number of surplus rural labourers who have left cultivation and other agricultural pursuits. Secondly, rapid urbanization is indirectly due to the policies which focus on the development of the coastal regions and reforms in the rural areas. Thirdly, parallel migration processes can be observed. There is the familiar rural to urban migration (to both towns and cities), and also the process of rural to rural migration from less to more prosperous regions. Fourthly, rapid urbanization and rural to rural migration are particularly noticeable in the more prosperous rural regions of China which are favoured destinations for those moving from the backward areas. Rural population from the prosperous regions is also likely to move from the rural areas to the towns and cities. Fifthly, rural to urban migration is likely to accelerate as regional differences increase. The proportion of rural individuals who will decide to try their fortunes in the cities can be expected to increase as the regulations on residential mobility are relaxed and the restructuring in the countryside continues. Larger numbers of rural-based individuals will want to seek opportunities in other spheres and the cities will be their favoured destinations. Sixthly, in the urban areas, social problems related to large number of new migrants are already emerging and can be expected to become more acute as more and more migrants flood into the cities.

Whether China's cities will experience the same problems which now grip most Third World cities depends on policy responses. System reforms, in particular rural reforms, and the policy of focusing on coastal development have contributed to significant economic growth for the nation, but the impacts have been spatially uneven. Unless the opportunities become more widespread, reaching to more regions, the migration flows to the cities can only be expected to surge. As other countries have found, preventing rural to urban migration seems futile. The issue is finding the means of encouraging orderly movement of migrants who can be absorbed into employment. The systematic recruitment of labour clearly indicates that the cities require more labour as economic growth continues, but the problem to be avoided is a flood of migrants swelling the ranks of the urban unemployed. Unless appropriate policies can be devised to cope with the deluge of migrants seeking opportunities unavailable in their home regions, the pilot study reported on here points to the spectre of a looming urban crisis.

8   The Spatial Structure of Shanghai City Proper

J. S. HYSLOP

SHANGHAI, China's largest municipality with a population of 12.5 million and an area of 6,200 km² in 1987, is located at the focus of the country's most productive economic region.   It has undergone substantial peripheral growth and spawned satellites, leading to the formation of Shanghai Municipality (of provincial status) which incorporates the inner city — the City Proper, now 351 km² — and an urban and rural hinterland.   Its core remains very compact, and its population densities at a broad, if not at a local scale, are among the world's highest.   The modernization and increased prosperity of Shanghai are placing considerable strain on its infrastructure and services.   The compact nature of the City Proper, while having many advantages, still presents numerous problems for city administrators, planners, and implementation agencies.   This chapter reviews recent planning initiatives in Shanghai, and then explores various aspects of urban spatial structure within the City, identifying some of the key issues to be addressed in urban renewal.

The Development of Shanghai

Urban settlement of the Changjiang (Yangtze) Delta near contemporary Shanghai began well before the twelfth century.   The old walled city in Nanshi district dates back to this period.   By 1832, when Westerners first settled in Shanghai, it was a walled city with fewer than 300,000 people.   Four foreign concessions were developed during the 1845–63 period; in 1930 these held a population of 1.4 million in an area of 32.8 km² and the Chinese district had a population of 1.7 million (Economic and Social Commission for Asia and the Pacific, 1982).   Mainly through expansion of the foreign concessions and further development, under Japanese and then Nationalist rule, Shanghai expanded from a small, walled settlement to an urban centre of metropolitan dimensions (Fung, 1981).

By 1949 the built-up area covered 80 km², and further accretional growth increased the total urban area to 116 km² by 1957.   During the 1950s there were administrative boundary changes embracing urban and suburban districts so that by 1958 the Shanghai Municipal Government had become responsible for an area of 5,910 km^2.

Chinese city development during the 1950s was greatly influenced by the Soviet model of industrial centrality, Soviet theories and principles of urban planning, and the desire of Chinese municipal officials to build large, modern socialist cities (Fung, 1981). Thus, in the case of Shanghai the Municipal Master Plan produced in 1953, with Russian technical assistance, included the idea of expanding the urban area to 600 km^2, with large-scale redevelopment of the city centre and construction of suburban industrial districts. A population density of 100 persons/ha was planned for the built-up area.

The 1959 revision of the Master Plan was influenced by British town-planning models. The aims were to control expansion of the built-up area of 140 km^2; make full use of existing urban facilities instead of renewing them; establish self-contained industrial new towns near the fringe of the city boundary; and revise the built-up area population density to 330 persons/ha. Between 1949 and 1980, 20 million m^2 of residential floor space were built for two million people in 156 housing estates, mostly on the fringe.

By 1980, the built-up area of the City Proper contained 5.8 million residents and 200,000 long-term visitors: the gross density was thus 429 persons/ha. In 1982 Shanghai City Proper had a population of 6,055,000 in 1,581,000 households, an average household size of 3.83. The housing stock totalled 46.8 million m^2 of floor space, providing an average of 7.74 m^2 per person, and an average living space — floor space excluding passageways and sanitary facilities — of 4.48 m^2 per person.

The 1983 City Plan

The 1983 Shanghai City Plan (Shanghai Municipal Urban Planning and Construction Bureau, 1983) provided a policy framework for inner area renewal. It proposed that the City Proper should be expanded from its existing 152 km^2 to 300 km^2 for 'economic development and the relief of overcrowding'. This was to consist of the existing urban area which had extended beyond the City Proper boundary (189 km^2); adjacent rural towns (30 km^2); and land for construction purposes (81 km^2). The population predicted for the year 2000 was 6.5 million as well as 500,000 transients. The expansion of the City Proper was considered necessary to provide each person with 8 m^2 living space. The gross urban density — which includes all land area — was then averaging 40,000 persons/km^2, and was to be reduced to 22,000 persons/km^2, while the gross residential land area per person was to increase from 12 to 23 m^2.

The City Proper was to be organized into eleven districts by applying a concept of 'multi-centres open structure' — a number of urban sub-centres were to be built, with lower building intensity in between — to replace the existing 'mono-centric closed circle' or single-centred city. Within these districts more land would be reserved for public use, for recreation activities, green areas, and retailing. The structure was to consist of a hierarchy of public activity centres — a city centre, eight district centres, twenty-four area centres, and other specialist centres according to local circumstances; small green areas in districts, and large and middle-size parks. Proposals included specialist centres such as the municipal administrative centre near People's Square and the nearby commercial trade centre.

The concept envisaged an outward dispersal from inner to adjacent outer districts, thus achieving population reduction in the City Proper. Some 2.5 million people would live in newly constructed peripheral residential areas. A main road network was to be developed based on existing roads that would be widened and improved as required. The plot-ratio plan — the allowable building floor area divided by the site area — for the city constrains the building area density, taking account of the protection of historic buildings, environment, and the landscape. Typically, the plot ratio varies from 0.5 to 2, but in business areas it is 3 to 10 and in the residential areas it averages 1.7. The intention is to increase land-use capacities, reduce overcrowding, and 'modify the skyline' by constructing more tall buildings.

Residential land-use proposals were formulated in terms of criteria such as building floor space and land area for the categories of new development, redevelopment, upgrading, and the maintenance of existing sound housing stock, totalling 97 million m^2 of floor space. The City Plan proposed that 14 million m^2 of old terrace floor space be 'reformed and modified'; that 20 million m^2 of modern buildings be 'maintained'; and that 17 million m^2 should be redeveloped on land gained by demolishing shanties and other old buildings. The development of new peripheral housing estates and related land uses would serve to accommodate people now living in poor housing conditions in the existing city, and would allow more scope for a comprehensive, city-wide programme of housing renewal. These proposals were based on broad estimates and excluded detailed consideration of the spatial distribution of housing renewal areas.

Further Growth on the Periphery

The 1983 City Plan envisaged that between 1982 and 2000 the population of the municipality would grow from 11.8 to 13.0 million (in 6,186 km^2), while the population of the City Proper would increase only slightly from 6.4 to 6.5 million but be distributed over 300 km^2 rather than 152km^2. The urban area would thus spread from an effective coverage of 189 km^2 in 1982 to 300 km^2 in the year 2000. By doing so the average population density would be thinned from 40,000 to 22,000 persons/km^2, and the per capita residential land area would increase from 12 to 23 m^2. Polluting industries would also be moved out of the urban area, with industrial districts in the suburbs becoming more compact and conveniently located in relation to residential accommodation.

One of the key factors motivating these proposals was the national goal of achieving a housing standard of 8 m^2 living space per person. The City Plan assessment and assumption for spatial distribution of land uses is that it will be necessary to have 2.5 million people living in the newly developing areas on the fringes. This would represent a massive movement of households and change in relationships between home, work place, and school for family members. People in Shanghai value the inner city and its attributes in terms of greater accessibility to a wider range of better services (education, shops, medical, and many other services). The idea of moving to the fringe is not popular, particularly for those family members whose jobs do not move. Other people, however, recognize the benefits of better and more spacious housing. Since the late 1970s, a substantial programme of new housing construction on the periphery has been implemented. At the same time, while there has been a programme to maintain old housing stock, little has been done about upgrading it although where shanties have been demolished limited residential redevelopment has occurred. A key strategy is to lead with the fringe development. There are two reasons. Inner city living is so popular that it would be more difficult to encourage people to move to the periphery if housing conditions there were significantly improved. Then there is the sheer difficulty of planning and implementing an effective and affordable renewal programme acceptable to the communities affected.

Shanghai Urban Studies

After China joined the World Bank in 1980, the Shanghai Municipal Government sought to borrow funds for an urban improvement programme mainly involving liquid waste management and the cleaning up of the Huangpu River which runs through the city. The Mayor had seen what had been achieved in cleaning up the River Thames, and was inspired to do the same for Shanghai. Following visits to Shanghai by the Bank President and other personnel during 1982, offers of assistance were made not only for liquid waste management, but also for housing and transport. An Urban Sector Memorandum was prepared as were terms of reference for further studies (World Bank, 1982). The sector memorandum examined Shanghai's growth and development issues, water supply, wastes and environment, transport and communications, housing, and the city gas system.

The municipality was advised that pre-feasibility and project preparation studies would have to be undertaken before a Bank loan could be arranged. The Australian Development Assistance Bureau (ADAB), now the Australian International Development Assistance Bureau (AIDAB), agreed to fund such an exercise through its Co-financing Facility with the Bank. In mid-1983, ADAB appointed consultants to carry out separate studies of liquid waste management, housing renewal, public transport, and traffic management, most of which were undertaken during 1984 and 1985. They were conducted through four separate specialist Shanghai municipal agencies with particular responsibilities in these fields. Each was seen as a separate infrastructure planning and development study so that there was virtually no opportunity to integrate them (see, for example, Maunsell & Partners Pty. Ltd. et al., 1986a).

Shanghai Housing Renewal Study

About half the City Proper's population live in old terrace houses constructed between 1890 and 1920. As much of this stock is in basically sound condition, upgrading was considered by the Capital Construction Commission to be important and could be treated at three levels: the block and house scale; the neighbourhood scale (with the prospect of upgrading a pilot neighbourhood); and the city-wide scale. As the study progressed, its direction shifted to a more comprehensive coverage of accommodation renewal embracing improvement through demolition and redevelopment where housing is no longer suitable for upgrading, as well as upgrading and maintenance. This was done within the context of city-wide housing needs and plans for urban expansion beyond the present boundaries of the City Proper.

The housing renewal study benefited from access to substantial demographic, housing, and other planning data for the 113 neighbourhoods of the City Proper. This was provided through the 1982 Census of Population and Housing and from other extensive surveys undertaken by the Housing Management Bureau (Maunsell & Partners Pty. Ltd. et al., 1986a).

The study emphasized the need for a renewal programme which would improve housing conditions at an affordable cost, while minimizing the number of households that would have to be relocated on the periphery of the city. The resulting programme recognized that the 8 m² living space per person standard would be too costly and disruptive if use of the existing housing stock were to be maximized, so that it was important to work on a household and dwelling unit basis rather than on per capita standards. (It should be noted, however, that household size is declining — 3.8 in 1982, 3.0/3.5 expected by 2000 depending on housing availability — adding to the number of dwelling units required.) People in Shanghai place more importance on having self-contained facilities than on increased space. All sound housing stock, the study argued, should be upgraded, but up to 40 per cent of old terraces would have to be demolished if the land is needed for redevelopment. Redevelopment at higher densities (higher plot ratios and less site coverage) will minimize the number of households which have to move and will provide more open space.

The Spatial Structure of Shanghai

These data also help to explain the urban structure of Shanghai, and could be used as a planning tool to help bring about beneficial change in the major restructuring which must inevitably occur as Shanghai develops into a modern city at the forefront of China's industrial expansion. The transport studies indicated that, although an extremely compact city, Shanghai suffers from a lack of significant internal structural features which could be used as the basis of some form of mass-transit system. It also seemed that well advanced efforts to develop a subway system could be aided by a knowledge of present and desirable future urban structure. Initially, attempts were made to use the planning data to establish patterns by ranking districts and neighbourhoods in terms of various density measures. In tabular format, this gave a limited understanding, but now it is possible to map these neighbourhoods efficiently and thus obtain a better understanding of spatial patterns.

Figure 8.1 Shanghai district and neighbourhood boundaries

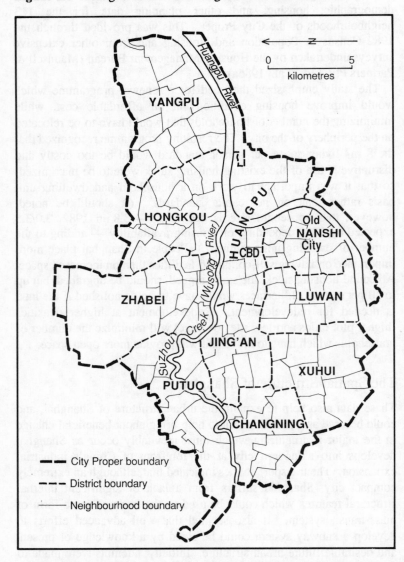

The chapter now turns to an analysis of the urban structure of Shanghai City Proper using the 1982 planning data on 113 neighbourhoods within the ten districts of the City, and briefly explores the implications of this structure for future planning and redevelopment.

The District Level

Data for each of the ten city districts delineated in Figure 8.1 show that the smaller and older ones tend to be more densely populated than the larger outer ones, but average household size is much the same. Surprisingly, the inner districts have more residential land use than the outer ones. Huangpu district has by far the largest amount of floor space devoted to public facilities, dominates the provision of retail employment and recreation places, but ranks lowest in terms of space devoted to educational institutions. The city's industrial floor space is concentrated in Yangpu, Putuo, and Zhabei districts, with the latter having much the highest densities of both population and employment.

Consideration of the characteristics of the city's districts, however, provides only a very limited idea of spatial patterns, so that an analysis at the neighbourhood level is needed to take account of the wider range of characteristics.

The Neighbourhood Level

Three of the measures of population or development intensity used were the densities of gross population, of residential area population, and of total floor space. The neighbourhoods in most of the inner districts have gross population densities above 500 persons/ha. Neighbourhoods with over 1,000 persons/ha are limited to a much smaller inner area in the old city and along part of Suzhou Creek: densities exceed 1,500 persons/ha in some neighbourhoods of Nanshi and Hongkou districts. All the others (except one) have a density of 250-500 persons/ha or less. Peak residential area densities of over 3,000 persons/ha are all in Huangpu district (maximum 5,120) (Figure 8.2). These high residential densities occur despite this being the business district with substantial public facilities. Otherwise the patterns again show the highest residential densities (>1,500 persons/ha) in the old city (Nanshi district), areas along Suzhou Creek, and the downstream sections on the Huangpu River.

Total built floor space densities in Shanghai are quite high with a value of 10,000 m²/ha representing a plot ratio of 1 over the whole area, including roads. The highest building intensity is concentrated around the junction of the Huangpu River and Suzhou Creek in Huangpu, and parts of Hongkou and Nanshi districts, where it exceeds 12,500 m²/ha. One outlying neighbourhood in Zhabei district is also in the range. Most inner areas have a built intensity exceeding 7,500 m²/ha. Elsewhere most neighbourhoods have greater than 500 m²/ha.

Figure 8.2   Shanghai residential area population density

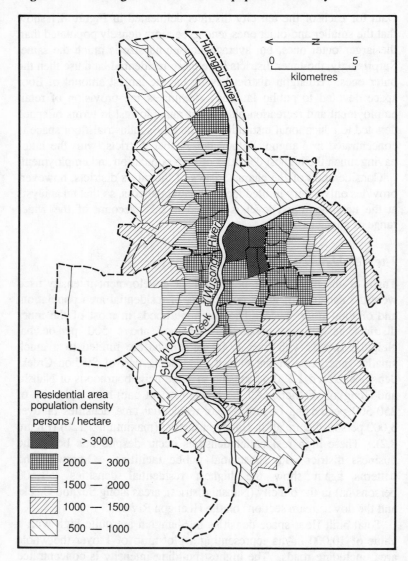

Residential area
population density

persons / hectare

> 3000

2000 — 3000

1500 — 2000

1000 — 1500

500 — 1000

Three measures of housing density have been used, based on
measures of floor space over the total neighbourhood land area. Areas
of high residential floor space density tend to be more confined,
reflecting other uses, mainly commercial and industrial (Figure 8.3).
The more intense areas (>5,000 m²/ha) are south of Suzhou Creek, and

highest in the old city, with smaller areas of high intensity north of Suzhou Creek and in Zhabei district.

Old terrace houses predominate in the old city (Nanshi district), Huangpu, Hongkou, and a small part of Zhabei districts. In the five most intense neighbourhoods there are over 8,000 m²/ha of old terraces. Other inner areas have 2,000-6,000 m²/ha. As with the shanty areas, there are opportunities for major change in old terrace areas through upgrading and demolition of poor stock to make way for redevelopment for other uses, including residential. Finally, shanties have largely been removed from the inner areas and are now more evident in the middle ring and outer neighbourhoods. However, they still remain at a density of over 1,000 m²/ha in Nanshi, Hongkou, and Zhabei districts.

Three measures of employment, industrial density, and distribution were used (Figure 8.4). Industrial floor-space density is higher in two major industrial nodes: one is the port area on the Huangpu downstream of the city, while the other is adjacent to the south of Suzhou Creek in Putuo and Jing'an districts. Most of these areas exceed 3,000 m²/ha with peak areas being over 5,000 m²/ha. In two peak neighbourhoods in the central business district (CBD) of Huangpu, employment density exceeds 1,200 persons/ha, and in another it exceeds 900 persons/ha. In the downstream port area and south of Suzhou Creek in Putuo district there are more than 600 employees/ha. Over about half of the rest of the City Proper, there are more than 300 employees/ha.

Another measure is the employment per resident in the neigbour-hood, an indication of the local availability of jobs. The average activity rate across the City Proper is 0.62 jobs per capita. Employment per resident tends to be higher at the extremities than in the inner and middle ring neighbourhoods (apart from one neighbourhood in the CBD). This is because there are high concentrations of employment and residential densities are lower.

Finally, four measures were used for the density or distribution of various forms of urban public services: retailing, schooling, recreation, and various public facilities. The latter includes buildings used for services, such as health, education, welfare, emergencies, public security, meeting places, retailing, and recreation, as well as government offices. The greatest concentration is in Huangpu district, the CBD-type area where public facilities exceed 10,000 m²/ha (Figure 8.5). There are other concentrations in Hongkou district and Jing'an/Luwan districts. In three neighbourhoods of Huangpu district,

Figure 8.3   Shanghai residential floor-space density

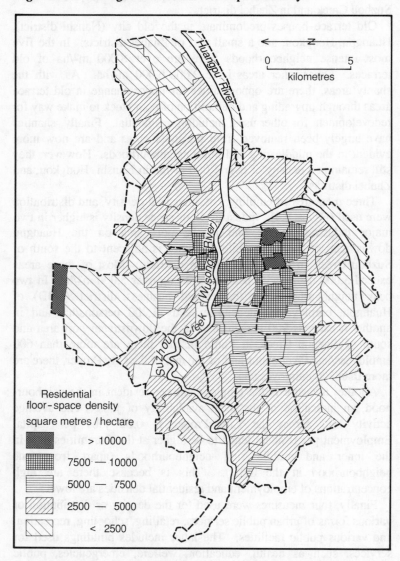

there are 20-75 retail employees/100 residents. Contiguous parts of
the Nanjing Road commercial area and one neighbourhood in Xuhui
district and one in Zhabei district have more than 10 retail
employees/100 residents. On average there are 5.13 school places/100
residents in the City Proper. Concentrations of school places tend to

Figure 8.4 Shanghai employment density

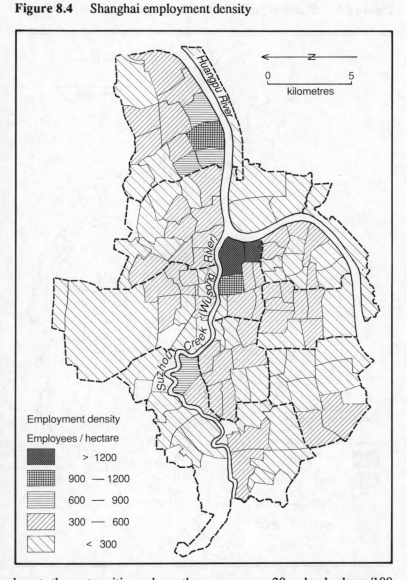

Employment density

Employees / hectare

> 1200

900 — 1200

600 — 900

300 — 600

< 300

be at the extremities where there are over 20 school places/100 residents. Cinema seats, sporting venues, parks, and other recreational facilities average 11.8 places per 100 residents. The greatest concentration, between 50 and 150 places per resident, is in the central parts in Huangpu and Luwan districts.

Figure 8.5   Shanghai public facility floor-space density

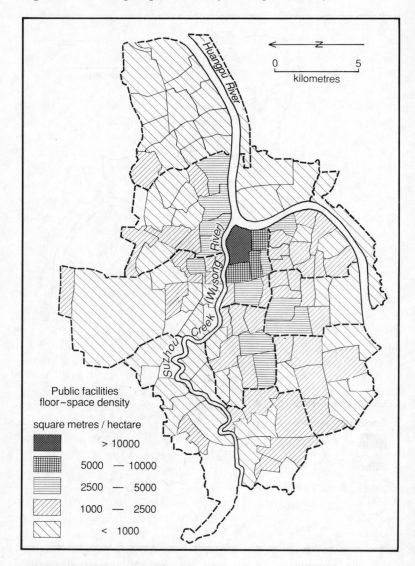

The Urban Form of Shanghai

Despite past planning efforts aimed at reducing population densities by expanding the fringe and creating satellites, densities in the older parts of Shanghai remain extremely high. The highest concentrations of above average density are wedge-shaped and centred on Suzhou Creek and its junction with the Huangpu River, reflecting the great importance of port-based activity. This area also reflects the intensity of the pre-1949 settlement pattern. It is remarkable that these population densities occur in areas which also dominate in central city activities such as retailing and other public facilities as well as recreation places.

Residential area (rather than gross area) densities reveal similar patterns. However the highest appear to be in the CBD at the junction of Suzhou Creek and the Huangpu River rather than in the old city. This could be related to the way in which residential land-use areas have been designated in a very mixed land-use area. The residential floor-space density pattern is less pronounced indicating a wider spread of higher intensity south of Suzhou Creek, and much less on the north side. The higher intensities are in the old city and part of the CBD. The intensity of built form as expressed by total floor-space density conforms to a similar wedge-shaped pattern around the Suzhou Creek/Huangpu River junction.

Work places are well distributed right through the City Proper. However, there are three major nodes — two industrial and one commercial/ community. The main industrial area is downstream on the Huangpu, with a major secondary centre located on the south side of a major bend in Suzhou Creek. The CBD south-west of the Huangpu/Suzhou junction is the dominant retail, business, administration and community node. When viewed in floor-space terms, the two industrial nodes appear more dominant, but this is probably more a measure of how much space industry occupies, particularly in specialized industrial areas. Employment opportunities related to residents are generally higher in the two major industrial nodes and in other areas near the periphery. This seems to be a reflection of local provision of housing for workers by work units in the newer industries since 1949.

Public facilities are concentrated in the CBD area, with lesser nodes to the north-east across Suzhou Creek and to the south-west in a significant secondary retailing area in Jing'an and Luwan districts. While recreation places are spread throughout City Proper, the CBD area and another location to the south-west of the centre tends to dominate. Other concentrations reflect major sports stadiums or cinemas.

The urban form of Shanghai was determined by its physiography and the trading patterns arising from its location on the Huangpu and

Suzhou Creek. With 500,000 km of waterways in Shanghai Municipality, movement by boat has been an important factor in the growth
of the city. Creeks and canals have also greatly influenced the street
pattern as they have created barriers to city expansion and produced a
very irregular pattern of narrow streets. The terrain is flat and low-
lying with no significant hills to constrain or otherwise influence the
urban form. Hitherto, the Huangpu has been a major barrier to urban
expansion on the east bank where there has been very little
development. The existing tunnel under the Huangpu is too remote
from the centre of the city to have had a great deal of influence on the
settlement pattern. However, a new tunnel on the alignment of Yan'an
Road, a major east-west route near the centre of the city, has recently
been opened and should provide opportunities for expansion quite
close to the centre of the city. Plans have recently been announced to
develop the area to the east of the Huangpu, known as Pudong, into a
major industrial, commercial, and financial zone. It is proposed to
invest about US$10,000 million converting 350 km^2 of farmland into a
high-technology industrial zone to be called the Pudong New Area.

The old walled city is still a significant element in the urban
structure: it is a very intense residential environment, while the foreign
settlements developed their own individual patterns largely unrelated
to one another. Shanghai's road system which emerged in the inner
areas does not serve the city well. It is rather better connected in the
east-west direction and advantage is being taken of this in traffic
management improvement schemes, including linked signal control
systems, which are being introduced. Walking and cycling are the
dominant travel modes, accounting respectively for 44 per cent and 13
per cent of all trips. For short trips walking predominates, and is
significant for journeys taking up to 35 minutes. Most cycling trips
are of 7 to 55 minutes duration. Bus travel only becomes significant
for journeys over 17 minutes and most trips are less than 75 minutes.
Many trips are unreasonably long for such a compact city. In 1986,
there were an average of twelve million bus boardings per day,
representing a doubling of demand in a decade. From the public
transport viewpoint Shanghai is a very inefficient city. Much of this
can be explained by the irregular and congested street network. The
relatively long distances which many people have to travel to work is
an added factor. Total daily travel times of two-and-a-half to three
hours are not uncommon.

The strongest travel 'desire lines' are either to or across the CBD
between the immediate south and the north-north-east. There is also a

strong 'desire line' between areas to the north and to the north-east, but because of barriers in the street system, such trips have to be made via the central area. Planners have displayed a strong commitment to building a subway system in Shanghai, consisting of seven lines to cover 176 km by 1995. The first 14.6-km line from the new Longhua airport to the new Shanghai railway station (which opened late in 1987) is under construction. Unfortunately the 'desire lines' along this north-south route are not particularly strong. The experience in Hong Kong and other cities is that a strong linear urban structure with intense corridors of development and strong travel demand are important requirements for a mass-transit system. In Shanghai a number of past and current shanty clearance and housing renewal schemes have incorporated road widening and other improvements to the street network. Future renewal to improve housing and other environmental conditions could provide opportunities to intensify certain desired corridors.

9 Urban Problems and Planning in Tianjin

D. K. FORBES AND D. WILMOTH

BEGINNING in the late 1970s, China entered a period of change as important as any in the previous thirty years. Initiated in Beijing, and with their primary focus on economic change, the reforms introduced under the banner of the 'open door' promised to have profound consequences for Chinese society and for both the built and natural environments. Though the economic reforms were introduced in stop-start fashion, and never had unanimous support within the ruling élite, planners began devising the strategies which would bring about the changes to the spatial structure of China that were required by its new outward-looking economic orientation.

Urban network development (see Murphey, 1980; Kirkby, 1985; Kojima, 1987; Wang, F., 1987) and China's large cities (see Sit, 1985; Schinz, 1989) were at the forefront of many of the new strategies. This chapter examines the case study of Tianjin Municipality (which includes Tianjin City), describing some of the problems it faces and the planning responses to them. The chapter first describes the growth and development of Tianjin; it then examines the overall urban and regional planning strategies, placing them in the context of the economic reforms in China; and finally it concentrates on particular problems and solutions in traffic and transport planning.

The Growth and Development of Tianjin Municipality

The Regional Context

Tianjin Municipality is an administrative region, equivalent in status to a province, of over 11,000 km² located on the northern edge of the Great North China Plain, about 130 km south-east of Beijing. The municipality is divided into eighteen administrative districts, six of which fall within Tianjin City (the so-called City Proper consists of thirteen districts). The City itself is located on the Haihe River, which empties into the Bohai Sea at Tanggu, about 50 km to the east.

Tianjin occupies a strategic location in contemporary China in what Li in Chapter 3 refers to as the Bohai Rim Economic Belt. The City has a hinterland extending deep into North China (Figure 9.1) due to its role as a transport centre. The port at Tanggu (called Xingang) was

Figure 9.1 The regional setting of Tianjin

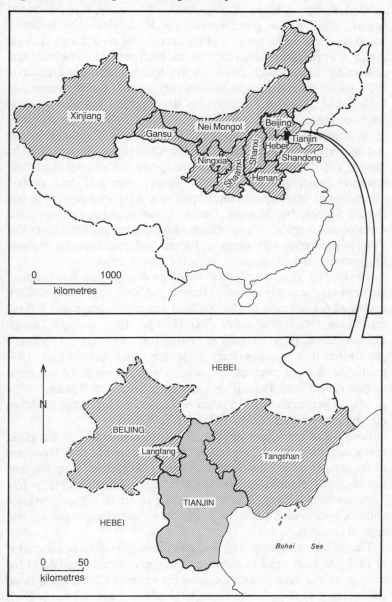

the seventh largest in China in 1987 (see Chapter 5) in terms of freight handled, though in terms of cargo-handling capacity, it ranks second largest. It is the main port for foreign trade (dominated by imports), which accounts for 80 per cent of the annual volume of cargo. Tianjin is also at a crucial junction of the national rail network. The main line connecting Beijing with the north via Shanhaiguan, constructed in 1901, passes through Tianjin Municipality, as does the line connecting Beijing and Shanghai. Tianjin has an important location *vis-à-vis* three economically powerful regions in China — the energy resources of the Shanxi Basin, the industrial concentration in Liaoning Province and the advanced development of the Changjiang (Yangtze) Delta region (Ye, 1984). Recently the municipality has also developed co-operative projects in such fields as energy, iron and steel, timber, cement, wool, leather, and mineral products in the Provinces of Hebei, Henan, Shanxi, Nei Mongol, Gansu, Liaoning, Jilin, and the Tibet Autonomous Region. Co-operation with the latter involved extensive shifts of productive technology and equipment, staff transfers, training programmes, and co-operative projects (Tianjin, 1985).

The Beijing-Tianjin-Langfang-Tangshan area (Figure 9.1) is one of the most economically advanced regions in China; by the mid-1980s it contained 6.1 per cent of China's total urban population and 9.5 per cent of the industrial share of GNP (Tianjin, 1985, p. 69). Though Tianjin Municipality contained only 0.8 per cent of China's population, it is a major force in industry and resources, in 1987 producing 2.9 per cent of the country's gross value of industrial output, valued at 40,450 million yuan (State Statistical Bureau, 1988a, p. 48). In per capita terms, Tianjin ranked second to Shanghai with an output of 2,730 yuan in 1982 (Wu, C-T., 1987b).

Local economies are already closely integrated. In Langfang Prefecture, for instance, 56 per cent of the town-owned and 70 per cent of the county-owned industrial enterprises have close economic and technological relations with Beijing and Tianjin (Tianjin, 1985, p. 69). Together with Beijing, Tianjin is a major centre of higher education within China, with a particular emphasis on science, technology, and applied research.

Tianjin's economic, population, and urban growth since Liberation in 1949 has been rapid in absolute and relative terms. As one of the main ports and manufacturing centres for northern China, it has faced continuing growth pressures irrespective of dominant national policies favouring agriculture or industry, big cities or small cities, political development or economic development. Tianjin has a very diversified manufacturing base: in 1984 there were 4,600 industrial enterprises with 1,400,000 employees making chemicals, petroleum products, engineering and metal goods, machine tools, motor vehicles and other transport equipment, bicycles, computers, electronics, television sets and other consumer durables, foodstuffs, building materials, textiles, fabrics, printing and dyeing, pharmaceuticals, and diversified light industry (Tianjin, 1985, p. 45).

Industrial development has been overwhelmingly concentrated in Tianjin City, which in the early 1980s accounted for 75 per cent of the municipality's enterprises and 84 per cent of its value of industrial output (Ye, 1984, p. 11). Although it is planned to give greater emphasis in industrial location to Tanggu and other satellite cities, Tianjin's tertiary sector is expected to grow rapidly and, together with non-polluting industries, light industry, and a range of other manufacturing establishments, will provide the economic base for the City. As a key open-door city, the economic growth pressures will remain strong, notwithstanding national policy towards restricting big city growth and the municipality's own policy favouring industrial relocation.

Urban Growth

The population of Tianjin City increased very quickly through the nineteenth and early twentieth centuries, assisted by the economic activity which stemmed from the establishment of foreign concessions there. At Liberation, the City had a population of 1,790,000. It has continued to grow although, since the early 1960s, natural increase has been slower than in China as a whole (Hsu, 1986; Li, J-N., 1987). Of the municipality's population of 8,310,000 in 1987, Tianjin City contained 41 per cent: thus 3,448,000 people were concentrated at an average density of 12,870 persons/km^2 that rises to 49,673 persons/km^2 in the central Heping district. Tanggu district (including Xingang) had an urban population of 331,200 in 1987, and is the site of the main seaport and the Tianjin Economic Technological Development Area (TEDA). Tanggu is closely linked to the satellite towns of Hangu (which had an urban population of 111,400), the focus of the salt and chemicals industry, and Dagang (174,300), a centre of oil, natural gas, and petrochemical developments. Other significant urban centres include Jixian in the north-east of the municipality, and Baodi, Wuqing, Yangliuqing, and Jinghai, all with populations between 10,000 and 50,000 (Tianjin Statistical Bureau, 1988, pp. 51–4).

In 1984 some 69 per cent of the total population of the municipality lived in urban areas (State Statistical Bureau, 1985a, p. 188). Tianjin City Proper is defined as consisting of six urban districts, three coastal districts, and four suburban districts: its total population in 1987 was 5,522,000, or 67 per cent of the municipality's population (Tianjin Statistical Bureau, 1988, pp. 51–4).

While the natural population increase has remained low, net in-migration has continued since 1980 at an annual rate of about 20,000 persons. Enterprises, institutions, and households are likely to continue to try to locate in Tianjin, and perhaps increase in numbers, as it specializes more in tertiary occupations for which some labour migration deregulation has occurred. Moreover, the success of the rural responsibility system has been greater near urban cash markets (Ye, 1984, p. 10), so that farmers are tending to relocate to suburban districts, thereby swelling the population of the City and increasing the pressure on urban services. The City's floating population — those without a residential permit or ration entitlement — has been estimated to number more than one million (Wilmoth, 1988, p. 6).

Urban growth in Tianjin has taken the form of uncoordinated expansion out from the old Chinese core and the various districts which had at one time housed the foreign population of the City. Rapid suburbanization of employment and associated housing occurred after Liberation with little attention being paid to the urban environment or environmental quality. Thus, 'new villages for workers' were built alongside their suburban factories in a haphazard fashion during the 1950s. The 1976 Tangshan earthquake killed about 30,000 Tianjin residents and destroyed or damaged much of the old building stock (Hersey, 1982). Since then there has been a concerted effort to rebuild in the suburbs and re-house the population at higher standards. The pattern of residential development has become higher-density and more compact, as the City's Housing Bureau takes over construction and management functions hitherto the responsibility of the various work units, and as inner-city urban renewal replaces old housing. With this change has come a better standard of urban planning, greater concern for environmental quality, and stronger interest in comprehensive urban renewal now that the space available for urban expansion has become very limited. Central government spending on urban construction in Tianjin — totalling 2,400 million yuan in 1985 (Edgington, 1985, p. 14) — has tended to be much higher per capita than cities such as Shanghai and Beijing, due to earthquake compensation and an active local political leadership.

Spatial Structure and the Tianjin Regional Plan

Economic Reform and the Seventh Five-year Plan

The first half of the 1970s saw a winding down of the influence of the Maoist views promoted during the Cultural Revolution, while the second half of the decade was the beginning of a period of transition. The landmark announcement in December 1978 proposed a series of reforms in the agricultural sector, including the gradual decollectivization of agriculture and the institution of a contract system which encouraged private peasant production of crops (Rozman, 1981).

Equally important, but of more direct relevance to the large cities, were a series of reforms under the banner of an open-door strategy (see Chapter 1). These were paralleled by changes to the way in which industries were to be managed. In October 1984 reforms in the urban industrial sector were proclaimed that were intended to shift decision making and financial responsibility to firms, encourage the development of private enterprise, and promote industrial democracy, in an attempt to improve the flexibility of firms and make them responsive to the market (Ellman, 1986).

The emphasis of China's Seventh Five-year Plan (1986–90) was on economic reform and development of the socialist economic structure, the promotion of growth through the technological skills of the population, and the improvement of living standards. The Plan emphasized consolidation, restructuring, and redevelopment: during the 1990s it was intended to give greater attention to economic revitalization and the development of productive forces (State Statistical Bureau, 1985b). The thrust of the Plan was to increase production, promote exports (which were targeted to grow by 40 per cent by the end of the decade), maintain full employment, and accelerate the construction of housing and public facilities. Foreign funds, including loans on preferential terms, were to be directed towards accelerating economic development, especially in energy, transport and communications (Chen, 1986).

The Sixth Plan (1981–5) achieved a steady growth in the economy, with industrial and agricultural production growing at 10 per cent per annum, energy (oil and coal) at better than 8 per cent per annum, and self-sufficiency achieved in grain and cotton production. The goal of the Seventh Plan was therefore to increase agricultural and industrial production by 38 per cent, which meant maintaining annual average growth at 6.7 per cent, and raising annual per capita consumption by between 4.2 per cent for urban residents and 5.1 per cent for those in rural areas (Chen, 1986; Pei, 1986; People's Republic of China, 1986, pp. 63–142). The Plan also sketched out some urban and spatial strategies:

We shall continue to adhere to the principle of controlling the size of large cities [over 1 million], developing medium-sized ones [200,000–500,000] moderately and small ones actively. Thus, we shall prevent overpopulation in large cities but will develop a number of small and selected medium-sized cities. In 1990, we expect there will be at least 400 cities and 10,000 towns. In this five-year period new urban housing with floor space totalling 650 million square metres will be completed. Efforts will be made to alleviate acute water shortages in urban areas and to basically meet the needs of country towns throughout the country for drinking water. We shall improve urban transport and build more roads and bridges. We shall rapidly increase gas supplies and central heating systems so that in 1990 an average of 40 percent of urban households will use gas for cooking, and more housing — a total floor space of 50 million square metres — will have central heating. We shall improve the environment by planting trees and grass and having better sanitation. In 1990 the tree- and grass-covered area will be four square metres per capita.

The main thrust of reform in China during the 1980s was economic, but this also had major spatial implications. The development of China's eastern coast was to be accelerated by the technological transformation of traditional industries and enterprises and the promotion of the larger coastal cities (though this was later broadened), the delta regions, and the Special Economic Zones (People's Republic of China, 1986, pp. 108–10). Yet, at the same time, urban policy favoured controlling the growth of large cities and concentrating development on medium and small towns and cities.

Regional Planning for Tianjin Municipality

Along with Shanghai and Beijing, Tianjin Municipality has the status, powers, and responsibilities of a province, including direct reporting to central government. As one of the fourteen coastal cities chosen in 1984 under the government's open-door policy on international trade, finance and investment, and as one of the four coastal cities which retained that status after a rationalization in 1985 (the others being Dalian, Shanghai, and Guangzhou), Tianjin was able directly to negotiate and implement economic agreements with foreign traders and investors and to approve quite large investment projects (Gu, 1985, p. 26). Although the 'open' coastal area was expanded in 1988 to include several hundred cities and counties, Tianjin's long history of trade and international development meant that it was quickly able to take advantage of its coastal city status.

By the mid-1980s, reforms to China's economic structure had started to have a marked impact on Tianjin's urban and regional planning and management. Party affairs had become more separated from government administration, which began to be streamlined. Agencies like the Housing and Land Management Bureau became more clearly distinguished in structure and function from new enterprises such as the Tianjin Construction Development Corporation. These enterprises were meant to be given more opportunities to make profits, and government organizations greater scope to manage the economy and plan the City's development. In addition to 9,000 collective enterprises, Tianjin had over 15,000 individually run enterprises in 1984, most of them in the service trades and most of them established with help from district governments and nearby cities (Edgington, 1985). The extension of the economic responsibility system to urban industries, a widening of the market sector, and greater opportunities for prices to reflect real costs had an influence on the urban planning and management system, as Tianjin was at the forefront in implementing national policies and reforms.

The current policy status of Tianjin does not permit strong urban growth commensurate with economic growth prospects. The PRC's national urban policy — as noted already — seeks to limit the growth of large cities and to encourage the growth of medium-size cities and small towns in rural areas (Ye, 1987). Tianjin is China's third largest city: its urban planning to the year 2000 is based on containing the City's population and its spread. With continued inter-regional controls over enterprise and residential location, the PRC may be more successful than other socialist or Third World countries at limiting city size, but one can predict increasing popular and international pressures to deregulate the labour market (for example, see World Bank, 1985, p. 89). Whether the whole municipality is caught under the policy of limiting large city size is not clear: the population forecast of 9,500,000 for the municipality as a whole by year 2000 suggests such a constraint, but the planned growth of satellite cities scattered throughout the municipality indicates an intention to deconcentrate industrial development within the municipality and perhaps even draw migrants from other parts of China to the satellite cities.

TEDA, at Tanggu, is one of the most important initiatives coming from the open-door policy. Near the mouth of the Haihe River, a large area is being developed for economic activities and residential facilities. Preferential treatment for foreign investment includes exemption from customs duty on re-exported inputs; exemption from industrial and commercial consolidated tax on materials and equipment; reductions of enterprise income taxes and exemptions in the early years; reduced personal income tax; tax-free remittance of capital and profits abroad; and accelerated depreciation of fixed assets such as machinery (Tianjin, Administrative Commission of Tianjin Economic Technological Development Area, 1985).

The overall regional plan for Tianjin Municipality focuses on the eight main urban areas, which have been designated as satellite cities and are intended to attract industrial development and population growth away from Tianjin City. However, apart from the Tanggu corridor and its two flanking urban areas of Dagang and Hangu, there is little indication of policies or programmes to implement the broader satellite cities concept. For example, in 1984 only 7.5 per cent of the investment in capital construction by state-owned units in Tianjin Municipality was outside Tianjin City, and only 0.1 per cent of that by collective units (State Statistical Bureau, 1985a).

A complementary alternative plan, based around the concept of a Tianjin–Tanggu corridor or 'T', seems to have greater acceptance among local planners. Given the restricted resources available to implement regional plans, the apparent neglect of the broader satellite city concept in favour of the corridor plan seems sensible. The plan for a corridor linking Tianjin with Tanggu therefore became the core of regional planning in the municipality. Land-use and transport proposals are key components of the comprehensive corridor plan adopted in the early 1980s by the Tianjin Municipal government (outlined in Figure 9.2). Its principle is the creation of a large port and industrial complex at Tanggu by the year 2000 with major new commercial, technological development, and residential areas, and the simultaneous restraint, already discussed, on the growth of Tianjin City. It is proposed that the population of the city of Tanggu will double to 600,000 by year 2000, with 200,000 people relocated from Tianjin City and another 100,000 people attracted from elsewhere or born in Tanggu. Tianjin City itself is expected to grow very slowly — from 3,400,000 people in 1986 to 3,800,000 by 2000. Tianjin and Tanggu will be linked by highway, railway, river, probably a freeway, and possibly some form of light-rail, rapid-transit link. They will be separated by green belts with open space, agricultural, and horticultural areas to maintain and increase food production. The

Figure 9.2 The Tianjin–Tanggu corridor plan

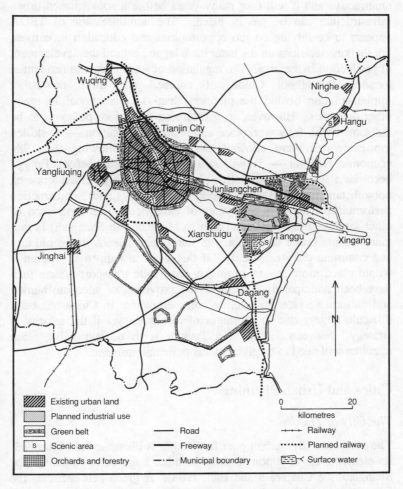

Source: Information provided by Tianjin Urban and Rural Construction Commission.

corridor will be part of the larger gateway to Beijing and much of north China. At the coast the pattern of development will trend north-south, to absorb the small centres of Dagang and Hangu into the conurbation, with north-south rail bypass routes emphasizing this 'T' shape.

It is unclear what methods will be used to relocate 200,000 people from Tianjin City to Tanggu, and how it is planned to gain their satisfaction with the new destination. The coastal region is physically unattractive and it will take many years before a sophisticated urban infrastructure can be put in place. The administration of TEDA appears to be relying on job opportunities and education incentives, but the key decisions on the latter have lagged behind the development of production in the area. The regulation of workplace and residential location throughout China, of course, puts more power of implementation behind the planners than is conventional in many other countries. However, if in future an open-door policy is to be associated with freer workplace and residential location — as skilled job categories were allowed more mobility following the 1984 economic reforms — it will still be a long time before Tanggu becomes a sufficiently attractive place to lure highly skilled workers, notwithstanding TEDA's sound economic and construction performance during its few years of existence. The experience of other satellite cities in China (such as Minghang in Shanghai) is that many people prefer to remain with family and friends in the old city and commute daily or weekly. If this were to happen in Tianjin it would place more severe strains on the public transport system than have been anticipated. Moreover, the provision of adequate human and cultural services to satellite cities elsewhere in China has been difficult, largely due to shortages of resources, yet if the relocation strategy between Tianjin and Tanggu is to be successful, close attention will need to be given to this potential problem.

Cities and Urban Planning

The City of Tianjin

The comprehensive urban plan for Tianjin is illustrated in Figure 9.3. Its elements are common to those of other large cities in China (for Shanghai, see Chapter 8 and Han, 1988). A green belt encircles the City; inner, middle, and outer ring roads are the main elements of the road transport system; an underground railway system is planned to increase public transport capacity; tertiary activities are dispersed throughout the City; advanced technology areas have been designated to build up Tianjin's high-technology industry; and inner-city residential areas are to be deconcentrated through extensive suburban housing development.

However, the plan has features that are specific to Tianjin. By comparison with other Chinese cities, Tianjin has a larger programme

Figure 9.3 The strategic plan for Tianjin City

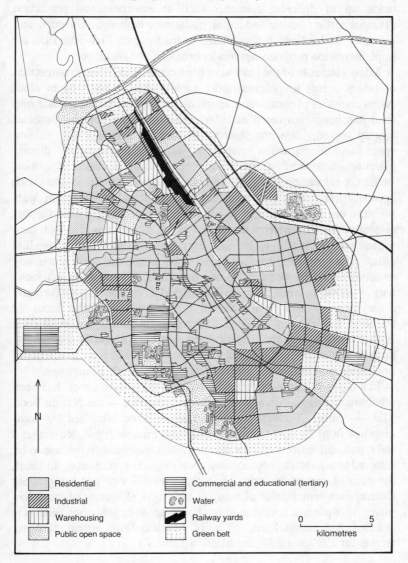

Residential

Industrial

Warehousing

Public open space

Commercial and educational (tertiary)

Water

Railway yards

Green belt

0   5

kilometres

Source: Tianjin (1985, p. 116).

of suburban housing development due to the legacy of the 1976 earthquake. The plan also makes provision for light industry, in keeping with the regional plan discussed earlier. The overall plan is made up of different elements such as environmental protection (Tianjin suffers severe industrial pollution), housing, transport, and greening, each of which was related to the Seventh Five-year Plan for implementation programmes, major projects, and budgets.

Many elements of the plan have been completed, while construction of others seems to progress more rapidly than is common in other Asian countries at comparable levels of development. The middle ring road has been completed and the post-earthquake housing problem largely solved, allowing planners to turn their attention to raising space and construction standards, more comprehensive district planning, and more compact urban expansion at higher densities. Industrial relocation has also been occurring as production units seek approval for expansion, and as the municipal government puts pressure on major polluters to clean up or be relocated. So far this relocation has been from the inner areas to the suburbs, but such moves will increasingly be to Tanggu and possibly other satellite cities. The green belt does not yet exist but negotiations are under way to acquire land for open space and orchards. However, an extensive park, generously treed, has been completed along the Haihe River, and other greening and environmental issues have been the focus of attention. Elaborate traffic interchanges (including the enormous Balitai overpass), a good traffic-light system, and traffic segregation arrangements have been installed. During the 1980s there was a boom in construction of offices, hotels, restaurants, and other buildings.

In a bid to attract more tourists, an 'ancient culture street' has been rehabilitated, and a downtown restaurant complex — the Nanshi Food Mall — built. Foreign concession areas, once inhabited by communities from Britain, Germany, Belgium, France, Japan, Russia, and Italy, and still reflecting their distinctive architectural styles, are to be restored to something approaching their original appearance. In short, the pace of capital construction during the 1980s helped bring about the early implementation of many of the physical aspects of the urban plan. This pace is bound to slow, however, as capital construction is reduced and rationalized. Tianjin Municipality's urban planning targets for 1990 and 2000 are listed in Table 9.1.

The Port City of Tanggu

The comprehensive plan for Tianjin Municipality gives attention to the development of Tanggu which, given its satellite status and centrality

Table 9.1 Targets for Tianjin City planning, 1990–2000

Service	Criterion	Unit	Target	
			1990	2000
Transport	Area of road/person	m²	3.0	4.1
	Area covered by roads	per cent	4.9	5.0
	Length of underground railway	km	14.6	27.5
	Network density of public roads	km/km²	2.0	2.5
Water supply	Capacity	m³ x 10,000/day	220	300
	Standard of use	m³/person-day	220	250
	Underground pipes	per cent	83	95
Green cover	Land in green cover	per cent	15	17
	Public open space	m²/person	2.0	3.8
Gas	Domestic gas use	per cent	70	98
Housing	Residential space	m²/person	7.0	9.0
Telephone	Telephone connections	per 100 persons	3.4	10.0
Postal	Value of business	yuan 10,000	5,900	13,400

Source: Tianjin Urban and Rural Construction Commission (1984, p. 10).

to the regional strategy, warrants further consideration (Yeh and Yuan, 1987). Until the early 1980s Tanggu was a small industrial and port city with housing of very mixed standard, congested interlocking transport routes, major problems with saline lands and environmental pollution, and land subsidence due to underground water depletion. It is being transformed by the massive port expansion at Xingang and the construction of the nearby TEDA.

The port currently has two international and two domestic passenger berths, five cargo berths, one bulk salt-loader, one bulk grain-loader, four container terminals, and various other general cargo areas. Altogether there are forty-six berths with depths ranging from 6 to 12.5 m. In 1987, total cargo throughput was 17,300,000 tonnes, of which 1,400,000 tonnes were containerized. In 1985, 60 per cent of the cargo to and from the port was transported by rail, 30 per cent by road and 10 per cent by water. However, it was planned that road transport would capture 50 per cent of cargo transport during the second half of the 1980s, and this share is likely to increase in the 1990s. A staged expansion on a massive scale will add many more berths (to 14 m in depth), iron and steel making and fabricating works, petrochemical plants, and new freshwater port facilities for river traffic on the Haihe River. Part of the Seventh Five-year Plan, it is estimated that it will cost US$2,000 million and will be partly financed by World Bank loans.

The nearby TEDA also has an ambitious expansion programme, based on manufacturing, but including residential, R. & D., and other areas. Some 33 km^2 of former salt-pan land are being utilized in stages, with the first 3 km^2 being developed over three years for a projected 100 to 150 enterprises with 30,000 workers and 2,400 million yuan industrial output. Targeted industries for the 'starting area' are small to medium enterprises engaged in electronics, new energy resources, optical communication, fine chemicals, offshore oil exploration, food preparation, paper-making and printing, instruments and assembly, building materials, and daily consumer goods. As the key part of Tianjin's open-door policy for economic expansion, TEDA has preferential access to infrastructural finance and, in turn, offers preferential treatment to offshore investors.

Although in the first years several project agreements were signed and new projects started, it remains to be seen whether TEDA will be successful in the long-term. Many countries in the Asia-Pacific region, and other cities and regions in China, are competing for limited foreign investment, while the PRC's political instability has helped to diminish the attractiveness of the country for foreign investors. The strategic relocation of industrial and urban growth from Tianjin City to Tanggu depends vitally on the success of the port development and TEDA and how the emerging Tanggu urban area is integrated. While the components of this area are likely to be well-planned and executed, the overall integration of physical, economic, and social development in Tanggu will also need close attention.

Transport and Traffic Planning

Although the development of the transport system has been a high priority for Tianjin Municipality, the pace of economic growth and increases in travel demand will keep pressure on the transport sector. Tianjin's pivotal role in the national transport system stems from its location at the junction of major rail lines, while China's first inter-urban freeway is under construction along the corridor linking Beijing, Tianjin, and Tanggu. The old system of canals (including the Grand Canal) links Tianjin with other regions via the Haihe River. Although river and canal shipping has declined markedly, due to the silting up of the Haihe, there is still some waterway traffic. Tianjin airport has direct international connections, and is designated as a reserve airport for nearby Beijing. The port at Xingang is of major strategic and economic importance, considering the proximity of Japan, China's largest trading partner (after Hong Kong and Macao), and South Korea, a major trading partner with which China deals indirectly.

The inter-regional dimension of Tianjin's transport system is of great significance to an understanding of its economy. For example, 91 (65 per cent) of the 140 million tonnes of rail freight handled in 1984 was through-traffic. Likewise eight million (53 per cent) of the fifteen million rail travellers were through-passengers (Wang, X-C., 1985). The status of inter-regional transport plans is not entirely clear, but they depend on which major projects can be funded, and on the role given to transport in national priorities. Currently, national priority for inter-regional transport is high, given the costs of the congestion and inefficiencies. As incomes rise, passenger demand for inter-regional travel is growing.

Municipal Transport

Within Tianjin Municipality transport is the key to the success of the Tianjin–Tanggu corridor plan, affecting the population relocation programme and, through the inter-modal freight system, the overall open-door economic policy. Present and proposed links between Tianjin City and Tanggu are shown in Figure 9.4. The existing highway is of adequate standard for current purposes, but it will be wholly inadequate to meet the demands proposed under the urban and economic plans. The Beijing–Tianjin–Tanggu freeway should meet the demand for through-traffic, but it may not be appropriate to satisfy short-movement demands that will increase with the industrialization of the coastal area and the gradual expansion of Tianjin City's tertiary activities. In the mid-1980s, passenger traffic constituted 32 per cent of the total highway volume, as compared with goods traffic which was over 60 per cent. For rail traffic, these ratios were reversed.

The proposed mass rapid-transit system will be essential for the likely daily and weekly cross-commuting generated by the relocation of people and work units. A rapid-transit system between Tianjin and Tanggu was investigated as part of the construction and economic development plan (Tianjin Public Utility Bureau, 1986). Average daily rail passenger volume between the two cities in the mid-1980s was 50-60,000 both ways; this is expected to grow beyond 130,000 by 1990 and 300,000 by 2000, more than half of which would be commuters. A 39-km line serving four stations is planned for the first stage, with a capacity of 10–15,000 passengers at peak hour in each direction and a speed of 60–80 km/hr.

Each transport mode in the corridor, it appears, has been planned and developed somewhat separately, without rigorous economic evaluation of inter-modal competition or full technical evaluation of alternative modes and technology, as is becoming increasingly the case in developed countries. Work on the mass rapid-transit system, for instance, could have usefully compared the economics of competing highway or freeway bus services including bus-only lanes or independent rights of way, or could consider other options for the corridor, such as the partial suburban electrification of the national railway line or the construction of a parallel passenger track. The ways in which the transport system links the cities, and in turn changes their form, is a planning problem that needs to be investigated more closely. Future potential savings in investment and operating efficiency might well be achieved, while avoiding rigidities in the urban system and consequential social and economic problems, if local planners gave greater attention to inter-modal issues and the transport/land-use nexus. The success of the corridor, or 'T' plan, hinges on the efficiency and effectiveness of the transport linkage between the two cities.

Urban Transport

Transport planning within Tianjin City has been made difficult by the unconnected and haphazard development of the city in the nineteenth century, including the foreign concessions, which bequeathed the city an old housing stock and an historic pattern of curved narrow streets. The decline in river transport from the middle of this century due to siltation, and the closure of the mouth of the Haihe River to large vessels, put increased pressure on road transport. Since Liberation, the pattern of joint industrial and residential development has added

Figure 9.4 The Tianjin–Tanggu rapid-rail transit alignment

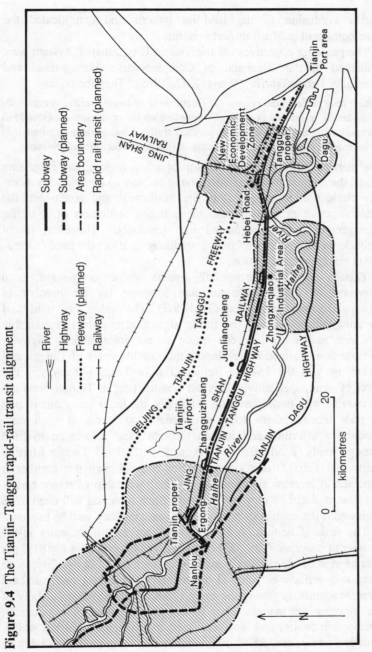

Source: Tianjin Public Utility Bureau (1986).

further confusion to the land-use pattern and complicated the development of public transport systems.

The planning objectives for the Tianjin City transport system were embodied in the 'Decision of Comprehensive Management and Control of Urban Traffic' (Wang, X-C., 1985). They included:

Setting up a perfect road system . . . Establishing an overall traffic system with public traffic in leading position . . . Speeding up the construction of rapid rail transport . . . Building up a modernised traffic administration system . . . Adjusting the city layout . . . Improving infrastructure facilities of the city.

The plan envisages the construction of inner, middle, and outer ring roads; the extension of the underground railway to complete an inner-city circle and to extend it to the north-west and south-east; the redevelopment of railway stations; and the institution of a traffic management system organized into precincts.   However, recent cutbacks in infrastructure funding are likely to affect the pace of intra-urban transport construction.

Though there is occasionally some traffic congestion, road provision in Tianjin is more than adequate for the number of motorized vehicles at present (Table 9.2). The middle ring road is, if anything, under-utilized, the traffic signalling system is reasonably efficient, and inner city congestion is not intolerable.   Highway construction is aimed at developing the satellite cities of Tanggu and Jixian, as will the 154-km Beijing–Tianjin–Tanggu freeway.   The level of municipal activity in road construction in Tianjin contrasts favourably with underprovision nationally, the latter being due in part to poor incentives for local governments to invest in such non-productive activities and in part through local reluctance to fund through-roads (World Bank, 1985, p. 83).   In 1984 Tianjin Munici-pality had 120,000 motorized vehicles and although this number is expected to increase substantially, private ownership of motor cars is not contemplated by current forecasts. Such forecasts will need to be reviewed if the open-door policy continues; they may well be too low.

The striking feature of traffic throughout the municipality is the number of bicycles: 4,050,000 owned in 1984 accounting for 81.2 per cent of trips by all modes (Wang, X-C., 1985, p. 1). In the City, there were two million bicycles (1.6 persons per bicycle) and numbers increased annually during the early 1980s by 10 per cent.   Many of the bicycles are manufactured in the municipality.   Consequently, intersection control and lane separation are difficult problems which, with prosperity, are likely to be exacerbated by greater ownership of motorcycles and mopeds.   Because of the principle of 'putting public

Table 9.2 Non-rail public transport vehicles, Tianjin City, *c*.1984

Mode	Number of Vehicles	Number of Passengers (million p.a.)	Per cent of Passengers	Route Length (km)
Buses	1,451	682.11	82.40	2,005
Trolley buses	184	116.49	14.07	73
Taxis	349	1.87	0.23	–
Long-distance buses	180	7.50	0.91	–
Boats	12	19.81	2.39	–
Total	2,164	827.78	100.00	–

Source: Tianjin Urban and Rural Construction Commission (1984, p. 4).

transport in [a] leading position and individual traffic in [an] auxiliary one', the share of trips by bicycle is expected to decline from 80 to 60 per cent by 1990 and to 40 per cent by 2000 (Wang, X-C., 1985, p. 7). Traffic planning and management is a major task for Tianjin, and a special research and planning organization has been set up to do this work. It is co-ordinated by the Tianjin Urban Transport Overall Research Group (TUTOR), with its counterparts in other cities, so that a specialized division of technological labour can emerge. Tianjin has had particular responsibility for transport modelling, software development, and industrial area transport planning. With the object of 'establishing an overall traffic system with public traffic in the leading position', the policy is as follows (Wang, X-C., 1985, p. 7):

During the period of the seventh five-year plan, place the conventional traffic on ground level in leading position, raise intensity of line networks . . . mean-while, develop rapid speed buses and electrified rail traffic to a certain degree. In the middle and distant future, electrified rapid rail traffic will be mainly de-veloped and an overall traffic network, in which traffic [at] . . . underground, ground . . . and elevated [levels] are combined together, will be formed.

The heavy rail system is congested with freight traffic and very heavily used for inter-urban passenger traffic. The greater use of rail for daily suburban passenger movement warrants serious consideration. Different state agencies control different tracks and sidings, suggesting there is scope for rationalization of use. However, even with present rail capacity so heavily used, and with a share of traffic moving on to roads as they are built or improved, better management would seem to be only a partial solution. New tracks will be needed. Construction of the present underground railway in Tianjin City began in 1970, but was interrupted by the 1976 earthquake. The second city underground in China after Beijing, Tianjin's system — 7.4 km and twelve power-coach trains — has not had much impact on total traffic, having a capacity of only 10,000 passengers daily. There are plans to extend the present Tianjin–Tanggu railway line in phase with the outer ring road. Thus a 'rapid rail transit frame of "one ring and two lines"' will be established (Wang, X-C., 1985, p. 7).

Conclusion

As has been noted in earlier chapters, the spatial development of China is both complex and critical. The large coastal cities, such as Tianjin, have been vital to the process because they are major centres of population and production and key components of the national transport network. The 1980s was a period during which the urban planners in Tianjin developed plans and strategies for enhancing the high-technology, light-industry, and service-sector role of Tianjin City, through extensive infrastructure development, while planning for limited population growth. At the same time, the 'T' plan for the municipality has the objective of making the Tanggu region a major national and international node for goods transport, the centre of heavy industry, and a city with a burgeoning population.

The suggested strategies were not without contradictions: developing sufficient infrastructure with a limited state budget; enticing people to move from large urban areas such as Tianjin to smaller, newer ones like Tanggu; and attracting sufficient foreign investment to make the TEDA scheme workable. However, such strategies could not possibly have achieved their goals within a decade. The importance of the period starting in the late-1970s stems from the fact that a beginning was made on trying to transform Tianjin into a municipality that reflected the open-door goals of the country's economic planners. Urban and regional planners formulated plans and strategies to enhance the efficiency of Tianjin, and with this its ability to expand the production and services located within the municipality.

10 China's Spatial Development: Issues and Prospects

D. K. FORBES AND G. J. R. LINGE

CHINA'S importance to its neighbouring Asia-Pacific countries and the wider world, now and in the future, is beyond question. Yet its turbulent past and the uncertainty which currently surrounds economic and social directions cloud the future and make speculation about progress during the 1990s risky. Shifts in such fundamentals as the balance of power following the Tiananmen Incident in June 1989 (though many, such as Gittings, 1989, would argue that the reform programme started to go awry as early as 1987) can result in complex, unpredictable outcomes.

China's guiding ethos since the late 1970s has been to search for practical solutions less influenced by ideological correctness than in the past. The chapters in this book have likewise looked at practical issues of spatial restructuring. This final chapter reviews recent influences on China's spatial structure; identifies key issues affecting the development of its space economy which suggest new research avenues; assesses prospects for the 1990s; and suggests alternative scenarios and their likely impacts on the country's future structure.

Spatial Structure in Retrospect

China's spatial structure is considerably more than a sideshow to the fundamental political, economic, and social directions which, conventionally, hold most interest for sinologists. A major theme of the chapters in this book is the significance of the spatial structure of the country in influencing the process of reform which began during the late 1970s and continued through much of the 1980s.

A corner-stone of the strategies prior to the open-door period had been a fundamental concern with regional self-sufficiency and the creation of a self-reliant socialist economy, in which small and medium-size cities were favoured over large ones, and 'productive' cities over 'consumptive' cities. Defence considerations were also significant in the third-line construction programme, while the prominence of the peasantry in the ideology of the time also helped to promote the special importance of the rural areas. The result was that the focus of state investment shifted further and further westwards from the early 1950s to the late 1970s.

The implementation of the programme of economic reform, including the open door, has required fundamental changes to the spatial structure of China. The particular emphasis given to the export-generating capacity of the coastal regions, involving expensive outlays on transport and infrastructural investments, and complex adjustments such as the easing of restrictions on the labour market still require many years to bring to fruition. The approach has underlined the importance of the cities — particularly the larger coastal ones — as a market for surplus rural produce, as providers of both formal and informal employment, and as centres of industrial production. Thus, during the 1980s the focus of new interest swung away from the interior and towards the coast, which, in Chapter 2, Fincher argues constituted the renaissance of a long and important historical pattern. The inland, not the coastal, emphasis he suggests was the aberration.

China's size has made economic planning, and spatial and regional policies in particular, both vital and exceedingly complex. China's large bureaucracy has not always been up to the mammoth tasks before it. This precipitated a major reorganization in May 1988 in which the State Planning Commission emerged with enlarged responsibilities for economic development, including short, medium, and long-term strategic economic planning. However, the shortage of skilled development planners at both the national and provincial (and sub-provincial) levels, combined with a large, complex, and still fragmented bureaucracy, remains a problem.

While overall economic growth was stimulated by the reforms, the regions which benefited most were in the richer parts of the country. It was estimated that in the mid-1980s some ninety-two million people lived in China's poorer regions — those with annual per capita incomes of less than 200 yuan — and these gained least from the reforms and therefore became relatively poor (Figure 3.1). It prompted the government to establish the Office of Development in the Poor Areas in 1984, and made it report directly to State Council. The Office is responsible both for policy formation and the management of resources for poverty-related projects, mainly in agriculture.

Regardless of future political and economic strategies, China's spatial structural adjustments have only just begun, suggesting some significant avenues for research in the 1990s. China's accelerated growth rate has reinforced concerns about how to cope with continued growth while also maintaining balanced regional development, and how to reconcile differences between regional and national needs, and between urban and rural areas. There is a challenge to conceptualize spatial strategies that are better suited to the 'socialist mixed economy' of the type now apparently coming into existence in Asia and Eastern Europe than the current, rather rigid, models based on principles of centralized control of all aspects of the economy. Moreover, questions of regional inequality and poverty should not be separated from environmental issues, such as land degradation, for there is a close dependent relationship between them. These problems will require an approach to economic geography which takes account of both *laissez-faire* and centrally planned solutions to spatial imbalances.

Spatial Issues

The increasing scale of regional economic integration attempted during the 1980s helped emphasize the inherent weaknesses in China's transport facilities. Transport and energy (particularly the transport *of* energy, in the form of coal), and the special transport requirements of an open-door strategy were identified as among the most important problems facing the PRC during the Seventh Five-year Plan.

To facilitate the transport of coal, it is essential to set up a transport network based on railways and incorporating highways, water routes and port facilities. To implement the policy of opening to the outside world and to link the coastal cities by maritime shipping, we have to set up another transport network, based on harbours and incorporating rail, highway, water and air routes (People's Republic of China, 1986, p. 98).

The lack of seaports and the inadequacy of existing facilities were major obstructions to the strategy of increasing China's exports. Port construction was pushed ahead after 1973, but it was only during the Sixth Five-year Plan (1981–5) that harbour construction received a high priority. There are still inadequate numbers of berths, and most ports require far better transport connections with their hinterlands. In mid-1990 the State Planning Commission, supported by the World Bank and the Australian International Development Assistance Bureau, began an extensive study of the transport needs of the Changjiang (Yangtze) Delta region (including Jiangsu, Zhejiang, and Anhui Provinces, and Shanghai Municipality), with the improvement of the linkages between the port and its hinterland being a major objective.

China has a freight-intensive economy compared to other large, developing countries. To reduce this there is a need for more investigation of the relationships, both nationally and regionally, between production, distribution, and transport facilities, and innovative solutions to reduce transport costs. More consideration is now being given to the freight burden associated with industrial location, and with the substitution of pipelines for rail freight for commodities such as oil. Changing patterns of energy production — China's planned nuclear energy capacity being an example — will influence the space economy and the environment. New transport and communication technologies, such as improved telecommunications and attempts at a higher level of inter-modal co-ordination, will also alter the demand for transport with spatial consequences worthy of examination. Underlying these major planning and investment issues is the question of how the expansion and upgrading of transport sector facilities, particularly those projects that include considerable foreign exchange costs, can be financed.

High levels of population growth occurred in China in the post-Liberation period, but these had declined dramatically by the 1980s. While the rates of decline in fertility occurred more or less uniformly across the entire country, they have reached their lowest absolute levels in the urbanized coastal municipalities (such as Shanghai and Tianjin) and provinces (such as Jiangsu). Nevertheless, population growth and distribution issues loom large for China and have a very significant impact on global population issues. Therefore, regional differences in natural population growth warrant close monitoring and further investigation.

For many years, internal migration was restricted by the internal pass system, reinforced by grain rationing and a shortage of available residential accommodation in attractive towns and cities. The growth of private markets in food and housing eased these indirect restrictions, while local government officials, encouraged by Beijing, became more tolerant of the movement of people. In 1988 it was announced that peasants could move to urban areas if they could provide their own staples and had the resources to establish an enterprise, although this has since been toned down because of urban unemployment. This has highlighted current concerns about urban growth and urbanization. While research on this question is growing, there is a need for better definitions of key concepts (see Appendix 1). Planners' and researchers' paramount need is for an objective, consistent definition of urban areas, not subject to political manipulation, and capable of reasonable use for international comparisons.

Population migration and labour-force changes are also important to the research agenda. There are emerging spatial consequences from the breaking of the 'iron rice bowl' — the practice whereby state enterprises guaranteed life-time employment — as a result of the easing of restrictions on personal mobility and the choice of residential location. In the past, urban planners could be fairly confident that their prescriptions on rates of population growth would be reasonably accurate, as long as the government did not mount a major rustication programme. Deregulation of population mobility will create greater uncertainties, forcing planners to develop new techniques of socio-demographic analysis.

The type of coastal big-city growth that inevitably resulted in China during the 1980s strained the infrastructure of large cities such as Shanghai, Tianjin, and Guangzhou, and their physical, economic, and social structures were generally unable to cope. Employment, housing, and physical and social infrastructure became overburdened. Planning solutions to the problems of these large cities were seldom straightforward. Shanghai highlights the difficulties posed for planners because of its extremely high population density and fragmented internal structure, while Tianjin's problems were compounded by the destruction caused by a massive earthquake in 1976, which has subsequently left its mark by influencing the form of the city's redevelopment.

The very ambitious strategic plans prepared for China's cities featured major attempts to improve the transport and communications infrastructure, build new housing, develop urban services (particularly water and energy), and set aside large areas for industrial development. Cities were physically bounded by green belts, and limits were imposed on future population growth. In part, the physical restrictions placed on urban expansion were an attempt to limit the alienation of arable rural land. The high level of investment required for urban redevelopment forced China to try to secure international finance from agencies, notably the World Bank.

Although China's urban planners have made impressive achievements, more thought is needed about ways of making cities more economically efficient — through changes to transport, housing, industrial location, and land use in general — but, at the same time, better places to live and work, and not just for the rich. These problems can be approached by examining the sorts of land, property, labour, and financial markets that can facilitate the development of urban areas. Yet it remains to be determined who is able to finance the rehabilitation of the deteriorating physical infrastructure in China's urban areas. It also needs to be asked what role planners should have either in regulating these markets or in distributing these kinds of resources.

The urban areas will provide one of the foundations of China's economic growth, but this will need to be managed without further damaging the quality of their natural and built environments. Trade-offs seem inevitable, but it is unclear what these will be. In some large Chinese cities efforts have been made to rebuild inner city streetscapes, but these have been primarily for tourists and fall well short of the kinds of urban heritage preservation plans required.

Finally, the sustainability of China's strategies of reform will depend almost as much on the ways in which key spatial and environmental processes are managed, as on their more prominent political support or economic performance. Concerns over food production and the loss of agricultural land, and land degradation — including salination, desertification, and deforestation — in the rural areas must remain high on the government's agenda. Air, water, and land pollution due to industrial growth in the towns and cities is also of major concern. The prospective impact of global environmental changes presents a further range of environmental problems of considerable importance to both rural and urban China. Environmental problems of this magnitude do not stand in a spatial vacuum — they are connected to parallel global concerns, and are closely linked to the domestic spatial economy, particularly to such issues as regional patterns of poverty and the location of production and new investment. As the World Commission on Environment and Development (1987, p. 261) has noted:

the traditional forms of national sovereignty are increasingly challenged by the realities of ecological and economic interdependence. Nowhere is this more true than in the shared ecosystems and "the global commons" — those parts of the planet that fall outside national jurisdictions.

Spatial Structure in Prospect

The pace of reform in China slowed in 1987 and virtually came to a halt in the second half of 1989 and early 1990, leading some to speculate that the period of reform had ended. The volatility of recent Chinese history makes speculation about the 1990s hazardous, though whether the PRC is more prone to abrupt shifts of policy direction than other countries at comparable levels of development is less clear. The political signals in the aftermath of the Tiananmen Incident are still mixed. For instance, the rise to more powerful positions in the second half of 1989 of the reformist former Mayors of Shanghai (Jiang Zemin became General Secretary of the Communist Party) and Tianjin (Li Ruihuan was elected to the Standing Committee of the Politburo) indicates to some that the reformist policies, particularly the open door, will survive. Yet this needs to be set against the vast majority of new strategies being discussed in the PRC which suggest that China has turned away from reform, underlined by the equally decisive fall from grace of senior reformers such as Zhao Ziyang and another former Mayor of Tianjin, Hu Qili.

While the internal politics of China are difficult to fathom, some of the context is less so. During the 1990s China will face a different international and domestic environment than in the 1960s or 1970s. While it can be assumed that China has not rejected 'socialism' in favour of 'capitalism', it must be asked what form of socialism is China likely to pursue. Zhao Ziyang's version of the 'primary stage of socialism' has been rejected by the present leadership (though not necessarily by the people), but the alternative is not clear.

Internationally it is unlikely that the PRC will continue to ignore the symbolic and practical significance of the political changes that have swept through Eastern Europe (Fincher, 1989a, pp. 5–7).

Domestically, China's economic reform programme led to a marked improvement in the country's economic performance, raising expectations of future policies. We should not ignore the fact, though, that China's economic performance was also good throughout much of the period since Liberation. Moreover, measures of economic growth alone are an incomplete indicator of economic development, and there seems to have been little improvement for many of the poorer groups in the country. Nevertheless, expectations have been raised of better access to a range of consumer goods: Zhao Ziyang's brand of reform policies made him 'the champion of both the most rapidly growing component of China's society — the "circulating" population drawn from home by opportunities to make money — and most of the urban population' (Fincher, 1989a, p. 21).

Spatial Futures

The evolving spatial structure of the country will also influence future possibilities. The physical endowments of the landscape and the distribution of population are spatial constraints on the pace of change, while major fixed investments in infrastructure take much longer to build or relocate than many other dimensions of economic policy set in Beijing. On balance, therefore, it is unlikely that the 1990s will witness a dramatic shift in the spatial structure of China back to what it was in the 1960s and 1970s. This is not to say that the spatial structure will not be seriously influenced by the direction the PRC's policy makers and planners set for the country.

Two Scenarios

Two scenarios can plausibly be envisaged for China during the decade. In the first — which we have labelled a *closing door* scenario, though we recognize this is a gross simplification — a slowdown in foreign direct investment and trade, and international concessional development finance, will result in economic brakes being applied. This, in turn, would force China to return to an emphasis on a more inward-looking strategy featuring a focus on self-reliance and regional self-sufficiency, while giving inter-regional trade more emphasis than international trade. There are many variations on this theme, but the key point is that China's political isolation results in a serious down-grading of the open-door strategy, and the stagnation or reversal of reform measures.

The second scenario — called an *opening door* scenario — is predicated on the assumption that the bitter experiences of the Cultural Revolution and its aftermath, and the generally beneficial liberalization that occurred after the death of Mao Zedong in 1976, changed China fundamentally. Expectations have been raised, and strengthened by reports of wholesale changes in Eastern Europe, precluding the PRC from turning back to economically self-sufficient socialism. It assumes, therefore, that the key aspects of economic reform, particularly the growth of the private sector and the extensive use of markets, together with the expansion of international economic relations including trade, foreign private investment, and concessional development finance, will continue as features of the PRC's economic strategy. Within this scenario might also be incorporated an extension of the existing reforms. The visits by Premier Li Peng and senior members of the Politburo to the Special Economic Zones in late 1989 and early 1990 are interpreted by some as evidence of a continued commitment to the opening door, sustained by the government even during a period of political consolidation and repression.

China's spatial structure is in a process of change, but because of the time and cost of transforming the built environment, the present structure arguably fits neatly into neither scenario. Whichever direction China opts for will require significant and sustained investment in the development of the spatial infrastructure of the country, such as the transport network, regional development, and the services offered in the towns and cities.

However, an export-orientated strategy consistent with an opening door will have different emphases and priorities from the essentially import-substituting and domestic self-sufficiency orientated approach of the closing door scenario. The former might naturally place greater stress on urban coastal development, especially labour-intensive exporting industries and specialized resource extraction for export. By comparison, the latter is likely to give more emphasis to rural development (especially food production) and industries geared to domestic consumption.

Internal migration and urbanization

Existing large city population projections assume a rigorous control on urban population growth will remain. The planners' year 2000 population for Shanghai City exceeds 6.5 million, for Tianjin City it is 3.8 million. In both cases most growth will be channelled to surrounding satellite cities.

A continuation of the reform programme could be expected to have a markedly different impact on population mobility and the functioning of the labour market than if the reforms are halted or reversed. Rural reforms, including the contract system, have underlined the existence of a large rural surplus population, estimated to reach 200 million in the year 2000. Clearly, then, there are pressures for large-scale population redistribution. During the last few years this pressure has been eased by a freeing of migration to the periphery of the cities, and into the cities to jobs in the informal sector and the construction industry, or else to unemployment.

Under a closing door scenario migration to the large cities might be stopped altogether. In early 1990 it was reported that an attempt to stem excessive migration to cities had led to ten million people being returned to the rural areas from the urban areas (*The Australian*, 21 February 1990, p. 9; *The Economist*, 17 February 1990, p. 28). Given the size of the surplus rural population, it is likely that the small and medium-size towns would be expected to absorb the surplus and create new employment, which is current policy.

However, while an opening door scenario would probably also see a continuation of the emphasis on small and medium towns, the pressures on the labour market could well result in an overall easing of restrictions on population migration to the larger cities, as began to occur in the late 1980s. Although the rapid growth of large cities creates a range of well-known problems, large cities play a key role in the economies of most Asian countries, not least because of their concentration of mobile labour, while governments find that restrictions on population movement are almost impossible to enforce in a *laissez-faire* economy. China is unlikely to be different.

Regional development

Regional problems might also be viewed differently under the two scenarios. The current emphasis on coastal development, consistent with the opening door scenario, parallels the growth pole strategies implemented in many Asian countries during the 1980s. New investments have been targeted on regions with high potential economic growth prospects, such as the key urban areas in the east of the country, in the expectation of a trickle-down of benefits to other areas, particularly in the west and central regions. Within such a strategy, regional inequalities might well increase in the early stages of development but may decline as the country develops.

In contrast, a closing door strategy might give greater emphasis to a more regionally even pattern of development, reminiscent of policies during the years before the open door. It would be recognized that there are only a limited number of locations that are capable of generating high levels of growth, given the shortages of investment capital. Therefore, it would be better to develop as many regions as possible by maximizing the use of local resources. The rural areas, as the source of food production, are important in underwriting the strategy, as limited foreign exchange precludes the option of importing food. Neither alternative is likely to provide a solution to China's core-periphery problems. The latter strategy is constrained by the shortage of local resources, while the possibility of a significant trickle-down from the core to the periphery flies in the face of the experience of most other countries which have adopted this developmental strategy.

Environmental implications

The environmental implications of the alternative strategies are also complex to assess. Persisting with a high-growth, open-door economy will put the greatest short-term stress on the physical environment. However, it could be argued that, in the long-term, economic growth will increase the resources available to China's planners and enable them to more effectively implement programmes to repair environmental damage. Moreover, the shift to greater reliance on the market in determining the price of resources will reduce price distortions and therefore might curb some of the worst effects of environmental exploitation, whilst increasing rural incomes — due to trickle-down effects — will begin to break down the nexus between poverty and land degradation. An alternative view is that environmental problems need to be addressed urgently and directly, and this is more likely to be achieved under the closing door strategy, which would be less concerned with maximizing growth rates, and more concerned with targeting poor regions and environmental problem areas. Realistically, though, in neither case is the environment guaranteed a high priority, yet in any circumstance it will remain central to sustainable social, economic, and spatial development.

Transport development

Regardless of the strategy adopted, the development of China's transport facilities will remain a priority. An emphasis on increasing output for the domestic market requires the expansion of the transport links between the provinces producing energy surpluses and the major industrial regions. Most of these will be rail links. Road transport must be improved, particularly between cities and their hinterlands, and between the towns and cities forming the urban system.

Persisting with the open-door strategy will require a similar improvement in transport facilities, in order to reduce the costs and to cope with the increased number of people and volume of freight being moved. In addition, it will require an increase in investment in the major ports and international airports, and in telecommunications. In recent years the major aid agencies have provided concessional finance for some of the big-ticket road, port, and railway investments required by China. While the global growth of demand for concessional finance is likely to increase due to events in Eastern Europe, it is probable that under the opening door scenario China will continue to draw on these sources in expanding transport facilities.

Conclusion

From the mid-1970s through to the late-1980s China experimented with new policies designed to reform the socialist economy. A debate continues as to whether these were too fast or too slow, although there is widespread acknowledgement that the failure to encompass political reforms jeopardized economic change. Inevitably, economic reform had begun to have an impact on China's space economy, by giving more prominence to the coast than the inland, stressing the potential of the south more than the north, and highlighting the exporting industries and the economically dynamic cities. However, the spatial economy is largely dependent on fixed infrastructure which takes time and resources to redirect. The PRC had embarked on this course, before its long-term commitment came into question during 1989.

No-one knows whether the PRC's leadership has the political will to continue with the economic reforms. Some believe that the growing significance of village and township enterprises will gradually undermine the powerful state-run urban enterprises, and therefore promote a 'bottom-up' reform programme. Others acknowledge that while a closing door scenario will lead to slower rates of growth, it will also reduce China's foreign debt and with it the debt-service ratio. In a country the size and complexity of China the choices are far from being clear-cut.

Whatever direction is eventually set for the 1990s, it promises to chart new territory in the quest to determine how spatial structure is related to economic and social policy in a large socialist developing country.

Appendix 1: Definition of Urban in the PRC

G. J. R. LINGE AND D. K. FORBES

A FUNDAMENTAL problem facing sinologists is the definition of urban in China. This is not merely of academic importance but colours views about whether China remains largely a rural peasant culture or, since the late 1970s, has been rapidly taking on the forms and functions of a technologically advanced society.

As indicated by the literature cited in this Appendix, a small army of scholars has tried to prepare coherent data sets that would facilitate a clearer understanding about urbanization processes in China but, as Chan (1987, p. 109) has noted, 'further research is urgently needed'. This note simply attempts to outline the problems and summarize some recent findings.

The Chinese authorities changed the definition of urban in 1955, 1963, and 1984. Boundaries have been successively narrowed and widened to exclude or include suburbs, nearby villages, rural areas, and regions under municipal control. In some cases the population designated as urban depended on whether people were residents or itinerants, whether they had non-agricultural or other jobs, and on the type of household registrations they carried. The minimum size and official status of settlements designated as urban also varied. The various criteria, set out in Kojima (1987), need not be detailed here because up to 1982 (and possibly afterwards) there is considerable doubt as to whether the definitions were strictly enforced or, in some cases, even applied at all.

Essentially there are two issues. The first is whether urban is better defined by using data on the total population of cities and towns (*shizhen zongrenkou* or *chengzhen zongrenkou*) or on the 'non-agricultural' population of cities and towns (*chengzhen feinongye renkou*). The former includes residents who are classified as 'agricultural' by household registration but who are actually engaged in non-agricultural jobs or who work as market gardeners supplying the local market on a day-to-day basis (an issue addressed, for instance, by Pannell, 1986, p. 298). K.W. Chan (pers. com.) notes, however, that these people should not be confused with the agricultural population in the *suburban* counties under municipal administration who were not considered part of the urban population. Arguably, in terms of function and lifestyle they should be considered as part of the *de facto* urban population. The non-agricultural population of cities and towns represents only the *de jure* urban residents eligible for urban rations. Although adopted by Kirkby (1985) and Ma and Noble (1986), the latter is seen by Chan and Xu (1985, p. 589) to be a less representative measure of the numbers of people actually living in urban conditions: in their view it understates the 1964 urban population by over twenty-nine million and that in 1982 by more than sixty million. The series prepared by Chan and Xu, and by Kojima based on similar principles, are shown in Table A1.1.

A further problem of interpretation is created by the fact that ninety-eight 'new' cities were included in the urban total from the beginning of 1978 through to the end of 1982. It is unclear whether these were places that had genuinely grown into urban status or whether at least some of them were promoted for other reasons. For example, thirty were among the 108 cities that had been abolished during the Mao Zedong period.

A similar kind of problem exists in relation to 'townships'. Before the creation of communes in 1958 the 'township was the basic level of both state and Party power in rural areas' (Ethridge, 1988, p. 162), but communes then assumed economic power over township areas as well as governmental and Party power. The shortcomings of the commune system led to the restoration of townships after 1979 but not on a one for one basis. By mid-1985 the 56,000 communes had been replaced by 92,000 rural township governments and 820,000 directly elected village committees.

While there is certainly room for argument at a detailed level about whether the figures shown in Table A1.1 up to 1982 are completely accurate (Chan, 1987; Scharping, 1987), further refinement seems risky and may change the order of magnitude only marginally. None the less, Kojima (1987, p. 14) bravely accepted the 1984 figure for *shizhen zongrenkou* — see discussion below — 'as the norm expressing the real state' and concluded that 'in previous years there had been hidden urban population in the areas surrounding the cities and towns and in the rural towns'. He used this argument as the basis to 'correct' the figures for previous years by using coefficients (the bases of which are not explained other than that they 'were determined in consideration of the severity of the criteria for recognition of cities and towns and open and hidden urbanization'). For what it is worth, this 'corrected' series has been included in Table A1.1.

There is, however, one important element of urban growth which is excluded from official data. As Banister (1987, p. 13) points out, after 1978 rural people were allowed to travel to cities for business, trade, or other reasons: as a result 'China's cities had a considerable number who had lived there for a year or more but had not been granted permanent resident status'. Her calculations suggest that in the 222 cities with populations greater than 100,000, a 'floating' or 'mobile' population (*liudong renkou*) of 930,000 should be added to the 1982 official total of 143,860,000.

During the early 1980s the upsurge of 'floating' population continued. In 1985, according to Ma and Noble (1986, p. 284), there was a further relaxation of controls on internal migration. Rural residents wanting to stay in a city or town for more than three months could obtain a 'temporary residence card' and those wanting to stay longer to establish stores, do building work, or engage in service activities could apply for a 'lodging card' (*juzhuzheng*). It is unclear what criteria were used to include or exclude these people in the urban total. Given the official policy to control the growth of very large cities while promoting the small and medium-size cities, it can be speculated that 'floaters' stood a better chance of gaining residential status in the latter places. Banister (1987, p. 15) suggests that the 1985 city population should be increased by 6,400,000 to take account of unregistered city dwellers: if anything, this may, however, be an overestimate of the numbers involved. For example, the *China Daily* (15 February 1986, p. 3) reported that there were more than 3,210,000 temporary residents in China's largest cities (Beijing, Tianjin, Shanghai, Guangzhou, Wuhan, Shenyang, Changchun, Harbin, Nanjing, and Xi'an), and that they made up 10.2 per cent of the total population of these cities. The temporary population of Shanghai alone was 1,100,000 at the end of 1985 (Floating Population Research Group, Fudan University, 1987). At the end of April 1986 more than 644,000 people from outside Beijing had registered there as temporary residents (*Beijing Review*, 1986, 29(35), pp. 26–7): these consisted of construction workers (174,000), sales people or purchasing agents (52,000), private traders (27,000), housemaids (15,000), and other workers (109,000). In addition there were about 144,000 visiting relatives or seeking hospitalization, 60,000 on official business, and 70,000 engaged in cultural activities. More than half the migrant population were from rural areas and their stay averaged three months.

The Xinhua News Agency (*News Bulletin*, 28 October 1989, p. 94) noted that new employment regulations had just been issued by the

Beijing Municipal Governnment:

Beijing will strictly control the employment of personnel from other provinces and cities in privately run enterprises [which] must give priority to hiring young people from Beijing . . . The new regulations also include getting 200,000 to 250,000 temporary workers from other provinces and cities out of the capital this year. By the end of last year, Beijing had more than 700,000 workers from other provinces and cities.

As part of this campaign, the Beijing Government also suggested to enterprises wishing to lay off workers that they should consider selecting those from 'outside the area' who should then be sent home.

Other major problems of interpretation arise after 1982. Firstly, forty-four *cities* were newly designated in 1983, six in 1984, twenty-nine in 1985, twenty-nine in 1986, twenty-eight in 1987, and fifty-three in 1988 bringing the total at the end of that year to 434. Some were simply upgraded from town status but others were amalgamations of towns and surrounding counties and thus included a high proportion of agricultural population. The 434 cities proclaimed by the end of 1988 included sixty-two that were named as being of 'historic or cultural interest' (Xinhua News Agency, *News Bulletin*, 27 October 1989, pp. 69–70). Secondly, it is unclear to what extent the increase in the number of *townships* from about 2,800 at the end of 1982 to about 8,600 at the end of 1988 (and the increase in their total population during this period by perhaps 110,000,000) represents 'real' urban *growth* as distinct from the reclassification of large numbers of places from one category to another, or a mixture of both. One component of the increase was the conversion of more communes to townships. New criteria, promulgated in 1984, led to the designation of 377 county seats as towns, and some 3,430 townships — previously classified as rural — were given town status and their populations added to the urban total. Another 1,300 towns were established during 1985, 953 during 1986, and 150 during 1987 and 1988. These administrative and definitional changes apparently underlie much of the sudden boost of China's (end of year) urban population from 212 million (20.8 per cent of the national total) in 1982, to 241 million (23.5 per cent) in 1983, 330 million (31.9 per cent) in 1984, 382 million (36.6 per cent) in 1985, 434 (40.8 per cent) in 1986 and 541 (49.3 per cent) in 1988. Thus, taken at face value, the official data would postulate that the annual rate of growth of the urban population jumped from 5.2 per cent in 1981 and 4.8 per cent in 1982 to 14.0 per cent in 1983, 36.8 per cent in 1984, 15.9 per cent in 1985 and 7.3 per cent in 1988.

Banister (1987) has attempted to analyse the components of the urban increase of 52,380,000 during 1985. Initially, the official data showed that the population of *cities* increased by 20,520,000 and of *towns* classified as urban by 31,860,000. Later the official figure for the increase in the city population during calendar year 1985 was revised to 21,121,000. Banister (1987, pp. 1–2) suggests that 73 per cent (15,400,000) of this increase resulted from the establishment of twenty-nine new cities, and 11 per cent (2,310,000) from the expansion of boundaries of existing cities. She further argues that, of the remaining 16 per cent (3,411,000), more than half (1,870,000) can be attributed to net permanent in-migration to previously established cities and only 1,540,000 to natural increase. Banister (1987, p. 2) also speculates that much of the thirty-two million increase in town population 'came from reclassification of rural places as incorporated towns' but that the data needed to determine the components of town growth are, as yet, unavailable. The basis for her contention is that if each of the 1,300 towns established in China during 1985 had 23,000 inhabitants (the average recorded for towns at the 1982 census) they would have accounted for nearly thirty million of the increase.

At the end of 1985 there were 324 cities with a total population of 212,900,000 (State Statistical Bureau, 1987, p. 197). During 1986 the State Council approved twenty-nine new cities, thus adding twenty-one million to the urban total; the incorporation of 1,590 more townships would have perhaps added a further thirty-six million.

The question that seems unresolvable, in the absence of further data, is the extent to which the 108 new cities and 6,300 townships created in the four years to the end of 1986 represent places that should have been included in the urban total in previous years (but were omitted possibly for political reasons), places that became urbanized during the economic boom of the early 1980s, or places that have been included simply because they are traditional cultural or minor administrative centres. However, to argue, as some scholars (for example, Fincher, 1989a, p. 20) have done, that the replacement of the 1982 figure of around 20 per cent with a 1987 figure of more than 46 per cent is an indication of 'just how far behind reality enumerations of China's urban population had fallen thanks to the rigidities of the household registration and internal passport system' seems to be pulling a very long bow. Others (such as K.W. Chan, pers. com.) consider that the urban figure has less to do with the household registration system and much more to do with the new town designation criteria and expanded city boundaries.

Table A1.1 Urban and total population of China, 1950–89[a]

Year	Total population (000)	Total urban (000)	Per cent urban
1950	551,960[b,c]	61,690[b,c]	11.2
1955	614,650[b,c]	82,850[b,c]	13.5
	614,650[c]	91,140[d]	14.8
1960	660,250[b]	130,730[b]	19.8
	662,070[c]	130,370[c]	19.7
	662,070[c]	143,800[d]	21.7
1964	691,220[b,j]	127,103[b,j]	18.4
	704,990[c]	129,500[c]	18.4
	704,990[c]	148,930[d]	21.1
1969	806,710[c]	141,170[c]	17.5
	806,710[c]	162,350[d]	20.1
1975	924,200[c,e]	160,300[c,e]	17.3
1978	962,590[c,e]	172,450[c,e]	17.9
	962,590[c]	189,700[d]	20.5
1980	987,050[c]	191,400[c]	19.4
	987,050[c]	210,540[d]	21.3
	987,050[e]	172,450[e]	19.4
1982	1,003,937[b,j]	206,589[b,j]	20.6
	1,015,410[c,e]	211,540[c,e]	20.8
	1,015,410[c]	232,690[d]	22.9
1983	1,024,950[c,e]	241,260[c,e]	23.5
1984	1,034,750[c,e]	330,060[c,e]	31.9
1985	1,045,320[e]	382,440[e]	36.6
1987	1,080,730[f]	503,620[f]	46.6
1988	1,096,140[g]	540,600[h]	49.3
1989	1,111,900[i]		

Note: [a] All figures are for end of year and include military unless otherwise indicated.
[b] Chan and Xu (1985, p. 597):   figures are for *shizhen zongrenkou* or *chengzhen zongrenkou*.
[c] Kojima (1987, pp. 12–13): figures are for *shizhen zongrenkou*.
[d] Kojima 'corrected total population for cities and towns' (1987, pp. 12–13): see text.
[e] Liu (1989, p. 10): figures are for 'population living in cities and towns'.
[f] State Statistical Bureau (1988a, p. 97).
[g] Li, C. (1989, p. 29).
[h] State Statistical Bureau (1989).
[i] *Beijing Review*, 1990, 33(9), p. viii.
[j] Mid-year census figures which exclude military.

Appendix 2: Industry in Liaoning Province

LIU YI AND ZHANG LEI

T H E industrialization of Liaoning Province began after Yingkou port was opened by the Treaty of Tianjin in 1858. Even so the economy largely remained dependent on hunting and pastoral activities for another fifty years, although some food processing, textiles, and light industries emerged.

In the 1930s use began to be made of the wide range of mineral resources. Moreover, its accessible location on the northern side of the Bohai Sea and its lengthy coastline contributed to its becoming the trading hub of north-east China. According to Liu (1988a, p. 76), 'in 1949, on the basis of 1970 constant prices, only Shanghai and Jiangsu and Liaoning Provinces were close to RMB 1 billion [1,000 million yuan] in industrial output value'.

After 1949 Liaoning was the obvious choice for the location of metal, chemical, and other processing plants when the PRC started to place greater emphasis on heavy industry which had remained backward and weakly developed. One of the first complexes to be built after 1949 was the Anben steel base: during the First Five-year Plan period (1953–7) this absorbed more than half the investment in the iron and steel industry (Liu, 1988b, p. 112). It consists of four major mines — Dong'anshan, Qidashan, Gongchangling, and Dagushan — and the Anshan and Benxi iron and steel works. Another example is the Liaohua petrochemical complex, 8 km south-east of Liaoyang, based on oil from the nearby Liaohe oilfield which produces 7 per cent of China's total output. Work on this enterprise began in 1974 using imported technology and equipment from France, West Germany, and Italy. When the first stage was completed in 1980 (along with residential accommodation, schools, and hospitals for 50,000 people), it was unusual — even by Western standards — in being a completely integrated plant taking in crude oil and turning out polyester, polyethylene, polypropylene, nylon, ethylene, and glycol products. During the Sixth Five-year Plan its capacity was increased and a plastic processing plant added: investment has continued.

Production became concentrated in a core area in central Liaoning of about 37,000 km^2 embracing the cities of Shenyang (the provincial capital), Fushun (oil refining, coal), Benxi (iron and steel), Anshan (iron and steel), and Liaoyang (petrochemicals, synthetic fibres). In 1987 this core contained over half the province's industry. Around it were Yingkou and Dandong (light industry, household appliances), Jinzhou (oil refining), Fuxin (coal), Tieling (coal), and Panjin (fertilizers). To the south, Dalian (oil refining, shipbuilding, transport equipment, electronics) was China's third busiest port in 1987.

Figure A2.1   Liaoning Province and the Liaodong Peninsula Economic Development Zone (shaded)

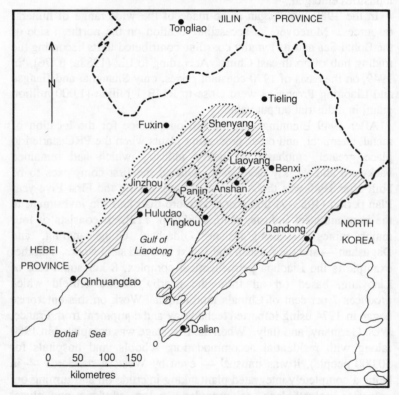

More than 10,000 small and medium-size enterprises are engaged in traditional activities, such as paper making (from reeds), food processing and textiles, and are widely spread among cities, towns, and villages. For example, Dandong is a milk-processing centre, while Dalian, Shenyang, and Yingkou have enterprises processing hemp, cotton, and wool.

During the 1980s Liaoning Province found itself in a dilemma. On the one hand, much of the investment had been designed to meet China's own needs. On the other, this meant that the province was less able to take advantage of the growing export markets such as textiles and clothing.

In March 1988 the State Council approved the formation of the Liaodong Peninsula Economic Development Zone encompassing the area from the port of Dalian to Shenyang 350 km to the north (Figure A2.1). The immediate task has been to adjust industrial policies to adapt to international competition. The authorities are trying to make the Zone more attractive to foreign investors by streamlining the bureaucracy and upgrading infrastructure. The ports of Dalian, Yingkou, and Dandong are already open to foreign ships, and construction is in hand at Jinzhou and Panjin: in 1990 the handling capacity was expected to be about 70 million tonnes (Li, R., 1988, p. 17).

The industrial development proposals face several problems. One is the growing demand for coal which is expected to increase from 70 million tonnes in 1987 to 100 million tonnes by the end of the century, and much of which will have to be brought in from other producing areas in Shanxi Province and the Nei Mongol Autonomous Region. One proposal is to ship Shanxi coal from Qinhuangdao to power stations on the coast of the Liaodong Peninsula; another is to build a special railway to transport Mongolian coal to Tongliao near the northern border of the Province.

Air and water pollution remain a problem, especially in heavy-industrial cities like Anshan and Benxi. Morever, despite the high annual precipitation, storage capacity is limited so that there is a need to share clean water between agricultural, industrial, urban, and household uses in some rational way.

References

Anon. (1968), 'Industrial development in China: a return to decentralisation', *Current Scene*, 6(22), pp. 11–8.

Anon. (1985), *Contemporary Seaport Planning* [in Chinese] (Harbin, People's Press of Heilongjiang).

Asian Development Bank (1990), *Asian Development Outlook 1990* (Manila, ADB).

Awanohara, S. (1990), 'No more favours: US lawmakers expected to maintain anti-China stand', *Far Eastern Economic Review*, 148(23), pp. 56–7.

Banister, J. (1987), 'China: components of recent city growth' (paper presented to the International Conference on Urbanisation and Urban Population Problems, Nankai University, Tianjin, October).

Blunden, C. and Elvin, M. (1983), *Cultural Atlas of China* (Oxford, Phaidon).

Brugger, W. (1986), 'From "revisionism" to "alienation", from Great Leaps to Third Wave', *The China Quarterly*, No. 108, pp. 643–51.

Chai, C.H. and Leung, C-K. (eds.) (1987), *China's Economic Reforms*, (Hong Kong, University of Hong Kong, Centre for Asian Studies).

Chan, K.W. (1987), 'Further information about China's urban population statistics: old and new', *The China Quarterly*, No. 109, pp. 104–9.

Chan, K.W. (1988), 'Rural-urban migration in China, 1950–1982: estimates and analysis', *Urban Geography*, 9(1), pp. 53–84.

Chan, K.W. and Xu, X. (1985), 'Urban population growth and urbanization in China since 1949: reconstructing a baseline', *The China Quarterly*, No. 104, pp. 583–613.

Chan, T.M.H. (1985), 'Financing Shenzhen's economic development: a preliminary analysis of sources of capital construction investments 1979–1984', *Asian Journal of Public Administration*, 7(2), pp. 170–97.

Chang, C. (1976), 'The changing system of Chinese cities', *Annals of the Association of American Geographers*, 66, pp. 398–415.

Chao, Q. and Gao, M. (1987), 'The opening of the labour market and the development of the north-west economy [in Chinese]', *Nongye Jingji Wenti*, No. 2, pp. 41–4.

Chen, H. (1984), 'The economic basis of seaport development and distribution [in Chinese]', *Geographical Science*, 4(2), pp. 125–31.

Chen, J. (1988), 'An analysis of the characteristics of rural surplus labour [in Chinese]', *Nongye Jingji Wenti*, No. 1, pp. 24–7.

Chen, R. (1986), 'The new five-year plan', *China Reconstructs*, 35(1), pp. 15–17.

Chen, S. (1983), 'Women's fertility in forty-two years from 1940 to 1981', *Population and Economics* (Special Issue), pp. 32–51.

Chen, Y. (1987), 'The new trends and models of the restructuring of the rural labour force [in Chinese]', *Jingji Yanjiu*, No. 10, pp. 77–80.

Cheng, E. (1989), 'Beggar thy neighbour: Peking tries to reduce Guangdong's privileged position', *Beijing Review*, 143(2), pp. 45–6.

Cheng, E. (1990), 'Now it's Bund aid: Shanghai gains at Guangdong's expense in wake of political reshuffle', *Far Eastern Economic Review*, 147(11), pp. 38–9.

Chiu, L.H.R. (1986), 'Modernization in China: the experiment of Shenzhen Special Economic Zone 1979–1984', unpublished Ph.D. dissertation (Canberra, The Australian National University, Department of Human Geography).

Chung, H. (1989), *Shouting From China* (2nd edn.) (Melbourne, Penguin).

Clark, A.L., Dorian, J., and Fridley, D. (1989), 'Problems and prospects for China's mineral and energy industries', in C.E. Morrison and R.F. Dernberger (eds.), *China in the Reform Era* (Honolulu, East West Center), pp. 75–82.

Coale, A. (1984), *Rapid Population Change in China, 1952–1982* (Washington DC, National Academy Press).

Coale, A. and Chen S.L. (1987), *Basic Data on Fertility in the Provinces of China, 1940–82* (Honolulu, East West Population Institute).

Dai, Y. (1988a), 'Nanjing opens its doors to the world', *Beijing Review*, 31(31), pp. 14–22.

Dai, Y., (1988b), 'Doing business by the seaside', *Beijing Review*, 31(32), pp. 16–24.

Delfs, R. (1989), 'Power to the party: centralised planning gains the upper hand', *Far Eastern Economic Review*, 146(49), pp. 23–5.

Deng Xiaoping (1984), *Selected Works of Deng Xiaoping (1975–1982)* (Beijing, Foreign Languages Press).

Ding, S. (1987), 'Harbour construction and its technical progress in China [in Chinese]', *China Ports and Waterway Engineering*, 1(1), pp. 3–9.

Ding, Y. (1988), 'A notable trend of the present shift of rural surplus labour [in Chinese]', *Zhongguo Jingji Wenti*, No. 2, pp. 52–6.

do Rosario, L. (1987), 'Models in a muddle: China's SEZs are struggling to justify their role', *Far Eastern Economic Review*, 140(40), pp. 102–3.

do Rosario, L. (1988), 'The envy of China: power and privilege prompt provincial jealousy', *Far Eastern Economic Review*, 142(49), pp. 60–2.

do Rosario, L. (1989), 'North wind doth blow: Peking sacks Hainan's governor and Guangdong trembles', *Far Eastern Economic Review*, 145(39), pp. 10–11.

Duan, J. (1986), 'Analysis of contraceptive use and abortion in China', *Population Dynamics*, 5, pp. 78–88.

du Guerny, J. (1978), *Migration and Rural Development* (Rome, Food and Agriculture Organization).

Duus, P., Myers, R., and Peattie, M.R. (eds.) (1989), *The Japanese Informal Empire in China, 1895–1937* (Princeton, Princeton University Press).

Economic and Social Commission for Asia and the Pacific (1982), 'Shanghai — China', *Physical Profile of Cities in the ESCAP Region*, (Yokohama,

Habitat), pp. 112–9.

Edgington, D.W. (1985), *Town Planning and Local Government Administration in Tianjin, China* (Melbourne, Monash University, Department of Geography, Working Paper 19).

Ellman, M. (1986), 'Economic reform in China', *International Affairs*, 62(3), pp. 423–42.

Environmental Science Committee, Academia Sinica and Environmental Protection Bureau, Tianjin (1986), *Atlas of Environmental Quality in Tianjin* [in Chinese] (Beijing, Science Press).

Ethridge, J.M. (1988), *Changing China: The New Revolution's First Decade, 1979–1988* (Beijing, New World Press).

Fincher, J. (1978), 'Land tenure in China: evidence from a Kwangtung hillside', *Ch'ing Shih Wenti*, 3(10), pp. 68–82.

Fincher, J. (1989a), 'Zhao's fall, China's loss', *Foreign Policy*, No. 76, pp. 3–25.

Fincher, J. (1989b), *Chinese Democracy: Statist Reform, the Self-government Movement and Republican Revolution* (Tokyo, Gai Kokugo University).

Fincher, J. (1989c), 'Urbanisation, repression and Deng's resignation', *New York Times*, 17 November, pp. 1 and 8.

Fincher, J. (forthcoming), 'Changing balances in population information, development planning, and population', in T. Hull and J.Y. Wang (eds.), *Population and Development* (Sydney, Allen & Unwin).

Floating Population Research Group, Fudan University (1987), 'A research and analysis of the floating population in the Municipality of Shanghai', in J. Li (ed.), *Presentations of the International Conference on Urbanisation and Urban Population Problems* (Tianjin, Nankai University), pp. 398–423.

Forbes, D.K. and Wilmoth D. (1986), *Urban Development Problems and Opportunities in Tianjin, China* (Canberra, Australian Institute of Urban Studies).

Forbes, D.K., Lloyd, R.J., and Nairn, R. (1987), *Transport and Communications in China: Sector Study and Recommendations for Australian Assistance* (Canberra, Australian International Development Assistance Bureau, Appraisals, Evaluation and Sectoral Studies Branch).

Freedman, R., Xiao, Z., Li, B., and Lavely, W. (1988), 'Local area variations in reproductive behaviour in the People's Republic of China', *Population Studies*, 42, pp. 39–57.

Fung, K. (1981), 'The spatial development of Shanghai', in C. Howe (ed.), *Shanghai: Revolution and Development in an Asian Metropolis* (Hong Kong, Cambridge University Press), pp. 269–99.

Ge, W. (1988), 'Urban reform experiment goes in depth', *Beijing Review*, 31(12), p. 4.

Geng, Y. (1988), 'The coast to intensify its export orientation', *Beijing Review*, 31(7–8), pp. 4–5.

Gittings, J. (1989), *China Changes Face: The Road from Revolution*

1949–1989 (Oxford, Oxford University Press).

Gränzer, R. (1989), 'The energy impediment to China's growth', *The OECD Observer*, No. 157, pp. 9–14.

Greenhalgh, S. (1986), 'Shifts in China's population policy, 1984–1986: views from the central, provincial and local levels', *Population and Development Review*, 12, pp. 491–515.

Gu, M. (1985), 'Coastal cities policies', in W. Su (ed.), *The Open Policy at Work* (Beijing, Beijing Review).

Han, B. (1988), 'Shanghai takes on a new look', *Beijing Review*, 31(9), pp. 14–20.

Han, J. (1987), 'The transition and policy issues related to rural labour occupational change [in Chinese]', *Zhongguo Nongcun Jingji*, No. 8, pp. 1–7.

Hardee-Cleaveland, K. and Banister, J. (1988), 'Fertility policy and implementation in China, 1986–88', *Population and Development Review*, 14, pp. 245–86.

He, Q. (1987), 'An investigation into the problem of peasants moving to the markets [in Chinese]', *Nongye Jingji Wenti*, No. 5, pp. 26–9.

Hersey, J. (1982), 'A reporter at large', *New Yorker*, 58, 10 May, pp. 49–79; 17 May, pp. 46–70; 24 May, pp. 44–66; 31 May, pp. 47–67.

Hoyle, B.S. and Hilling, D. (eds.) (1984), *Seaport Systems and Spatial Change: Technology, Industry and Development Strategies* (Oxford, Pergamon).

Hoyle, B.S. and Pinder, D. (eds.) (1981), *Cityport Industrialization and Regional Development: Spatial Analysis and Planning Strategies* (Chichester, Wiley).

Hsu, M. (1986), 'Chinese cities: controlled growth and employment problems', *Urban Geography*, 7(4), pp. 336–69.

Huang, D. (1987), 'A study on ports and the international port-city of Shanghai [in Chinese]', *Chinese Ports*, 3, pp. 20–2.

Hull, T.H. and Yang, Q-H. (1987), 'High production or low reproduction? Conflicts between China's reforms and population planning' (paper presented to the Annual Meeting of the Population Association of America, Chicago).

Jao, Y.C. and Leung, C-K. (1986), *China's Special Economic Zones: Policies, Problems and Prospects* (Hong Kong, Oxford University Press).

Jiang, D. (1988), 'Classification and development research of poor areas in China [in Chinese]', *Geographical Research*, 7(3), pp. 1–15.

Jiang, H.K. (1986), 'The rural employment problem in the new historic context', *Fujian Luntan*, No. 11, pp. 44–6.

Jiang, J. (ed.) (1987), *Confucianism and Modernisation: A Symposium* (Taipei, Wu Nan Pub. Co.).

Jing, W. (1988), 'Wuxi: combining agriculture & industry', *Beijing Review*, 31(30), pp. 14–18.

Jowett, A.J. (1986), 'China's water crisis: the case of Tianjin (Tientsin)', *The*

Geographical Journal, 152(1), pp. 9–18.

Kane, P. (1987), *The Second Billion: Population and Family Planning in China* (Ringwood, Penguin).

Keuh, Y.Y. (1987), 'Economic decentralization and foreign trade expansion in China', in J.C.H. Chai and C-K. Leung (eds.), *China's Economic Reforms* (Hong Kong, University of Hong Kong, Selected Seminar Papers on Contemporary China, VII), pp. 444–81.

Kinzelbach, W.H. (1987), 'Energy and environment in China', in B. Glaeser (ed.), *Learning from China? Development and Environment in Third World Countries* (London, Allen & Unwin), pp. 173–84.

Kirkby, R.J.R. (1985), *Urbanisation in China: Town and Country in a Developing Economy, 1949–2000 AD* (London, Croom Helm).

Kirkby, R. and Cannon, T. (1989), 'Introduction', in D.S.G. Goodman (ed.), *China's Regional Development* (London, Routledge), pp. 1–19.

Kojima, R. (1987), *Urbanization and Urban Problems in China* (Tokyo, Institute of Developing Economies, Occasional Paper Series No. 22).

Li, C. (1989), 'Only socialism can develop China', *Beijing Review*, 32(40), pp. 19–34.

Li, D., Wu, C., and Liu, H. (1988), 'The migration of agricultural labour from Wenzhou and policy implications [in Chinese]', *Renkou Yanjiu*, No. 2, pp. 32–7.

Li, J-N. (ed.) (1987), *China's Population (Tianjin Branch)* [in Chinese] (Beijing, Economic Financial Publishers).

Li, N. (1989), 'More steam for shipping trade', *Beijing Review*, 32(1), p. 30.

Li, Q. (1986), 'On the problem of rural surplus labour in China [in Chinese]', *Nongye Jingji Wenti*, No. 10, pp. 8–11.

Li, R. (1987), 'Surveys find out population momentum', *China Population* (English edn.), 12 July, p. 3.

Li, R. (1988), 'Liaodong looks towards world markets', *Beijing Review*, 31(33), pp. 17–18.

Li, S-M. (1988), 'Labour mobility, migration and urbanization in the Pearl River Delta Area' (paper presented to the International Conference on Environment and Spatial Development of the Pearl River Delta, Guangzhou, August 2–4).

Li, W-Y. (1986), 'Development strategy of China's energy resources [in Chinese]', *Economic Geography*, 6(2), pp. 86–91.

Li, W-Y. (1987), 'Changing industrial allocation and industrial management in the People's Republic of China' (paper presented to the Conference on Urban and Regional Development in Britain and China, Manchester, University of Manchester, 26–8 November).

Li, W-Y. (1988), 'Industrialisation in peripheral China with special reference to the Greater Northwest', in G.J.R. Linge (ed.), *Peripheralisation and Industrial Change: Impacts on Nations, Regions, Firms and People* (London, Croom Helm), pp. 94–112.

Li, W-Y. (1990), 'Towards a better system for managing China's industry', in

D.C. Rich and G.J.R. Linge (eds.), *The State and the Spatial Management of Industrial Change* (London, Routledge), pp. 22–39.

Lin, S., Zhou, S., and Qi, M. (1984), 'Industry and transport' in G. Yu (ed.), *China's Socialist Modernization* (Beijing, Foreign Languages Press), pp. 271–349.

Lin, Z-Q. (1987), 'Comments' (International Symposium on the Role of the Public Sector in Human Settlements, Yokohama and Kobe, 23 October–3 November).

Lin, Z-Z. (1987), 'The importance of overseas Chinese investment in the development of coastal cities and Chinese modernization' (unpublished paper, Xiamen University).

Liu, C. (1987), 'On the urbanisation of China's villages [in Chinese]', *Zhongguo Nongcun Jingji*, No. 9, pp. 37–41.

Liu, S. and Wu, Q. (1986), *China's Socialist Economy: An Outline History (1949–1984)* (Beijing, Beijing Review).

Liu, W.T. (ed.) (1989), *China Social Statistics 1986* (New York, Praeger).

Liu, Z. (1988a), 'The development and distribution of industry since 1949', in J. Sun (ed.), *The Economic Geography of China* (Hong Kong, Oxford University Press), pp. 70–82.

Liu, Z. (1988b), 'The metallurgy industry' in J. Sun (ed.), *The Economic Geography of China* (Hong Kong, Oxford University Press), pp. 109–27.

Lu, D. (1987), 'The microstrategy of regional development in China', *Acta Geographica Sinica*, 42(2), pp. 97–105.

Lu, L. and Wang, X. (1984), 'On examining the flow of builders from village to town as a mode of urbanization [in Chinese]', *Renkou yu Jingji*, No. 6, pp. 34–7 [translated in *Chinese Sociology and Anthropology*, 1989, 21(2), pp. 85–91].

Lu Y. (1987), 'War industry turns out civilian goods', *Beijing Review*, 30(3), pp 14–16.

Ma, L.J.C. and Noble, A.G. (1986), 'Chinese cities: a research agenda', *Urban Geography*, 7(4), pp. 279–90.

Ma, X. (1984), 'On the temporary movement of the rural population [in Chinese]', *Renkou yu Jingji*, No. 1, pp. 10–13 [translated in *Chinese Sociology and Anthropology*, 1989, 21(2), pp. 78–84].

Ma, X. and Wang, W. (1988), 'Migration and the urbanization of small towns in China [in Chinese]', *Renkou Yanjiu*, No. 2, pp. 1–7.

Mao Zedong (1965), 'On practice: on the relation between knowledge and practice, between knowing and doing. July 1937', *Selected Works of Mao Tse-tung*, vol. 1 (Beijing, Foreign Languages Press), pp. 295–309.

Maunsell & Partners Pty. Ltd. and Pak Poy & Kneebone Pty. Ltd. (1986a), *Shanghai Urban Studies Project* — Volume 3 and 3A — Housing Renewal Report (Canberra, Australian Development Assistance Bureau and World Bank).

Maunsell & Partners Pty. Ltd. and Pak Poy & Kneebone Pty. Ltd. (1986b),

Shanghai Urban Studies Project — Volume 4 and 4A — Public Transport Report (Canberra, Australian Development Assistance Bureau and World Bank).

McNeill, W. H. (1987), 'The eccentricity of wheels, or Eurasian transportation in historical perspective', *American Historical Review*, 92(5), pp. 1111–26.

Ministry of Public Health (1985), *Public Health Yearbook 1985* [in Chinese] (Beijing).

Murphey, R. (1980), *The Fading of the Maoist Vision: City and Country in China's Development* (New York, Methuen).

Nairn, R.J. & Partners Pty. Ltd. (1987), 'Comparative analysis of home interview travel surveys in Sydney, Melbourne and Canberra' (unpublished report, Canberra).

Nakajima, M. (1988), 'Summary report' (unpublished commentary presented to Symposium on Comparative Studies on East Asia, Oiso, Japan, 16–18 September).

Naughton, B. (1988), 'The Third Front: defence industrialization in the Chinese interior', *The China Quarterly*, No. 115, pp. 351–86.

Nickum, K. and Dixon, J. (1989), 'Environmental problems and economic modernization', in C.E. Morrison and R.F. Dernberger (eds.), *China in the Reform Era* (Honolulu, East West Center), pp. 83–91.

Pak Poy & Kneebone Pty. Ltd., Travers Morgan, R.J. Nairn and Partners Pty. Ltd. Joint Venture (1987), *Liaoning Urban Transport Project Home Interview Surveys* — *Technical Paper No. 1* (Canberra, Australian Development Assistance Bureau).

Pannell, C.W. (1986), 'Recent increase in Chinese urbanization', *Urban Geography*, 7(4), pp. 291–310.

Pei, Y. (1986), 'Development priorities of China's Seventh Five Year Plan, 1986–90', in J. Fincher and C-L. Pan (eds.), *In Business with China: Planning and Managing Sino-Australian Cooperation* (Canberra, The Australian National University, Contemporary China Centre), pp. 13–18.

Peng, X. (1987), 'Demographic consequences of the Great Leap Forward in China's Provinces', *Population and Development Review*, 13, pp. 639–70.

People's Republic of China (1986), *The Fourth Session of the Sixth National People's Congress.   Main Documents* (Beijing, Foreign Languages Press).

Population Research Centre, Academy of Social Sciences (1987), *Chinese Population Yearbook 1986* [in Chinese] (Beijing, Publishing House of Social Science Literature).

Portes, A. (1988), 'One field, many views: competing theories of international migration', in J.T. Fawcett and B.V. Carino (eds.), *Pacific Bridges: The New Immigration from Asia and the Pacific Islands* (New York, Center for Migration Studies).

Poston, D.L. and Gu, B. (1987), 'Socioeconomic development, family planning and fertility in China', *Demography*, 24, pp. 531–51.

Roll, R. and Yeh, K.C. (1975), 'Balance in coastal and inland industrial development', in US Congress, Joint Economic Committee, *China: A Reassessment of the Economy* (Washington, D.C., US Government Publishing Service), pp. 81–93.

Rozman, G. (ed.) (1981), *The Modernization of China* (New York, The Free Press).

Scharping, T. (1987), 'Urbanization in China since 1949', *The China Quarterly*, No. 109, pp. 101–4.

Schinz, A. (1989), *Cities in China* (Berlin, Gebrüder Borntraeger).

Selden, M. (1988), *China's Socio-Economic Development* (New York, M.E. Sharpe).

Shanghai Municipal Urban Planning and Construction Bureau (1983), *Shanghai Municipal Overall Urban Planning* (Shanghai, The Bureau).

Shao, Q. (1987), 'The formation of three economic zones [in Japanese]', in K. Murata (ed.), *Spatial Organisation of Industry* (Tokyo, Chuo University Press), pp. 25–34.

Shen, D. (1987), 'New features and problems in the urbanization of the economically developed region of the Yangtze Delta', *Chinese Sociology and Anthropology*, 19(3–4), pp. 54–72.

Short, R.V. (1986), 'Today's and tomorrow's contraceptives', in C.R. Austin and R.V. Short (eds.), *Reproduction in Mammals, Book 5, Manipulating Reproduction* (2nd edn.) (Cambridge, Cambridge University Press), pp. 48–89.

Sit, V.F.S. (ed.) (1985), *Chinese Cities: The Growth of the Metropolis Since 1949* (Hong Kong, Oxford University Press).

Sit, V.S.F. (1988), 'Industrial out-processing – Hong Kong's new relationship with the Pearl River delta' (paper presented to the International Conference on Environment and Spatial Development of the Pearl River Delta, Guangzhou, August 2–4).

State Statistical Bureau (1985a), *China Urban Statistics 1985* (Beijing, China Statistical Information and Consulting Service Centre).

State Statistical Bureau (1985b), *Statistical Yearbook of China 1985* (Beijing, China Statistical Information and Consulting Service Centre).

State Statistical Bureau (1986a), *Statistical Yearbook of China 1986* (Beijing, China Statistical Information and Consulting Service Centre).

State Statistical Bureau (1986b), 'Preliminary report on China's first phase fertility survey', *Population Research*, 3, pp. 8–15.

State Statistical Bureau (1987), *China Urban Statistics 1986* (Beijing, China Statistical Information and Consultancy Service Centre; and Hong Kong, Longman Group Ltd.).

State Statistical Bureau (1988a) *Statistical Yearbook of China 1987* [in Chinese] (Beijing, China Statistical Information and Consulting Service Centre).

State Statistical Bureau (1988b), *Transportation Yearbook of China* [in Chinese] (Beijing, China Statistical Information and Consulting Service Centre).

State Statistical Bureau (1988c), *China Urban Statistics 1987* [in Chinese] (Beijing, China Statistical Information and Consulting Service Centre).

State Statistical Bureau (1989), *China Urban Statistics 1988* [in Chinese] (Beijing, China Statistical Information and Consulting Service Centre).

Sun, S. and Chen, S. (1984), 'Setup of production', in G. Yu (ed.), *China's Socialist Modernisation* (Beijing, Foreign Languages Press), pp. 147–205.

Thomson, E.B. (1988), 'China's energy programme up to the year 2000: aspiration or reality?', *The China Quarterly*, No. 115, pp. 467–72.

Tianjin (1985), *Tianjin Opening to the World* (Beijing, The Red Flag Publishing House).

Tianjin, Administrative Commission of Tianjin Economic Technological Development Area (1985), *Handbook of Tianjin Economic Technological Development Area Teda, Tanggu* (Tianjin, TEDA).

Tianjin Public Utility Bureau (1986), *Brief Introduction of the Project of Tianjin–Tanggu Rapid Rail Transit System* (Tianjin, TPUB).

Tianjin Statistical Bureau (1988), *Statistical Yearbook of Tianjin 1988* [in Chinese] (Beijing, China Statistical Information and Consultancy Service Centre).

Tianjin Urban and Rural Construction Commission (1984), *The General Condition of Urban Construction in Tianjin Municipality* [in Chinese] (Tianjin, TURCC).

Unger, J. (1987), 'The struggle to dictate China's administration: the conflict of branches vs areas vs reform', *The Australian Journal of Chinese Affairs*, No. 18, pp. 14–45.

Walker, K.R. (1984), 'Chinese agriculture during the period of the readjustment, 1978–83', *The China Quarterly*, No. 100, pp. 783–812.

Wang, D. (1985), 'Developing road and river shipping', *Beijing Review*, 28(28), pp. 4–5.

Wang, F. (1987), 'China, People's Republic of' in *Asian Development Bank Urban Policy Issues. Regional Seminar on Major National Urban Policy Issues Manila, 3–7 February 1987*, (Manila, ADB), pp. 315–36.

Wang, H. (1987), 'The independence of non-agriculture rural population [in Chinese]', *Zhongguo Nongcun Jingji*, No. 12, pp. 19–22.

Wang, X. (1988), 'Impacts of population migration and movement on the urbanization process [in Chinese]', *Population and Economy*, 2, pp. 19–24.

Wang, X-C. (1985), *Comprehensive Management and Control of Metropolitan Traffic of Tianjin* (Tianjin, Tianjin Urban Transport Overall Research Group).

Wei, L. (1988), 'Torch plan outlined', *Beijing Review*, 31(34), p. 5.

Whyte, M.K. and Gu, S.Z. (1987), 'Popular response to China's fertility transition', *Population and Development Review*, 13, pp. 471–93.

Wilmoth, D. (1988), 'Current urbanisation issues in China' (unpublished report on the International Conference on Urbanization and Urban Population Problems, Tianjin, October 1987).

Wilmoth, D. and Forbes D.K. (1988), 'Opportunities for urban planning in Tianjin, China', *Australian Planner*, 26(4), pp. 19–33.

World Bank (1982), *Shanghai Sector Memorandum* (Washington, World Bank Projects Department, Urban and Water Supply Division, East Asia and Pacific Regional Office).

World Bank (1985), *China Long-Term Development Issues and Options* (Baltimore, Johns Hopkins University Press).

World Commission on Environment and Development [the Brundtland Report] (1987), *Our Common Future* (Oxford, Oxford University Press).

Wu, C-J. (1986), 'Discussions among Chinese geographers about the development of the Eastern, Middle and Western economic zones in China [in Chinese]', *Geographical Knowledge*, 4, pp. 2–6.

Wu, C–J. (1987), 'Territorial development in China', in L.A. Kosiński, W.R.D. Sewell, and C.J. Wu (eds.), *Land and Water Management: Chinese and Canadian Perspectives* (Edmonton, University of Alberta), pp. 19–28.

Wu, C-T. (1987a), 'Impacts of rural reforms', in J.C.H. Chai and C-K. Leung (eds.), *China's Economic Reforms* (Hong Kong, University of Hong Kong, Centre for Asian Studies), pp. 265–92.

Wu, C-T. (1987b), 'Chinese socialism and uneven development', in D.K. Forbes and N.J. Thrift (eds.), *The Socialist Third World: Urban Development and Territorial Planning* (Oxford, Basil Blackwell), pp. 53–97.

Wu, C-T. (1989), 'The special economic zones and the development of the Zhujiang delta', *Asian Geographer*, 8(1–2), pp. 71–87.

Xia, Z. and Li, X. (1988), 'Urbanization and the stages and group direct natures of rural labour occupational changes [in Chinese]', *Nongye Jingji Wenti*, No. 1, pp. 19–23.

Xu, B. (1988), 'The special characteristics and policy of control towards migration to Beijing [in Chinese]', *Renkou Yanjiu*, No. 2, pp. 28–31.

Xu, G. (1988), 'China reform affects Asia-Pacific region', *Beijing Review*, 31(29), pp. 27–8.

Xu, X. and Zhang, W. (1984), 'A preliminary study of the driving force behind rural urbanization in areas open to the outside world [in Chinese]', *Redai Dili*, 6(2), pp. 108–19 [translated in *Chinese Sociology and Anthropology*, 1989, 21(2), pp. 35–51].

Xue, M. (ed.) (1984), *Almanac of China's Economy 1983* (Hong Kong, Modern Cultural Company).

Yang, L. (1987), 'The development of port construction in China during the Sixth Five-year Plan [in Chinese]', *China Ports and Waterway*

Engineering, 1(2), pp. 1–7.

Ye, S. (1984), 'Regional perspectives of the relationship of development of two metropolises: Beijing and Tianjin' (unpublished paper, Beijing, Academia Sinica, Institute of Geography).

Ye, S. (1987), 'Urban policies and urban housing programs in China', in R. Fuchs, G. Jones, and E. Pernia (eds.), *Urbanization and Urban Policies in Pacific Asia* (Boulder, Westview), pp. 301–18.

Yeh, A.G.O. and Yuan, H-Q. (1987), 'Satellite town development in China: problems and prospects', *Tijdschrift voor Economische en Sociale Geografie*, 78(3), pp. 190–200.

Yeh, K.C. (1984), 'Macroeconomic changes in the Chinese economy during the readjustment', *The China Quarterly*, No. 100, pp. 691–716.

Yenny, J. (1986), 'Modernizing China's transport system', *China Business Review*, July-August, pp. 20–3.

Yu, M. (1987), 'On the transition of rural labour force and surplus labour [in Chinese]', *Zhongguo Nongcun Jingji*, No. 12, pp. 23–8.

Yue, H. (1988), 'Export-oriented economy in South Jiangsu', *Beijing Review*, 31(36), pp. 17–21.

Zhang, L. (1981), 'Birth control and late marriage', in Z. Liu and J. Song et al. (eds.), *China's Population: Problems and Prospects* (Beijing, New World Press), pp. 111–18.

Zhang, W-G., Yang S-Z., and Grau, L-Q. (eds.) (1987), *Regional Co-operation and Economic Networks* (Beijing, Economic Sciences Press).

Zhang, Z. (1987a), 'The characteristics and trend of the new stage of occupational changes amongst the surplus rural labour force [in Chinese]', *Renkou Yanjiu*, No. 4, pp. 2–8.

Zhang, Z. (1987b), 'The mechanics of the new stage of occupational change amongst the rural labour force and policy issues [in Chinese]', *Renkou Yanjiu*, No. 5, pp. 11–19.

Zhang, Z. (1988), 'China's ocean-going fleets', *Beijing Review*, 31(15), pp. 22–3.

Zhao, W. and Yu, H. (1983), 'Changes in age at first marriage of Chinese women after Liberation', *Population and Economics* (Special Issue), pp. 124–5.

Zhejiangsheng, Nongcun Zhengce Janjiushi (1988), 'The characteristics and problems of rural labour occupational change in Zhejiang province [in Chinese]', *Nongye Jingji Wenti*, No. 1, pp. 28–30.

Zheng, H. and Gu, C. (1987), 'A study on the coastal urban system in China [in Chinese]', *Journal of Natural Resources*, 2(3), pp. 213–27.

Zhou, Q. and Li, D. (1987), 'A comparison of the movement of people into small towns in the Suxi and Yancheng regions [in Chinese]', *Renkou Yanjiu*, No. 4, pp. 22–3.

Index